ABOUT TI

Ariel Salleh is a founding men

Sustainability; visiting professor in culture, philosophy and environment at Nelson Mandela University; 2013 senior fellow in post-growth societies at Friedrich Schiller University Jena; and research associate in political economy at the University of Sydney. She taught in social ecology at the University of Western Sydney for a number of years and has lectured at many schools, including New York University; ICS, Manila; York University, Toronto; and Lund.

Salleh's theoretical work builds on activist experience in anti-nuclear politics, water catchments, biodiversity protection, and support for Asia-Pacific women's eco-sufficient community alternatives. She co-founded the Movement Against Uranium Mining in Australia and The Greens, and she has served on the Australian Government's Gene Technology Ethics Committee, the International Sociological Association Research Committee for Environment and Society, and various journal editorial boards. Her publications include *Eco-Sufficiency and Global Justice: Women Write Political Ecology* (2009) and some two hundred chapters and articles in *Capitalism Nature Socialism, Globalizations, Environmental Ethics, Arena, Journal of World Systems Research, New Left Review, Organization and Environment, Environmental Politics,* and *The Commoner*. Salleh's transdisciplinary analysis is seminal to political ecology as the study of humanity-nature relations. As an early eco-socialist formulation, her embodied materialism emphasises the political economy of reproductive or regenerative labour in the world system. By restoring value to local everyday care-giving and indigenous livelihood skills, she re-orients social justice and sustainability debates on water, climate, and the neoliberal green economy.

ECOFEMINISM AS POLITICS

SECOND EDITION

NATURE, MARX AND THE POSTMODERN

ARIEL SALLEH

WITH FOREWORDS BY
VANDANA SHIVA AND JOHN CLARK

ZED

Zed Books
LONDON

Ecofeminism as Politics: Nature, Marx and the Postmodern was first published in 1997 by Zed Books Ltd, The Foundry, 17 Oval Way, London SE11 5RR, UK.

This edition was published in 2017.

www.zedbooks.net

A catalogue record for this book is available from the British Library.

ISBN 978-1-78699-097-6 hb
ISBN 978-1-78699-040-2 pb
ISBN 978-1-78699-041-9 pdf
ISBN 978-1-78699-042-6 epub
ISBN 978-1-78699-043-3 mobi

Dedicated to courageous women worldwide in their struggle for life-on-earth. As Timorese anti-mine activist Mama Aleta Baun says:

That stone is our bone
Water is our blood
Land is our flesh

And to the memory of Berta Cáceres of Honduras, assassinated 3 March 2016 for leading her community against the Agua Zarca Hydroelectric Dam.

CONTENTS

ACKNOWLEDGEMENTS

I would like to acknowledge several organisations that have sustained my work in ways big and small since *Ecofeminism as Politics* first appeared: the Humanities and Social Science Council of Taiwan; Political Science Department, York University, Toronto; Women's Studies Research Consortium, Amherst; Linkoping University, Sweden; Lyman Briggs School of Science, Michigan State University; the 5th EU Framework Programme; International Society for Ecological Economics; Centro di Ecologia Alpina, Trento; Circolo Culturale e Politico Cicip & Ciciap, Milan; Institute for Environmental Politics, Shandong University, Jinan; Institute for Social Analysis, Rosa Luxemburg Foundation, Berlin, and RLS, Brussels; Asia Pacific Research Network, Manila; South-South Forum, Hong Kong and Beijing; Transdisciplinary Studies program, University of Poznan; the GDF Research Group in Post-Growth Societies, Friedrich Schiller University Jena; the World March of Women, Sao Paulo; Nelson Mandela Metropolitan University, Port Elizabeth; Transform Europe!, Copenhagen; and the KNA Foundation for Education, Bangalore.

I am grateful too, for the creative energies of comrades and co-authors: John Clark, Saed Engel-diMauro, John Bellamy Foster, Shannon Bell, Lauren Langman, Jackie Smith, Greta Gaard, Silvia Federici, Ana Isla, Patrick Curry, Mary Mellor, Maria Mies, Saral Sarkar, Kate Farrell, Frigga Haug, Clive Spash, Ulrich Brand, Nora Rathzel, Federico Demaria, Patrick Bond, Inge Konik, Vandana Shiva, Ashish Kothari, Nalini Nayak, Lau

Kin Chi, Qingzhi Huan, Shuji Ozeki, Motoi Fuse, Gustavo Esteva, Arturo Escobar, Hans Baer, Anitra Nelson, Ted Trainer, James Goodman, Hamed Hosseini, Frank Hutchinson, Shé Hawke, and Political Economy colleagues.

The editors of *Polygraph* at Duke University, have kindly given permission to reproduce the following article as a final chapter in this book:

Gerry Canavan, Lisa Klarr, and Ryan Vu, 'Embodied Materialism in Action: An Interview with Ariel Salleh', *Polygraph: special issue on Ecology and Ideology*, 2010, No. 22, 183–99: www.duke.edu/web/polygraph/cfp.html.

FOREWORD

BY JOHN CLARK

Whenever anyone has expressed curiosity concerning the meaning of ecofeminism, I have without hesitation suggested this book. It was a major theoretical breakthrough when it appeared two decades ago, and has since then been an enduring point of reference for me. In fact, it was the inspiration for my article on 'the lessons of ecofeminism' in *Capitalism Nature Socialism*, a journal with which both Ariel Salleh and I have a long association.* As a dialectical philosopher and social ecological activist, I have used *Ecofeminism as Politics* as a guide to the integrative role of ecofeminism, not only in political ecology, but in any transformative ecological politics, and especially in the growing global eco-socialist movement. I can only begin to summarise here the many reasons why it deserves careful attention.

We must always be prepared for the moment when politics begins to catch up with vision. Salleh helps us do so by showing that in recent decades, a vast new history of grassroots global struggles for social and ecological justice is being led by caring workers – mothers and grandmothers, peasants and indigenous peoples. Today, we see significant advances in this historical process. For example, the degrowth movement in Europe has grasped the central relevance of the care revolution. In Rojava,

* John Clark, 'The Matter of Freedom: Ecofeminist Lessons for Social Ecology', *Capitalism Nature Socialism*, 2000, No. 43, 62–80.

several million people have blended life-affirming ecofeminist principles with deeply-rooted local traditions to guide their women's militias and communal assemblies. 'Intersectionality' is now a major theme on the left, echoing Salleh's dialectical view of how diverse forms of oppression deeply condition one another, and how sex-gender is systemically interconnected with other forms of domination and exploitation in the lives of women around the world. Such a view reveals how capitalist patriarchal attitudes and values penetrate every aspect of the social whole, giving rise to a patriarchal state, a patriarchal science, and unfortunately, even patriarchal radicalisms.

Ecofeminists reject the hierarchical dualisms that have plagued the legacy of domination we call 'History' and the system of domination we call 'Civilization'. This book demolishes those dualisms, and especially the primordial ones that place 'humanity over and above nature' and 'men over and above women'. Salleh challenges us to examine the rigid culturally constructed hierarchical sensibility that has prevailed, and to rethink, reperceive, and reimagine social and ecological relations dialectically. Twenty years ago, she was inviting us to look at sex and gender, not as stark binaries, but as a continuum, and urging us to abandon the extremes of both instrumental and romanticised ideas of nature. Nevertheless, she underscores the importance of retaining a radical conception of 'the wild', as that which 'escapes control', explodes essentialising and manipulative ideological categories, and defies domination.

Ecofeminism as Politics: Nature, Marx and the Postmodern contains an incisive critique of the patriarchal bias in both orthodox Marxist thought and in most red–green activism. Salleh notes a contradiction between Marx's authentic dialectic, which has radically ecological and feminist implications, and the perpetuation of traditional Western dualisms in the distinction between a feminine, embodied, reproductive realm of necessity, and a masculine, creative, productive realm of freedom. She notes the blindness of many left radicals to the masculinist instrumentalism inherent in the preoccupation with production and exchange value, and the neglect for nature's intrinsic or 'metabolic value'. Salleh's ten ecofeminist criticisms of Marx's methodology remain one of the best summaries of what must be confronted and overcome to achieve a truly ecological marxism or socialist ecology.

The book makes an enormous contribution to understanding what an 'embodied materialism' will look like. Such a perspective, like that of the majority of activists in the global South, is not only feminist but 'womanist', in that it is an expression of engagement in 'social reproduction'. It differs fundamentally from bourgeois feminism, which relies on abstract rights to legitimate the participation of women in the neoliberal system. Salleh sees the care-giving labour of marginalised women, subsistence farmers, fishers and gatherers as the creation and practice of an alternative ontology and epistemology in humanity-nature relations. The ecofeminism that arises out of such practice is in no way 'essentialist', as critics would label it, but is firmly grounded in material and historical realities, the work of 'a meta-industrial class' that is skilled in facing the exigencies of everyday life.

World-system thinkers have begun to acknowledge that capitalism relies on a massive free appropriation of material nature, including women's labour, which is conventionally treated as part of 'nature'. In rethinking marxism, Salleh asks how a segment of humanity that is responsible for two-thirds of global labour, and yet receives only ten percent of the world's pay, could be excluded from 'the proletariat', the supposed world-historical subject of revolution. This raises the disruptive and absolutely necessary question of how the revolutionary imaginary is an extension of the reigning patriarchal imaginary. Salleh argues that the conventional concept of a vanguard class is too narrow, both anthropocentric and androcentric, and that human survival will require an ecocentric politics. This is why the global majority of women, subsistence farmers, and indigenous peoples are a critical force. The emancipation from hierarchical humanity–nature relations is inherent in their meta-industrial form of labour.

In tying global change to personal responsibility and action, ecofeminism challenges the problematic of masculine entitlement, since deep cultural change will mean undoing the domineering ego-identity that is deeply implicated in capitalist patriarchal civilization. The institutions that maintain hierarchical power perpetuate a massive addiction and a systemic deception. As Salleh points out, while this system oppresses and inflicts suffering on women disproportionally in both the global North and South, it also makes men unhappy. Their increasing misery is one of the factors that leads them into violence against women, against ethnic others, and against the natural world. Ecofeminism is not only a movement for the liberation of women, but for the liberation of all human beings, and indeed, of all living beings.

Many of us, both men and women, were inspired as far back as the 1970s by great feminist thinkers like Dorothy Dinnerstein and Nancy Chodorow who focused on care. Many of us dreamed that we were helping to create a renewed and regenerated world, in which nurturing would become ubiquitous, the very foundation of all social practices and institutions. Then we saw that dream crushed in a wave of cultural reaction that produced a resurgence of capitalist values and oppressive character structures. As was the case twenty years ago, *Ecofeminism as Politics* appears now in

2017 as a beacon of hope reaffirming and, indeed, expanding the vision of a politics and ethos of care. We will need this transformative vision more than ever over the *next* twenty years, if our children and beleaguered Earth are to be saved.

John Clark, emeritus professor of philosophy, Loyola University, author and activist, director of La Terre Institute for Community and Ecology, New Orleans

FOREWORD

BY VANDANA SHIVA

This anniversary edition of Ariel Salleh's *Ecofeminism as Politics*, twenty years after first publication, holds much-needed insights for making the paradigm shift from capitalist patriarchal globalisation to a world of non-violence – in our minds and in our lives. As Ronnie Lessem and Alexander Schieffer say:

> if the fathers of capitalist theory had chosen a mother rather than a single bourgeois male as the smallest economic unit for their theoretical constructions, they would not have been able to formulate the axiom of the selfish nature of human beings in the way they did.*

Capitalism is gendered, racialised, and anti-nature in both cultural assumptions and economic instruments. Its anthropocentric reasoning denies the creativity of nature, and hence Rights of Mother Earth. Meanwhile, women, Indigenous people, farmers and peasant workers are defined as less than human. Big Money is based on rules that reward only those who exploit the Earth, minimising the material contribution of workers. Think of the billions of women whose care giving sustains society, yet whose work is not counted in the economy. More, women's

* Ronnie Lessem and Alexander Schieffer, *Integral Economies* (Farnham: Ashgate/Gower, 2010), p. 124.

burden increases as the ruling 1% appropriates resources and wealth, leaving them to sustain families and communities with ever fewer resources.

Why do women lead ecology movements against deforestation and water pollution, against toxic and nuclear hazards? It is not due to any so-called inborn feminine 'essentialism'. It is a necessity that is learned through the sexual division of labour, as women are left to look after sustenance – providing food and water, health and care. When it comes to the regenerative economy, women are the experts – albeit unacknowledged as such. Even though provision of sustenance is the most vital human activity, a masculinist economy that understands only the market, treats it as non-work. This model of the economy is dominated by one number, GDP, measured on the basis of an artificially created production boundary. By this inverted logic, if you produce what you consume, you do not 'produce'. When an anti-nature, ecologically blind economic paradigm leads to the disappearance of forests and water, or spreads disease because of poisoned air and soil, it is women who waken society to the threat to life and survival. In an era of global crisis, women defend the Earth – and all our lives through their lives. Women are leading the paradigm shift to align economy with ecology. After all, both are rooted in the word *oikos* – our home.

Not only are women experts in the life giving economy. They are experts in ecological science through their daily participation in, and management of natural processes that provide sustenance. Their expertise is rooted in experience, not abstract and reductive disciplines disconnected from the web of life. The rise of European science with Bacon, Descartes and Newton led to new forms of domination by treating nature and bodies as machines. It subjugated both women's and indigenous knowledge systems based on relations rather than objects. The most violent display of mechanistic science is the promotion of industrial agriculture, using chemicals developed for warfare as inputs. As soils fail under this abuse, GMOs are introduced as 'a solution' to world hunger and malnutrition. Genetic engineering rests on the idea of genes as 'master molecules' giving unidirectional commands to the rest of the organism. The reality is that living systems are self-organised, interactive, dynamic, and the genome is fluid.

As poverty generated by global market economies undermines every society, it is the local alternatives women bring through their care giving protection of biodiversity that offer real solutions to the food and nutrition crisis. As I have learnt over forty-five years of ecological activism and research with women, and thirty years of building the movement called Navdanya, meaning Nine Seeds (www.navdanya.org), domestic polycultures produce more than monocultures. In the global South, family farms based on women's participation provide most of the food eaten in the world. Navdanya research makes a paradigm shift from the monoculture measure of 'yield per acre', to our criterion of 'nutrition per acre'. Small farmers growing food ecologically with their own seeds can feed two India's and increase incomes tenfold. This is 'true wealth per acre'. Industrial agriculture reliant on mechanistic science produces only 25 per cent of the world's food while using and destroying 75 per cent of the Earth's resources – the soil, the water, the biodiversity. As I point out in *Soil, Not Oil*, industrial agriculture and globalised food trade contributes to 50 per cent of atmospheric pollution, with greenhouse gases driving climate chaos.* By acknowledging women and nature-centred agriculture, humanity could address

* Vandana Shiva, *Soil, Not Oil* (London: Zed Books, 2016).

the problem of climate change, while simultaneously increasing nutrition and health – and democracy.

Women managed traditional farming systems use more than 10,000 species of plants. And with it goes the knowledge of food processing and nutrition, bodily care giving and health. The capitalist patriarchal market-oriented food base has shrunk to twelve globally traded, nutritionally empty toxic commodities. The likely outcome of this irrational economic logic is life-threatening disease epidemics. When it comes to real solutions to real problems faced by the planet and people, it is subjugated knowledges and invisible non-violent co-production with nature that shows the way to human survival, peace and well-being in the future. This is what Ariel Salleh's challenge to eco-socialists and postmodern liberals refers to as an 'embodied materialism'. As she puts it in her opening remarks to *Ecofeminism as Politics*, this book is about:

> giving historical significance to 'othered labour', that unnamed class of hands-on workers who catalyse natural processes so enabling life-on-earth to flourish. Unless radical politics is grounded in the experience of this global labour majority ... it will simply reinforce the instrumental culture that treats the Earth and its peoples as an endless economic resource.

Vandana Shiva, director of the Research Foundation for Science, Technology, and Ecology, New Delhi; ecofeminist author and recipient of the Alternative Nobel Prize

PREFACE TO THE FIRST EDITION

AN INTEGRATING POLITICS

In a time of ecological crisis, ecofeminists worldwide have become agents of history/nature. They give voice to a subversive politics, aware of its own situatedness and transitionality. In epistemological terms, I would say that ecofeminism expresses an embodied materialism. Its first move is to interrogate the eurocentric convention that positions Man over and above Woman and Nature. This book conveys the misplaced concreteness or essentialism of that hegemony with the ironically positivist formula Man/Woman=Nature. Unravelling the contradictory identities and unlivable exploitations embedded in this ideology, I hope to show how socialism, ecology, feminism and postcolonial struggle can be grounded, unified and empowered by an ecofeminist dialectic of internal relations.

I began thinking about the integrative potential of ecofeminism as a theory of domination and as a strategy for change twenty years ago. An activist in ecology and social justice campaigns, I saw feminist friends close to burnout in their endless work to undo women's lot. Men on the left were fixated on a gender- and nature-blind marxist tradition and, having lost the chosen proletariat, were refusing to look in new places for allies. By contrast, environmentalists had no preconceived theory, though global crisis was provoking them to question the social system.

It seemed that here was a movement women might work with in opposing the status quo. In fact, this alliance is just what women have quietly chosen to build over the last decade; women at large, that is, as distinct from a minority feminist establishment. Many feminists *per se* remain wary of green politics, especially a globally egalitarian agenda, racing ahead as they are for their turn on the info superhighway.

So, it is important to make clear at the outset that the embodied materialism of ecofeminism is a 'womanist' rather than a feminist politics. It theorises an intuitive historical choice of re/sisters around the world to put life before freedom. Focusing as ecofeminism does on social reproduction, it transcends differences of class, age, and ethnicity between women. I include in this groundswell men and women who would not necessarily name themselves 'ecofeminist' but who act in ways that promote the same complex of objectives. Ecofeminism is more than an identity politics, it reaches for an earth democracy, across cultures and species. It reframes environment and peace, gender, socialist, and postcolonial concerns beyond the single-issue approach fostered by bourgeois right and its institutions.

As against the glazed eye of liberal pluralism, social movement objectives are not separate-but-equal issues spread across a flat political plane. Some kinds of domination penetrate the conditions of life more deeply than others. Yet if ecofeminists reject the canon of postmodern pluralism, against Marx they insist that it is false to reduce all power to the economics of class. A given woman, after all, may suffer on account of gender, class predation, environmental poisoning, and postcolonial status. In fact, the global majority of women live out their lives right at the bottom of a hierarchy of oppressions, inhabiting the contradictory space where Women and Nature meet. The situation is made worse as eurocentric M/W=N assumptions are exported everywhere in the name of development.

We live in a time when despite its economic and cultural bankruptcy, the United States still asserts itself as the leading nation on Earth. Yet, having failed to convert military production to good civilian use after World War Two, the free world's first republic is not a people's government, but a welfare system for the brotherhood in suits who direct a complex of tele--pharmo-nuclear corporations. The international economy is now governed by bourses, banks and supercartels. This ruling class of men annuls democracies worldwide with lavish funds to both sides of politics. Real government is no longer accountable to constitutions, but hidden away inside a transnational order of some five hundred firms controlling global trade.

Notions like 'national sovereignty' and 'free trade' have now become hollow. Old economies based on land, labour, and capital are displaced by highly mobile information processes and products. In an era of bio-resourcing, conventional social movement ideologies have little to say. Globalisation is a colonising force that literally drives the contradictions of late capitalist patriarchal relations right down to our body cells. In this expanded material reality new questions are posed. What is North and South? Who is a subaltern? Is there a subject whose labour, and therefore political sensibility, is not implicated in industrialism and its parcels of administered time? Who is equipped to design an ethical constellation that is workable beyond commodity production? I will argue that ecofeminists are doing this.

Today, an insidious international business greenwash neutralises the discourse of government and nongovernmental organisations (NGOs) alike. Everywhere, feminists and ecological activists are obliged to think and talk and dress like technocratic men. Without doubt, this totalisation is 'the main enemy' for all women and men who care. Postmodern critique is ill equipped to deal with such things. First, its anti-realism becomes defeatism by assuming the relation between words and actions to be unknowable. Second, its micro-political focus on texts distracts attention from the New World Order and its materiality. Third, as a discursive pluralism it has no way of grounding an alternative vision. We might well ask whether the glossy marketing of this castrated academic philosophy is not more than accidental? For already, the postmodern style has called one generation of students off the streets and into the salon.

The oppression/s of Man over Man, of Man over Woman, and of Man over Nature so-called are triangulated like a Boromean knot and will only be dismantled together. But even our revolutionary brothers sometimes take on ecofeminist insights kicking and screaming. From the outset, Françoise d'Eaubonne's pathbreaking contribution *Le feminism ou la mort* was attacked as 'dangerous exaggeration'. Like feminists everywhere, she was accused of setting up 'women's power' over men. Lately, residual masculine fears of control by 'mother' have been excited by the rhetoric of Naomi Wolfe. Yet her liberal feminist slogan 'Women are the First Sex!' deforms the idea of gender equity in a very masculinist way. I suspect the message of her counsel on competitiveness is really something more like 'The USA is the First World!' Mainstream liberal feminism is highly conservative.

In the early days, ecofeminists thought that greens would seize the historical moment and work cooperatively with women on terms that they, as the Other half of humanity, are so well qualified to spell out. We are older and wiser now. Objections to ecofeminist analyses have also come from emerging ecophilosophies such as deep ecology, social ecology, eco-socialism. This is no surprise, since each has developed within an unexamined androcentric framework. Accordingly, each has tried to suppress the subaltern voice of ecofeminism by trivialisation. The insult of 'essentialism' or 'biological reductionism' is one tack, dismissal as 'goddess worship' is another. My website (www.arielsalleh.info) carries detailed deconstructions of these misleading claims.

Androcentrism is forceful: for as d'Eaubonne's brilliant metaphor of the capitalist patriarchal ego has it, 'one cannot stop a vehicle careening at a hundred miles an hour toward a brick wall when one is only sixty feet away from it'.* The prevailing ecological and sexual crisis is symptomatic of the profound hold that eurocentric gender enculturation has. Perhaps the strength of men's resistance to ecofeminism is the measure of how correct we are in identifying gender as lowest common denominator of all dominations. This would be so since, by Freud's dialectical insight, in denying an interpretation, the patient affirms its accuracy. Surely, there must arrive a point when the penny drops: when our detractors will reconnect and come to recognise how environmental struggle is socialist struggle is feminist struggle?

In a reflexive politics, *working with* also means *confronting* comrades on gender where necessary. Recently, a favourite Reichian friend suggested that ecofeminism should aim at helping men in their relations with each other. Coming from a married and therefore serviced man, this innocent proposal inflames the sense of gender justice. Should women activists, often already burdened with single parenting in conditions of poverty, further take responsibility for mothering adult men's new consciousness too? When I pointed to this reactionary implication, he replied,

* Françoise d'Eaubonne, 'The Time for Ecofeminism', in C. Merchant (ed.), *Ecology* (New Jersey: Humanities Press, 1994), p. 177. The extract is from d'Eaubonne's *Le feminism ou la mort* (Paris: Horay, 1974).

'You talk as if politics were therapy.' Yes, a quite non-Reichian refusal to see how the personal is political! Ecofeminism does, of course, point to how men can move beyond deforming capitalist patriarchal relations. Building bridges with progressive elements in the men's movement is an important part of our politics.

It is said that every new idea passes through three stages before its final acceptance: ridicule, then argument and debate, and finally legitimation. Perhaps this generation is still too much enmeshed in the diehard attitudes of an earlier time to see the sense of an ecofeminist position. D'Eaubonne, for one, looks to the future for action, claiming, 'youth of both sexes come more and more to the realisation that their cause is not only that of the Mother but of all women the world over'.* It would be politically expedient to make this point without reference to 'the mother', given the well of unresolved social hostility directed at mothers in general. On the other hand, discovering the deep structural meaning of that collective negativity may be the first healing step towards life-affirmative social relations.

WHO SPEAKS AND HOW?

This is a book of ideology critique, but its writing has been as much a personal and political journey as an academic one. In a sense, it is a collective biography from two decades of sharing the struggles of an international ecopolitical community. Even as I type these words in Australia, letters from women activist friends trickle in from overseas, despondent for the future of life-on-earth, outraged by experiences of displacement and exile after trying to bring change. From Finland to Fiji, it is always the same letter. These ecofeminist

* Ibid., p. 192.

re/sisters are too numerous to acknowledge here, but their names and activities are woven into the text that follows. It is their story and I tell it with love; encountering these women has brought joy, and validation, to my own 'damaged life'.

My need to situate ecofeminism as politics occurred in the spring of 1989, when I was teaching Environmental Ethics in the Unitarian Theological School on campus at Chicago. I am indebted to a lively crowd of Midwest graduate students and colleague Ron Engel as catalysts. The project was sustained by the collegial support of Tom Colwell in the Environmental Conservation Education Program at New York University, during my 1990-92 sojourn there as visiting scholar. David Watson *at fifth estate,* Patrick Murphy, editor of *Isle,* and Jay Levin of *LA Weekly* gave encouragement and feedback. Other ecopolitical activists have become supportive friends in the comings and goings of New York City: Silvia Federici, Bertell and Paule Ollman, John Brentlinger, Roz Boyd, Guy Chichester, Kirk Sale, Lorna Salzman, Susantha and Hema Goonatilake, Minna Barrett, Joan Shapiro, Trent Schroyer and Lavinia Padarath. To the Women's International Policy Action Committee in New York I owe a special thanks for a travel grant enabling me to attend the Earth Summit held in Rio de Janeiro in June 1992.

In the Antipodes – a harsh climate for ecofeminism – my commitment has been nurtured by Barbara Whiteman, Jo Immig, Kathryn Squires and Clare Henderson, co-editors of *ecofeminist actions.* Frances Lovejoy made it possible for me to teach the first ecofeminist course in Australia, to Women's Studies graduates at the University of New South Wales in 1984. This opportunity has been extended by colleagues at the University of Western Sydney, Hawkesbury. Over time, academic friends – Lynette Dumble, Alastair Davidson, Frank Fisher, Ted Trainer, Andrew Dutney,

Charles Sampford; in Britain, Les Levidow and Chris Rootes; in France, Martin O'Connor – have sharpened my pen. When little writing got done because of corporate and technocratic bloody-mindedness over a patch of forest, streams and beach at Wombarra, neighbourhood rebel Ian Miles, engineer Jim Irish and Sid Walker from the Nature Conservation Council steered me back to the book. Salleh ben Joned, father of my children, supplied postcard enthusiasms from Kuala Lumpur. Finally, for believing that I had something to say, I owe an eternal debt to two dear people no longer with us: tireless anti-imperialist Alex Carey and the mischievous George Munster of *Nation Review*.

In a dialectical world, tensions are constructive. So to the boys in Science for People, the Movement Against Uranium Mining, the Australian Labor Party, the *Arena* collective, the Society for Social Responsibility in Engineering, the Glebe Greens, and others whose intransigence has helped grow my dissident ecofeminist senses over the years, I give a vote of gratitude in retrospect. As Luce Irigaray has noted:

> Being denied the right to speak can have several meanings and take several forms. It can be a conscious effort to ban someone from institutions, or to banish him or her from the polis. Such an action can mean, if only in part: I don't understand what you're doing so I reject it ... writing allows your thought to be put on hold, to be available to those women and men who sooner or later will be able to understand it. This applies to some areas of knowledge more than others ... the discourse seeking to establish a new sexed culture is one of them.*

* Luce Irigaray, *Je, tu, nous* (London: Routledge, 1993), p. 52.

Dialectics teaches that subjectivity is not encapsulated by the identitarian either/or logic of the M/W=N ideology. The sociology of knowledge teaches that what people see and feel is shaped by their experiences. For my part, I speak from the position of a white working-class adopted child of Irish-German-Jewish extraction, later academic and single mother of mixed-race Malay-Muslim children. Further, the Land of Oz is a postcolonial enclave of Britain, currently colonised by the USA, and itself a coloniser of Aboriginal, Asian and Pacific Island peoples. My perspective privileges and celebrates voices that are usually unheard, being historically located outside of commodity production – they happen to be mainly voices of women and indigenous people. This book is written for an English publisher to counter US territorialisation of ecopolitical theory.

Questions of identity/non-identity can be complex for an Australian. Colonisations give way to dualisms which in turn threaten to become contradictions. Sometimes only irony can say what needs to be said. My hope is that this postcolonial critique winds in and out of these layered livings and double binds with some integrity. But there is yet a further level of discursive complexity that should be made explicit. In a text whose agenda is to challenge the artificial separation of Humanity and Nature, many words will carry both current and potential liberatory senses. Given the linearity of the print medium, only context can tell which sense is implied. Readers are asked to be aware of this and so enjoy a dialectical process of thought. I use the image of a Mobius strip for envisaging these paradoxical transformations of meaning through time.

I expect people will receive my narrative in many ways. Cynical postmoderns may treat it as another language game, while ecotheologians find a salvational quality in women's environmental commitment. Marxists may dismiss the text as parody; and political pragmatists argue that it does not matter whether history is a meaningful totality or not, but simply that we need a coherent myth for making a future. Certainly, most people can do with help in making sense of violences carried out in the name of Enlightened reason, universality and natural law. Moreover, given the rough contingency of feminine existence in so many cultures designed at men's convenience, a unifying anticipation such as ecofeminism is a source of affirmation and solidarity for women.

But ecofeminism is more than a manifesto, it already lives in the actions of women. Even so, as a specific body of knowledge and practice, it is an absence in the mainstream consciousness. Neither the public at large, nor activists, nor academics are yet making all the connections – libidinal, ideological, organisational – needed for an equitable and sustaining political agenda. This book translates the ecofeminist idea into ecopolitical discourse, suggesting implications for epistemology and ethics along the way. Connections are made across several interlocking fields: the sociology of knowledge, the politics of social movements, and environmental ethics. The argument is about links that are often invisible, so being asked to recognise them may unsettle some readers.

Even so, I do not write simply to challenge intellectually. I am driven by many mournings. Among them is the fact that my birthplace is a stolen land, nurturing me at unspeakable cost to displaced indigenous Australians:

Mordja Amari Boardadja
Ngu Borngga Amari Mordja

Forgotten I lost dreaming
Country I left forgotten lost
He who loses his dreaming is lost.*

Another source of this book is joy for all that walks and flies and swims and stands: the regent honey eater, pig-footed bandicoot, the barramundi and ocean waves, rufous bristlebird, crescent-tailed wallaby, sandstone cliffs, and scraggly eucalyptus.

* Charles Mountford, *The First Sunrise* (Melbourne: Rigby, 1971), p. 9.

INTRODUCTION

IS ANOTHER ECO-SOCIALISM POSSIBLE? REFLECTIONS ON THE TWENTIETH-ANNIVERSARY EDITION

Two decades from its original 1997 publication, the intuitions of *Ecofeminism as Politics* are affirmed by trends in green politics, European calls for degrowth, North American eco-socialisms, livelihood models from the global South, a feminist 'care revolution', and diverse alter-globalisation movements. Subtitled *Nature, Marx and the Postmodern*, the book makes an eco-socialist argument that is at once decolonial and feminist. It calls for an embodied materialism, asking thinkers and activists to recognise the historical significance of 'othered labour', that unnamed class of hands-on workers who catalyse natural processes, so enabling life-on-earth to flourish.[1] Unless radical politics is grounded in the experience of this global labour majority constituted by women, peasants and indigenous peoples, it will too readily reinforce the dominant instrumental culture that treats the Earth and its peoples as an endless economic resource. This means that a reductive reading of the book through 'actually existing' socialist, postcolonial, feminist or environmental theory will miss what is unique here – a triangulated analysis, teasing out a common foundation shared by each political oppression.

Today, public interest in the Anthropocene idea shows wide acceptance of the urgent need for social change.[2] Yet too many ethically committed people, even climate activists, still take industrial production for granted as 'the way to do an economy'. Sadly, the international capitalist system cannot be repaired, rationalised or even regulated, as twentieth century social democrats believed. This is rarely admitted, although a noisy implosion of blogs, NGOs and global conferences speaks disorientation and uncertainty. Conversely, many women in the so-called global North and rural workers in the global South look beyond the model of linear development to a life-affirming future where feminist, decolonial and ecological values converge.[3] This book adopts their vision of an 'earth democracy' and as 'another' eco-socialism, it turns from the conventional marxist interface between capital and labour to the neglected interface between labour and nature. At the domestic and geopolitical peripheries of capital, other agents of history are discovered, workers beyond the proletariat. Yet attempts to explain this shift drop the book right back into the key dilemma of politics at large. That is to say, the relative power and privilege enjoyed by men of all classes and ethnicities does not encourage their reflection on the sex-gendered dynamics of worldwide capitalist patriarchal practices. Even on the left and among academics, critical feminist scholarship is still routinely erased, or put to one side as 'women's stuff'. But innovations in environmental ethics or economic degrowth or eco-socialism really must start at square one by examining the premises of an embodied materialism.[4]

PRAXIS

The integrative logic of *Ecofeminism as Politics* was expressed in nascent form at the famous 1999 Battle for Seattle when an international coalition of street fighters – workers, women, indigenes and youthful supporters – challenged the World Trade Organization agenda. In 2001, this new conjuncture would quicken in two directions. Top down: in response to 9/11, an intensified imperial plan for securitisation sent the tele-pharmo-nuclear complex into a Middle East war. Bottom up: a people's World Social Forum (WSF) was created at Porto Alegre, Brazil; subsequent gatherings would be held in Mumbai 2004, in Tunis, and locally in cities like Atlanta. In North America, this 'movement of movements' was joined by a committed network of Sociologists Without Borders and gave fresh impetus to the *Journal of World-Systems Research.*[5] It was fostered by left-wing think tanks like the Netherlands-based Transnational Institute and by Focus on the Global South in Thailand. An emerging literature on globalism was matched by monographs on Karl Marx's ecological insights. More movement transversalism came in 2006 with ecological feminist efforts to en/gender eco-socialist thought in the journal *Capitalism Nature Socialism.*[6] If working-class unions in industrialised metropolitan societies were paralysed by the loss of jobs offshore to low-wage manufacturing zones, a vibrant Landless People's Movement from the periphery was talking eco-villages and food sovereignty.[7]

Alter-globalisation movements were thriving, but so was the transnational ruling class. In tandem with the World Bank and International Monetary Fund (IMF), the Business Council for Sustainable Development, so proactive at the 1992 Rio Earth Summit, now formed a broader alliance of corporate executives and diplomats. Their regular World Economic Forum get-together at Davos, Switzerland would go on to enlist G20 states and BRICS (Brazil, Russia, India, China, South Africa) leaders to consider an ideal of world governance through the United Nations as a public–private partnership.[8] That said, big politics in the early years of the new millennium was also preoccupied with intractable oil wars and corruption closer to home, the 2008 global financial crisis being a symptom of that dysfunctionality. As middle-range social alternatives like solidarity economies and transition towns were being promoted in the suburbs of Britain, Canada and Australia, China convened an Environmental Politics conference at Jinan University featuring both eco-socialism and ecofeminism.[9] Polish anarchists blogged autonomous marxism, deep and social ecology; and governments in Venezuela and Brazil inspired alter-globalisation movements for decolonisation.

In a path-breaking move, the constitutional assembly of Ecuador voted to give nature, or *Pachamama*, legal standing. Later, Bolivia introduced this way of thinking at the UN, and eco-theologians from Ireland to South Africa and beyond nurtured a network for Wild Law.[10] At this time, the global commons – earth, air, fire, water and biodiversity – was being privately appropriated behind an international policy mask of 'economic scarcity'. However, the capitalist overproduction crisis driving climate change simply spiralled on with market mechanisms and geo-engineering – profitable but false solutions. The first Earth Summit had brought big pharma and bio-piracy of indigenous knowledge to centre stage. Now it was the Kyoto Protocol and UN Framework Convention on Climate Change (UNFCCC) that tied the activist community in knots. The global ruling class manages climate policy with an economic logic that does not correspond to natural processes. Thus debate over emissions trading keeps environmentalists on the back foot, obliged to negotiate in a language that is alien to them. This manipulated contest shows why high-level talks about 'sustainable development' terminate at an oxymoron. The ecological crisis can only be remedied outside of capitalism.[11]

Given grassroots disillusion with UNFCCC negotiations, climate networks multiplied on every continent. Swedish feminist research and German women activists from GenderCC highlighted a major obstacle to progress in the fact that climate change is sex-gendered in its causes, effects and solutions. Uruguay women started their own World Rainforest Movement. In North America, an Indigenous Environmental Network (IEN) coalesced, soon to protest against the direct access pipeline scheduled to carry fracked oil across Sioux land in Dakota to Illinois. In 2009, the international peasant union Via Campesina, coordinated from Indonesia, stepped up with the claim that 'our way of life is cooling down the earth'. Another common-sense approach to global warming was spelled out at the 2010 Cochabamba People's Climate Summit, whose hosts asserted that their *buen vivir* economies already model a clean alternative to high-tech consumerism.[12] At official UNFCCC negotiations like Copenhagen and on the streets outside Davos or G20 summits, movement voices continued to reject climate policy based on the tech fixes of business as usual. The demand for social justice, tied together with environmental justice, eventually led to a people's Tribunal for the Rights of Mother Nature, concurrent with COP21 proceedings in Paris.

As Mediterranean nation-states faltered under European Union austerity programmes, Spanish citizens known as *indignados* inspired a chain reaction of populist revolt against neoliberalism. By 2011, urban youth called Occupy had set up camp near Wall Street stock exchange, railing against the wealthy global 1 per cent on behalf of the 99 per cent. Occupy prefigured a future horizontalist politics of spontaneity and mutuality – a commons.[13] The German left now began to blockade the dodgy Frankfurt banking sector. In Japan, mothers affected by the

Fukushima meltdown were fighting government plans for new nuclear reactors, as their Australian indigenous sisters were trying to halt a radioactive waste dump enterprise on sacred country.[14] At Rio+20 in 2012, business, politicians and the United Nations Environment Programme (UNEP) turned the anniversary of the first Earth Summit into a public relations exercise for the next wave of capital accumulation. Earlier corporate proposals for a 'green new deal' were revamped as a 'bio-economy'. The new technocratic platform, reinforced by European aspirations for Earth System Governance, was entitled *The Future We Want.* Conversely, the alter-globalisation movement, bolstered by the Canadian people's science monitor ETC (Erosion, Technology, Convergence), replied that *Another Future is Possible*! and pitched for nothing less than a 'bio-civilisation'.[15]

In 2013, the World March of Women moved headquarters to Mozambique and African women impacted daily by mining near their homes established Wo-Min, a continental anti-extractivist network with an office in Johannesburg. In the United States, Appalachian mothers took direct action against mountaintop removal by the local coal industry, and Californian women from Code Pink maintained the rage for Israeli peace in Palestine. Ecofeminists from the Navdanya school in India were building up 'banks' of traditional seeds around the country; their efforts mirrored by the Melbourne group MADGE (Mothers Are Demystifying Genetic Engineering). In Sichuan, women farmers were revitalising customary organic agriculture methods; and housewives around London were volunteering their time to repair the Thames River catchment from centuries of industrial abuse.[16] In 2015, *Laudato si'*, a passionate statement from Pope Francis, identified productivism as a threat to all species and called for a new global alliance of the poor.[17] But the year 2016 has seen women in former communist, now conservative Poland struggle to reclaim rights over their own fertility, and women in Argentina organise a National Strike over ongoing gang rape-murders of teenage girls. Femicide is becoming an international epidemic, inside the home and out. Children's bodies, too, are felled by confused and immature predators.

Environmental damage is often explained as an effect of 'over-population'.[18] But it is corporate extractivism and the militarism that supports it which lay forests bare, poison water and displace refugee populations, whose desperation is then targeted by police. In France, all-night street demonstrations known as Nuit Debout are demanding amnesty for migrant *sans papiers*, closure of the sex-gender pay gap, and an end to anti-democratic free trade treaties.[19] But freedom of assembly and electronic communications are increasingly monitored by the neoliberal state. Students at neoliberal universities become 'clients' and research centres serve as auxiliaries of industry. Applied studies of the socio-ecological crisis using geography, environmental sociology, ecological economics, governance, policy and risk analysis rarely examine the white, middle-class masculinist origins of their 'ecological modernist' constructs and methodologies.[20] Those 'softer' disciplines as survive the pacification of academia – environmental humanities, cultural studies – encourage the deconstruction of eurocentrism, even as digital hardware secures the monoculture of mastery. Meanwhile, a brand of post-feminism in the global North markets itself as 'the new materialism'.[21]

On the positive side, the second millennium has seen a new wave of research into alter-globalisation movements, and activists in Hong Kong are using the internet to launch a Global University for Sustainability.[22] An international conference, Minding Animals, is now held regularly, and an ethics of veganism has been formulated by ecofeminists in the United States.[23] In the years 2013–16, professionals have gathered in Leipzig and in Budapest to explore degrowth and the Boell Foundation debated the commons idea. The organisation Transform Europe! is looking at the viability of red–green politics and the Rosa Luxemburg Foundation in Brussels has a working group, Beyond Development, drawing on localised notions like *ubuntu*, *buen vivir* and *swaraj*. Major publishing houses are increasingly interested in ecofeminist writing.[24] Feminist re-visionings of marxism continue, notably through the Institute for Critical Theory in Berlin, which puts out *Das Argument*.[25] There is no doubt that the historical diminishment of women 'as closer to nature' remains the foundational social contradiction of capitalist patriarchalism. The mainstream economy is fully reliant on a surplus appropriated from women's unpaid and underpaid labours at the humanity/nature interface. The language of care work is entering economics and law, though often in ways that make it GDP-compatible and management friendly. In the affluent global North and in communities of the South, women's bodies remain de facto shock absorbers for the collateral damage of engineered progress. Capital owes an 'embodied debt' to those whose caring labour protects biological growth and cycles of regeneration.[26] But for structural change to happen, it is critical that socialist, decolonial and ecological politics respond to what Karl Marx and Friedrich Engels saw as 'the woman question'. In fact, public inertia here suggests a material dependency so shameful that it cannot be uttered.

Re-reading *Ecofeminism as Politics* twenty years after the book was written, we may well ask: has politics been 're-framed'? True, there are moves to integrate social justice with environmental protection, although these initiatives encounter resistance from powerful class interests. Demands for sustainability policy in the global South are re-packaged by the global North in self-serving foreign aid programmes or as the 'green economy'.[27] At the UN, the upgrade of Millennium Development Goals into Sustainable Development Goals is a barely disguised neocolonial project for technology transfer. Even the Anthropocene conversation veers close to a repressive tolerance, wherein a scientific establishment acknowledges the global crisis, and yet underscores its inevitability as if there were no alternatives. Then again, as the contours and fractures of neoliberal capitalism sharpen, alter-globalisation movements become more sensitive to the eurocentric default position of international politics. *Taking hold of the sex-gendered genesis of that default position is another matter.*

THEORY

This is why *Ecofeminism as Politics* remains as salient a handbook for re-thinking change today as it was in 1997. Since the dynamics of sex-gender underlies all oppressions, the first half of the book is devoted to exploring how and why this is so. To demonstrate the intractability of the problem, *Chapter 1*, 'Ecology reframes history', surveys pioneering examples of twentieth century green thought revealing a rather inward-looking white middle-class masculinist literature with an assortment of ideas on the sociological conditions for historical agency. It is plain that assumptions about class, ethnicity and sex-gender must be challenged for environmental politics to move forward. One way to begin this is by asking: which groupings around the world are most under pressure from the anti-life orientation of capitalist patriarchal institutions? Second, do these potential agents of history possess the skills for building a life-affirming politics? These questions are answered in *Chapter 2*, 'Ecofeminist actions', where the exclusionary character of green thought, its inability to make sense of women's political activities, is juxtaposed with a brief international history of their ecological praxis and theory: an outline of the first twenty-five years of the movement.

To help explain just why women's political initiatives are systematically marginalised, *Chapter* 3, 'Body logic: 1/0 culture', opens the case for an embodied materialism. The uncompromised judgement of early radical feminist thinkers and feminist psychoanalysts is that men's enduring structural control of women is achieved by the same libidinal dissociation and 'alienative consciousness' as the social positioning of Man over Nature (1/0). This primal contradiction, neatly articulated in Aristotle's Great Chain of Being, is both energised every day in the embodied actions of individual men, and sublimated historically in eurocentric institutions. *Chapter* 4, 'Man/Woman=Nature', amplifies this thesis through four classic ecofeminist statements. Rosemary Ruether and Carolyn Merchant from the US, Maria Mies from Germany and Vandana Shiva from India each demonstrate how the compulsive cultural hierarchy of humanity over nature, man over woman, capitalist over worker, white over black is conveniently denied, displaced and mystified as religion, law, economics and science.[28] The hegemony is carried forward in radical politics too.

In *Chapter* 5, 'For and against Marx', the irreducible importance of marxist thought for deconstructing capitalism is a given. However, the marxist dialogue with other social movements – women's, indigenous and ecological struggles – is undermined by dualist habits of reasoning. In the present era of neoliberal globalisation, Marx's analysis is necessary but not sufficient. This is because, historically speaking, patriarchal practices extend back thousands of years, while their latest manifestation in capitalism is but a few hundred years old. Masculinist structures of domination are all but universal, but marxist analyses reverse this level of abstraction and posit capitalist relations of production as *a priori*. The manoeuvre makes no sense. If one level of Marx's thought encompassed the great metabolism of nature, it lacked any vantage point on the cultures of sex-gender politics. As a consequence, marxism 'naturalises' relations of reproduction in an ideological way just as liberal political economy does. Women's and indigenous people's labours exist as economic externalities, even though capitalism is fully reliant on their regenerative services. Getting to the libidinal roots of this systemic international appropriation is central to a transversal movement wherein socialist, postcolonial, feminist and ecological objectives merge.

Most socialists still treat 'the woman question' as liberals do – an add-on, a matter of equal rights. The ecofeminist analysis that could re-frame and integrate their politics is not grasped. *Chapter 6*, 'The deepest contradiction', revisits the 'free gifts' of reproductive labour at the domestic and geographic peripheries of capital. The structure of capital accumulation is kept in place by societal violence on and workplace harassment of female and black bodies. In global North and South, most women's standing in this predatory system is one of inclusion/exclusion – structurally essential to capital yet ambiguously defined as not quite labour, a condition of production or a natural resource. This said, some actually existing feminism also has shortcomings. *Chapter 7*, 'When feminism fails', queries the regressive character of liberal and postmodern feminisms with their emphasis on individualism. In the 1990s, Women's Studies departments in universities, influenced by the intellectual fashion for poststructuralism, took a 'linguistic turn'. But the focus on discourse provided no tools for dealing with *the living metabolism of human bodies embedded in ecological processes.* The discussion of m/othering labour was almost taboo – and in this respect, middle-class equality feminism came to reflect the wider culture of misogyny. In a related vein, the international policy trend towards 'mainstreaming' women has held back feminist political unity cross-culturally, and held back collaboration of movements in the struggle for global alternatives.

Chapter 8, 'Terra nullius', takes up neocolonialism and its multiple tensions. Since the mid-twentieth century, capital accumulation strategies in the name of 'development' have intensified the interlocking crises of indigenous displacement, loss of livelihood and environmental breakdown. The Earth Summit at Rio de Janeiro in 1992 primed both Climate and Biodiversity Conventions, oppressive new agencies like the World Trade Organization and neoliberal propositions such as the ultimately defeated Multilateral Agreement on Investment. The century closed with corporate elites, guided by public relations agencies, having discovered how to manipulate the United Nations in the further pursuit of profit. In Australia, the introduction of 'regional agreements' following Rio threatened Native Title law by legitimating trade-offs over mining rights on indigenous land and patents on traditional knowledge of medicinal plants. At this point, potent new terms like 'bio-colonisation' enter the lexicon.

Chapter 9, 'A barefoot epistemology', might be seen as a subaltern version of the 'positivism dispute'. An embodied materialist assumes that human consciousness emerges in the phenomenology of subject–object interaction.[29] A parallel pattern of reciprocity occurs at the interface of human labour and natural matter, where a worker's non-alienated attunement to 'living time' wards off entropy. No dualism here, but a relational logic empowering both human and natural agency. In parts of the global South that are still free of industrialisation, intact meta-industrial livelihood economies already model ecological sustainability and communal solidarity. Likewise, in the global North, women's socially ascribed domestic labours provide them with a unique skill set for managing natural living cycles – in this case, embodied ones. This materialist transvaluation of marginality prepares the way for a fresh dialectical interrogation of marxist ideas about labour and class.

Thus *Chapter 10*, 'As energy/labour flows', revisits the ideological dualisms that occur unconsciously in Marx's text and consequent lapses of ethnocentrism, sexism and speciesism in twentieth century political economy. The accepted theorisation of use value and exchange value gives primacy to the exploitation of industrial men's 'productive' labour while women's domestic 'reproductive' labour is not factored into the production equation. Twentieth-century socialist feminists tried to theorise the unspoken appropriation of that surplus, but to little effect. Here, taking an embodied materialist perspective, it is argued that the standard 'economic laws of motion' reflect a symptomatic silence, a profound disconnect from life flows. Instead, the eurocentric patriarchal imaginary cascades with illusions of rational control over matter and mystification of technological progress. An ecofeminist analysis can enjoin the marxist emphasis on labour as the medium through which humans know their world and their own species' capacities. But a sex-gendered ecological focus is the hands-on provisioning that prevents entropy – care giving, subsistence farming, foraging and fishing.[30] The book names this labour 'meta-industrial', since it is *sui generis*, existing both alongside capitalist production yet also over and above it. Just as humans are 'nature in embodied form', so reproductive labour is the capacity for meeting needs while 'holding' together material/energetic exchanges in ecological systems. A bioenergetic theory of value makes more sense than the vanities of man-to-man exchange and, for this, Marx's dialectic can come into play, read as a holographic model of internal relations in a multi-dimensional field.[31]

The phenomenological features of meta-industrial mediation are outlined in *Chapter 11*, 'Agents of complexity'. In a time of post-normal science and post-normal politics, vital thinking is necessarily triangulated – and by definition, a socially grounded standpoint like ecofeminism cannot be essentialist as some critics fear.[32] The transgression that ecofeminist women speak stems from living an absurd historical contradiction – the 'non-identity' of being positioned under a masculinist culture as both human subject and natural resource. The tension resolves as women and indigenous peoples sense the intimate link between abuse of 'nature' and their own condition. This critical 'epistemology from below' is experienced by a majority of alter-globalisation actors, but still the politics of solidarity and care remains out of reach. What is needed now is for socialists to enter their reflective praxis on the other side of the political/personal coin, by contemplating 'the securitisation' of masculine identity and how it undermines all efforts for an earth democracy. A maturation of the movement of movements will be predicated on this intimate disarmament.

The title of *Chapter 12*, 'Beyond virtual movements', speaks to the fact that conventional eurocentric sociologies and neoliberal policies, formulated under a humanity versus nature divide, are based on fictitious ideological assumptions. Ecological crisis means re-framing modernist political practices and challenging virtual nation-states. Recovering the common ground of oppressions is a first step in this direction. So too, the critique of specialised disciplines, including scientific methods, can draw on the experiential epistemology of meta-industrial labour. It is time for a new mode of production/reproduction worthy of human identity with nature. As the neoliberal economy of militarist excess and social austerity unravels, it will be precautionary values and skills that hold things together by minimising risk and reconciling differences. And this same labour – intrinsically and immediately political – is indispensable to building the future commons.

In reaching for an eco-socialism that is at once feminist and decolonial, embedded in a new bio-epistemic field, this book is inevitably transdisciplinary. A continuum of analytic levels traces the flow of energies from unconscious embodiment, to conscious subjectivity, to individual action, to class structure, to economic institutions, to cultural hegemony, and back again through the discursive sediment of social construction. The reader is asked to move between philosophy, political economy, psychoanalysis and biology – each vantage point a set of causalities active in the overdetermination of our politics. The reading forces new concepts up against the premature closure of older hegemonic ones in order to shift from an anthropocentric to ecocentric frame, and then to dissolve that old dualism too. The dialectical interplay may unsettle readers expecting a conventional linear argument lodged inside the parameters of a single discipline. But intellectual constructs are always provisional, the more so when theory and praxis are joined.

PART I

WOMEN AND ECOPOLITICS

1

ECOLOGY REFRAMES HISTORY

THE GREEN CONJUNCTURE

Ecological crisis displaces modernist political analyses – liberalism, socialism, feminism. It provokes us to reframe our history, to inscribe a new understanding of ourselves in relation to Nature, so-called, and to ask how can we get to live this new sensibility in practical ways.[1] That political moment is long due. The bourgeois and proletarian revolutions evaporated before realising their full potential; feminists now fight hegemony from within and backlash without; indigenous peoples, ecologists, anarchists and new movement activists disperse their energies piecemeal. While fashionable postmoderns enjoy this flux, safe in a world of ideas, transnational capital tightens its grip and life is hurting. Against a backdrop of political disorientation and despair, this book argues that most women already live an alternative relation to nature, one that activists engaged in reframing our history and renewing our politics might look to.

Could women, still invisible as a global majority, actually be the missing agents of History, and therefore Nature, in our troubled times? As a radical stance, this ecofeminist proposition dissents from Marx's premise that the working class owns a special transformative role. Equally, it defies liberal or post-modern claims that there are as many political actors to bring about social change as there are sites of resistance in society. The ecofeminist idea of women's unique agency in an era of ecological crisis may antagonise readers schooled in these established habits of thought. Some may be tempted to pull ideological rank and wave it off as simplistic. Perhaps at least they will first grapple with the multiple levels of argument that support the thesis.

Even Jacques Derrida has come to concede that 'Marxism remains at once indispensable and structurally insufficient.'[2] For with the rise of a tele-pharmo-nuclear complex, we face new material givens. Among them, the concept of property is biologised; and colonisation of wilderness is matched, literally, by the conveyancing of blood, sweat and tears. Sadly, most men's ongoing desire for acknowledgement by other men is embedded in these new conditions, both in the worried West and for those in a 'developing world' who mimic its fraternity. Emerging green movements are a major political intervention in this conjuncture. However, greens assume that since environmental damage impacts on people universally, it is to everyone's advantage to solve it. In other words, no particular social grouping is seen to be better placed than any other to save the Earth from human excess.

Socialists, by contrast, see this kind of thinking as misguided and utopian; the following passage from the *Manifesto of the Communist Party*, in which Marx and Engels comment on the utopian socialists of their day, explains why.

> [They] consider themselves far superior to all class antagonisms. They want to improve the condition of every member of society, even that of the most favoured. Hence, they habitually appeal to society at large, without distinction of class; nay, by preference to the ruling class ... they reject all political, especially revolutionary, action; they wish to attain their ends by peaceful means, and endeavour, by small experiments,

> necessarily doomed to failure, and by the force of example, to pave the way for the new social Gospel.[3]

Andrew Dobson's well-reasoned account of 'green political thought' concedes this utopian tendency within ecologism and affirms Marx's materialist line that it is conditions, not simply people themselves, that must change.[4] Of course, from a dialectical point of view, the two elements are interrelated in the formation of a specific revolutionary class.

Utopianism then, is a kind of liberalism by default, but sometimes old-style liberal thinking among greens is explicit. In his *Seeing Green*, Jonathon Porritt, for example, downplays capitalist responsibility for environmental degradation, recommending that

> the post-industrial revolution is likely to be pioneered by middle-class people. The reasons are simple: such people not only have more chance of working out where their own *genuine* self-interest lies, but they also have the flexibility and security to act upon such insights.[5]

There is a certain plausibility to this, but it does tend to pull ecopolitical strategy back to the ideology of the seventeenth century bourgeoisie who established the Western tradition of urban representative government. Liberalism inevitably celebrates the middle class as political actor. Moreover, removed as that class is from the lessons of physical labour, it treats community transformation much like a religious conversion: as if ideas alone can do the trick.

The spiritual wing of ecopolitics represented by *Resurgence* magazine or Charles Birch's *Regaining Compassion for Humanity and Nature* is a case in point. The deep ecology of Warwick Fox's

Toward a Transpersonal Ecology with its search for another way of being in the world is also tacitly housed within the liberal individualist political tradition.[6] Criticism of such trends is not intended to deny the importance of empathy and spiritual vitality in a barren, secular age, but to plead that personal readjustments are not enough. Hans Magnus Enzensberger observed very early in the career of green politics that the middle-class character of the ecology movement and its idealist emphasis on change through right thinking are likely to hold up substantive developments.[7] The middle class is also culturally advantaged by prevailing political practices, not to mention economic arrangements and gender traditions. A light-green middle class can coexist quite comfortably with capitalist despoliation of the world, because it can afford to eat organically grown food and buy houses in unpolluted places. The progressive home-gardening image of British royals illustrates the contradiction nicely, since much of their fortune comes from investment in the environmental crimes of a multinational mining industry.

Yet this claim, in turn, needs amplification. For the middle class, as most people understand it, is made up of distinct economic interests, and is also segmented by gender, ethnicity, age, and ableness.[8] Small business, on the one hand, and corporate executives, on the other, are two competing fractions of capital. Porritt selects small entrepreneurs as possible catalysts for eco-political change, but given the relentless expansion of transnational corporations (TNCs), it is fairly hard to see small businesses remaining 'secure and flexible', as Porritt's agents of change are said to be. In addition, the survival of small businesses largely depends on manufacture of products demanded by the existing consumer system. And, in the name of efficiency, they may well be tempted to cut corners by externalising environmental and human costs.

Beyond this is the middle class of scientists, technocrats, consultants, bureaucrats. Not owners of the means of production, these 'operatives' and 'co-preneurs' are heavily implicated in preserving the nation-state that services capital. As technicians and service workers, they materially constitute the industrial mode of production through their daily actions, or as white-collar salariat they help legitimate it. Not owners, though occasional shareholders, they are utterly financially dependent for a living wage on the capitalist patriarchal economy. Though technocrats often express genuine concern over green issues, the social position of this sector is inherently anti-ecological. This is why policies of the self-styled Business Council for Sustainable Development, including Agenda 21 devised for the Rio Earth Summit, are so intent on 'technology transfer' and 'capacity enhancement'.[9] A new trans-ethnic middle class is being cultivated by these transfers. Establishment of this technocratic elite in the South is especially urgent from the point of view of the global expansion of corporate enterprise and its complement of salaried consumers.

The other segment of middle-class wage workers consists of humanist-educated professionals, teachers, welfare workers, journalists. Often poorly paid and relatively low in status, they may have marginally less ego investment in the capitalist order, but they remain economically bound to it. The political attitudes of this humanist middle class tend to be tempered by the presence among its professionals of women, many of whom also work as mothers. Now, it is plain that the concerns of men in an industry-based productive system are quite different from those of women in a daily round of domestic reproductive labours. A handful of women, often liberal feminists, do arrive at high-status positions in the public workforce, but the stakes for them generally become identical with men's more technocratic commitment.

Such women are unlikely to upset the capitalist patriarchal status quo. However, the greater portion of women, middle- or working-class, or peasant, remain unpaid. Rudolf Bahro's *Socialism and Survival* is unusual on the left in valuing the longer-term 'species interest' of such women – 'outside' the system.[10] The tendency on the part of both liberals and socialists has been to suppress gender difference in the name of a greater humanity, community or class. Utopianism in a different guise, perhaps?

The suppression of gender difference is counterproductive, especially if theorists are trying to work out how to facilitate the growth of a mass ecological consciousness. Greens go so far as to acknowledge that their values are typically 'feminine' – care, modesty, connectedness – but they do not take the next step by asking: Who in society already acts on these values? If they did, they would encounter the exciting fact that half of the world's population is already educated into feminine behaviours. True, liberal and socialist women in the feminist movement may want to assert that there are no fundamental differences between women and men, but this does not affect the practical ecofeminist argument being made here. Feminist arguments for an 'androgynous equality' come from a statistically unrepresentative grouping of women globally speaking. And second, so far as political action is concerned, it does not matter whether sexed differences are ontological fact or historical accident. The case for women as historical actors in a time of environmental crisis rests not on universal essences but on how the majority of women actually work and think now.

Nor is this an idealist proposition in the sense that social change might come about simply by learning from feminine attitudes and ideas. Those marxists who see feminists as 'bourgeois individualists' sometimes toss off this kind of objection. As David

Pepper's book *eco-socialism* urges, good ideas are not enough; a shift in the economic organisation of society is crucial. The green movement must use a materialist analysis.[11] This accords beautifully with an ecofeminist premise for women's historical agency, because on an international scale women, undertaking 65 per cent of the world's work for 5 per cent of its pay, effectively are 'the proletariat'. To bring the logic of historical materialism home to eco-socialism: since the interest of women as a global majority lies in challenging existing productivist structures, women as an economic underclass are astonishingly well placed to bring about the social changes requisite for ecological revolution.

The question is, do ordinary women as domestic labour, factory workers or subsistence farmers have what the Club of Rome describes as a 'global perspective that extends far into the future'?[12] An ecofeminist response to this is yes, and that claim to intergenerational awareness will be enlarged on in due course. Even so, there is more than a touch of utopian idealism about the Club of Rome's concern. It is desirable from a humanist perspective for the subject of history to have a big picture, but it may not be strictly necessary structurally speaking. Sociologically, people located at an appropriate place in the system form an aggregate of actors who by carrying out their socially inscribed interests come to constitute a political force. It is actions, not words and ideas, that make change.

SPECIES, GENDERED AND POSTCOLONIAL OTHERS

Ever since the 1930s, marxism has been said to be in crisis because the working class failed to embrace its historical mission of overturning capital. Meanwhile, actually existing socialism in Eastern

Europe proved a travesty of Marx's original vision. Recent efforts to devise an eco-socialism are an implicit acknowledgment of the tragic fate of the socialist ideal. Even so, ecomarxists such as Joe Weston or James O'Connor of the journal *Capitalism Nature Socialism* still champion the political agency of trade unions, although O'Connor is open to a possible alliance of labour and new social movements. Weston, meanwhile, wonders about the radical potential of the 'disenfranchised', free as they are of party affiliation.[13] After all, green activists from Jeremy Seabrook to Jonathon Porritt agree that it is working-class people who are most likely to suffer from unhealthy jobs and polluted living environments.

Less often raised as an issue for concern is the situation for people of colour. When it comes to labour, distinctions between class and race are often blurred in the public imagination. Thankfully, a new politics of environmental racism articulated by Robert Bullard and others is sharpening up the debate in North America.[14] But given the feminisation of poverty that follows from capitalist patriarchal economic 'development' North and South, where does the impact of class or race end, and gender effect begin? Dobson, who is keen to integrate socialist theoretical insights within ecologism, responds to the question of historical agency by looking out for who in contemporary societies is most thoroughly 'disengaged' from the general interest – a grouping that 'profoundly questions the presuppositions on which present social practices depend':

> it might be argued from a Green perspective that the external limits imposed on the production process by the Earth itself are beginning to shape a class that is more or less permanently marginalised from the process of consumption.[15]

Dobson turns away from a possible ecofeminist reading of this outsider status to a thesis based on consumption potential. Hence, he picks the unemployed as the force most likely to usher in social change in the late twentieth century. According to neo-marxist André Gorz's *Paths to Paradise*, these 'post industrial neo-proletarians', cruelly marginalised, may even be majorities, as formerly in South Africa, 'deemed to be socially inferior and inadequate and effectively denied all participation and activity. They remain outcasts and objects of resentment'.[16]

Gorz, like Bahro, includes Third World people among the 'disaffected', but in doing so both authors conflate class factors with ethnicity or postcolonial difference. And gender is simply ignored by Gorz. Moreover, in any such analysis it is crucial to distinguish economic interests of investor elites in newly industrialising countries (NICs) from those of ghetto dwellers and rural subsistence producers. Poor Third World metropolitans are usually reluctant consumers, having lost their autonomy through government-sponsored land enclosures.

On the other hand, unemployed people in the North may not be readily able to buy things, but is this grounds for concluding that they are disengaged from the prevailing capitalist system of accumulation? Have they truly dropped out in the countercultural sense endorsed by Bahro? Certainly, Gorz's agenda suggests this grouping is still mightily into productivism:

> the mass of dis-affected non-workers is the possible social subject of the struggle for work sharing, generalised reduction of work-time, gradual reduction of waged work by the expansion of autoproduction, and for a living income for all.[17]

Against Gorz, Boris Frankel, author of *The Post-industrial Utopians*, queries whether the unemployed actually have the numbers to make any political impact.[18] It is also debatable whether the unemployed are really as 'alienated' as Dobson believes. But in any case they are likely to lack alternative insights by which to formulate a constructive future option. In fact, Dobson more or less admits this, by proposing that middle-class ecologists might have a vanguardist role in helping make the unemployed aware of social alternatives.

Another contender for the vanguard role might be women, North or South. Whether farmers or domestic labour, their inscribed gender difference has left them historically outside of industrial commodity production and focused on reproducing the conditions of daily life. Their hands-on domestic and subsistence skills provide a means of resisting the irrational excess of a capitalist patriarchal system that they have little egoic need to preserve. Yet Dobson seems to share economist Herman Daly's pessimism that it is unrealistic to think anyone would choose 'simplicity and frugality' unless under great duress.[19] He is left wondering how to make a start towards revolution, while Frankel complains there is not enough advice in the green literature on getting from 'here to there'.

Since the 1970s, postmodernism has eclipsed the popularity of socialism among radical thinkers. Inspired by Michel Foucault, Derrida and others, the trend began as a movement concerned with the elucidation of texts.[20] However, the tenets of deconstructive practice have been catechised and used as political rhetoric, resulting in an impractical nihilism when applied to everyday life. While structural analysis is useful for exposing hidden agendas in writing, the overall effect of its verbal circuitousness – a schism between idealist and materialist spheres – is to massage the liberal political status quo. A politics locked into the cultural realm like this simply cannot go anywhere; it is ahistorical.

Andrew Ross's treatment of ecology in *Strange Weather* typifies the dissociated textual production that ensues.[21] Like democracy in America, the postmodern paradigm celebrates openness, diversity and liberal pluralism. Its systemic underpinnings downplay any notion of an existential subject, actively working for change. Humanist marxism or feminism are treated as *passé*. The very idea of a totalising theory or 'metanarrative' positing a specific agent of history is met with contempt. Foucault himself was active in prisoner and gay rights campaigns, but the disconnection between his own political engagement, on the one hand, and the absence of 'universal' guiding principles, on the other, exemplifies the classic self-contradiction of discourse politics.

A postmodern theory of identity politics has been developed by Ernesto Laclau and Chantal Mouffe in *Hegemony and Socialist Strategy*. They, along with ecologist Fritjof Capra, sociologists Carl Boggs and Stanley Aronowicz, and libertarian Dennis Altman all bank on the new social movements as catalysts for revolution. Herbert Marcuse's neo-marxism included marginals and students here.[22] Similarly anarchists, along with social ecologist Murray Bookchin in *The Modern Crisis*, favour the political agency of 'new classes' such as 'ethnics, women, countercultural people, environmentalists, the aged, the *déclassé*, unemployables or unemployed'.[23] Most of these authors have remarked on the parallel between 'feminine' and green ideals. However, the collapse of these assorted groupings together as historical actor is both unsociological and eurocentric. The making of an earth democracy must take into account subsistence farmers and indigenous hunter-gatherers as participating citizens.

Jürgen Habermas swells the list of new activists with a couple more: tax protesters and fundamentalist religious groups. But with respect to far-reaching ecopolitical transformation, it is essential to distinguish between groups with particular aims and those seeking 'fundamental change from a universalistic viewpoint'. Habermas does this, finding that the women's movement alone qualifies on both counts. Sociologist Anthony Giddens names movements against capital accumulation, surveillance, military power, and industrialisation, and is surprised to find that feminist objectives cut across each of these categories. This contrasts with Frankel's rather jaundiced view of movements, including feminism, which he sees as lacking a formed identity.[24] It is encouraging to find Alain Lipietz, French Green Party cadre and author of *Green Hopes*, commenting on the 'blind spot' covering feminine oppression in both liberal and socialist writing. But Lipietz too goes no further; feminism is merely 'a component' of political ecology.[25]

AN OLD BLIND SPOT

Women dissolve away again in Werner Hülsberg's book, *The German Greens*, in which the social basis of the Grünen is said to be made up of romantic nationalists, anthroposophists, reformist Christians, democratic socialists, and left and hippie subcultures. Hülsberg does acknowledge a 'crisis in the reproduction sector' and makes occasional reference to the women's movement, but he does not perceive the subculture of femininity as a salient motivational structure. For the truth is that most women can only enter politics on a capitalist patriarchal agenda.[26] It is unusual to find a Trotskyite like Hülsberg giving the nod to the movements and accepting that civilisation itself is on the wrong path. Nevertheless, with social democrats Habermas and Claus Offe, his own political practice remains eurocentric, masculinist, and 'realo', based on global planning and industrial compromise.

Meanwhile, P. Lowe and W. Rudig, writing in the *British Journal of Political Science*, surmise that the green movement is 'a totally new political cleavage'.[27] But the technocratic thesis that scientific knowledge is central to environmentalism remains very popular. Developers and greens both use risk analysis and science-trained experts to fill the upper echelons of the ecological establishment. Yet science is neither a necessary nor a sufficient condition for protest against the destruction of livelihood. Commonsense observation of the spread of sickness and plant deformities is sufficient for women and indigenous groups to challenge the capitalist patriarchal growth ethic. More often than not, the scientific fraternity is concerned to suppress dangerous findings in order to protect free enterprise. The mystifications surrounding the spread of mad cow disease in Britain and the 1995 escape of the rabbit *calici* virus from field tests in South Australia are typical.

Sociologist Leslie Sklair adopts Timothy O'Riordan's taxonomy: of dry greens wanting self-regulation and tech fixes; shallow greens wanting regulation via 'user pay' instruments; and deep greens wanting a fundamental shift from consumer-based society. On the assumption that any genuine challenge to capital lacks majority appeal, Sklair advocates green consumerism with TNCs and nongovernment organisations (NGOs) working together. Although he personally admires deep ecology, Sklair overlooks its androcentric limitations – a major ecofeminist concern. He does recognise the presence of women service workers in the ecology movement, but not the unique habitus of women as a source of countercultural values. Thus, he claims:

'The only counter-cultures that present potential threats to global capitalism, now that Stalinist communism is thoroughly discredited, are Islamic fundamentalism and the "green" or environmentalist movement.'[28]

The difficulty ecopolitical analysts have in acknowledging ecofeminist politics and its literature is telling. Michael Redclift and Ted Benton, in the introduction to their anthology *Social Theory and the Global Environment* make this observation:

> One consequence of the absence of gender analysis in the environmentalist discourses is the failure to recognise that the environmental relations of women reflect prevailing gender ideologies and struggles. ... Another consequence of the absence of gender analysis is that the assertion that environmental degradation is caused by 'poverty' remains unchallenged and unqualified.[29]

Even when women are visible, their contribution is processed in bourgeois liberal terms as a special interest; in fact, though, the ecofeminist thesis offers everybody a clean way out of a very confused historical conjuncture.

Dobson's account is refreshing for its early attention to ecofeminism, but it still repeats this tendency. What happens is that the terrain of ecofeminism is reduced to a specific feminist controversy over whether women's politics should be guided by a principle of 'equality' modelled on male-devised institutions or by a principle of gender 'difference'. Accordingly, exchanges between ecologism and socialism are characterised by Dobson as 'a debate between ways of thinking and acting', while ecofeminism is 'a debate within a way of thinking and acting'. In other words, ecofeminism has no wider contribution.[30] This has two effects: one is to miss the implication of ecofeminist epistemological critique for eurocentric culture at large; and the second is to disregard the value of ecofeminist *exposés* of undemocratic masculinism in the grassroots green movement itself. To ecofeminists, all ecologism appears light-green, partial and particularistic. Thus, according to Petra Kelly, men speak of peace as 'paying dividends', while ecofeminists think that nonviolence 'means that men are reconciled to themselves, with their own species, with nature and the cosmos ... disarmament means exposing one's own vulverability'.[31]

Steven Yearley's interpretation of women's ecopolitics also leads to their containment. He comments that the environmental movement has special reasons for being international in scope because threats readily flow across sovereign boundaries. Feminist issues on the other hand, while encountered in a variety of societies, are characterised as turning inward with a politics of the personal – employer, husband. However, as Swasti Mitter's *Common Fate, Common Bond* and Cynthia Enloe's *Bananas, Beaches and Bases* indicate, women's exploitation is intrinsically bound up with global politics through sex tourism, military bases, cash cropping, offshore manufacture, domestic servicing, and forced consumerism.[32] Women as an unpaid labour force are resourced by transnational capital just as if they were a natural commons.

Luke Martell's treatment of women's historical agency carries things a little further. His argument in *Ecology and Society* teases out different levels of linkage between feminism and ecology in ecofeminist thought. He writes that 'women' and 'nature' are both victims of men's abuse; both are ideological products of the Enlightenment culture of control; and both are constituted as identities by similar discursive processes and exploitations. Martell is uncommon among those outside ecofeminism in grasping women's relation to nature in a non-essentialising way. He notes that since 'ecofeminists aspire to [the practices of] femininity becoming more generalised throughout the population as a whole, [this] suggests that they do not assume femininity is biologically determined and fixed.'[33] Yet Martell does not use ecofeminist epistemology critique to frame his own discussion of green politics. If he did, he could not dismiss ecology as failing to break with old-paradigm thought.

Part of the difficulty in working toward a green synthesis is that both ecology and feminism are split internally between old and new movement tendencies – 'composites', in Alberto Melucci's terms.[34] Hence, liberal environmentalists lobby for licences to pollute and feminists lobby for anti-discrimination legislation – a piece of the same stale pie. Conversely, radical ecologists and ecofeminists envision appropriate technology and communal governance – a fresh pie. Deflected by the liberal element, Martell suggests that the feminist and peace movements are simply concerned with women's liberation and peace. His judgement thus falls back into a single-issue reading that is unduly pessimistic. For work on gender violence at women's refuges is not separate from work for a just green future. Second, the peace movement itself is highly gendered, a large portion of cadres being women of ecofeminist persuasion.

Ultimately, Martell prefers not to talk of any 'subject of history'. He faces a middle class weakened by divisions between humanists and the scientifically trained, a working class divided between workers and unemployed. He sees movements as too much 'issue based', and apparently not universally environmentalist.[35] Along with green liberal philosopher Robert Goodin, he argues that 'ideas' count more than materially determined groupings. Yet, at the same time, Martell leans to the left, recommending a practical alliance of greens with social democrats. This collapse of green politics into left reformism is quite pervasive and was the reason for Bahro's 'fundi' split from the Grünen. The corresponding choice for women activists is to join the green–left compromise; to build on the power base of liberal feminism; or to collaborate with indigenous movements. The last option is the one I would prioritise in an era of globalisation.

AGENTS OF HISTORY/NATURE

The basic premise of ecofeminist political analysis is that ecological crisis is the inevitable effect of a eurocentric capitalist patriarchal culture built on the domination of Nature, and domination of Woman 'as nature'. Or, to turn the subliminal Man/Woman=Nature equation around the other way, it is the inevitable effect of a culture constructed on the domination of women, and domination of Nature 'as feminine'. Equality feminists from liberal and socialist traditions are wary of discussing women in connection with nature, because it is precisely this loaded truism that men have used over the centuries to keep women in their place as 'closer to nature'. 'No Difference between the Sexes' is the catchcry of equality feminists mentored by Simone de Beauvoir. They fear that drawing attention to any gender difference will play into men's hands, reinforcing the standard repressive move. In this respect, greens such as Dobson are quite right to see ecofeminism as part of a debate within feminism.

Ecofeminism interrogates the very foundations of mainstream feminism, by pointing to its complicity with the Western androcentric colonisation of the life world by instrumental reason. But ecofeminism is far more than this, it confronts several self-styled radical political ideologies that stand at 'the end of history'.[36] Because they refuse to look below the surface to 'difference' as epistemology critique, many feminists, socialists, and greens see women environmental activists as locked in a dualist double bind with no escape. Dobson recounts the dilemma thus: 'either women side with nature and face the possibility of tightening their own subordination, or they seek liberation in terms disconnected from nature and abandon it to its fate as a resource'.[37] But this commonly expressed predicament is surely an artefact of one-dimensional thought habits.

The way out of any double bind is to recontextualise or reframe the problem, thinking it through dialectically. This is what a paradigm shift means. By moving to another level of abstraction, the contradictory tension between two static options can be resolved. Ecofeminism is just such a synthesis. This is not to say that ecofeminist women must think like philosophers. On the contrary, judging from the movement's global history, women North and South tend to arrive quite readily at ecofeminist insights as a result of the conditions they live in and the physical work they do. As distinct from men's lot, women's labouring activities are designed to protect life.

Women are not 'closer to nature' than men in any ontological sense. Both women and men are 'in/with/of nature', but attaining the prize of masculine identity depends on men distancing themselves from that fact. Ecofeminists explore the political consequences of this culturally elaborated gender difference. To valorise women's life-affirming orientations is not a reactionary turn 'back to nature'; rather, to quote Hazel Henderson: 'the maintaining of comfortable habitats and cohesive communities [is] the most highly *productive* work of society – rather than the most de-valued, as under patriarchal values and economics where the tasks are ignored and unpaid'.[38]

Taking rationality and autonomy out of the lexicon of bourgeois individualism and reframing them in a context of land-based cultures and domestic economies is a move towards subsistence and sharing. But exposing the frailty of high-tech development depends on finding a balance between prevailing masculine and historically undervalued 'feminine' skills. With a view to setting this change in motion, Marx's account of historical agency is helpful.

> A class must be formed which has *radical chains*, a class in civil society which is not a class of civil society, a class which is the dissolution of all classes, a sphere of society which has a universal character because its sufferings are universal, and which does not claim a *particular redress* because the wrong which is done to it is not a *particular wrong*, but *wrong in general* ... a sphere which finally cannot emancipate itself without therefore emancipating all those other spheres.[39]

Women do indeed have radical chains: their social containment in a sexualised reproductive sphere is bolstered by exclusion and harassment from male-controlled institutions. Women are indeed a class *in* civil society, which is not *of* civil society; the vote was not fully available to women in Switzerland until the 1990s. Women's restorative labours and knowledges cut across all classes – middle, working, peasant – and may yet prove the dissolution of old industrial concepts of class as such. Feminine suffering is universal because wrong done to women and its ongoing denial fuel the psychosexual abuse of all Others – races, children, animals, plants, rocks, water, and air. Ecofeminists make no particular claim for themselves, but a claim in general. An emancipation of the relational sensibility of women and its reclamation by men will release Earth energies.

2

ECOFEMINIST ACTIONS

A GLOBAL TAPESTRY

Ecofeminism is found in initiatives like women's legal challenges to giant nuclear corporations in the USA and tree-hugging protests against loggers in north India. These actions express a materially embodied standpoint grounded in working women's commonsense understanding of everyday needs. Despite cultural differences between women around the world, this new politics reflects a common intuition that somehow the struggle for a feminine voice to be heard is joined to the struggle for a nurturant, protective attitude towards our living environment. The word 'ecofeminism', turning up spontaneously across several continents during the 1970s, reflects that doubleedged political perspective.[1]

Women's ecological commitment is fed by an intimate biocentric understanding of how people's survival links in to the future of the planet at large. It is no surprise that reproductive risks, and dangers to public and occupational health arising from reckless use of technology were prominent early concerns. In the USA as far back as 1962 an astonishing series of law suits against the corporate world came from the kitchens of mothers and grandmothers: *Mary Hays v. Consolidated Edison, Rose Gaffney v. Pacific Gas, Jeannie Honicker v. Nuclear Regulatory Commission, Kay Drey v. Dresden Nuclear Power Plant, Dolly Weinhold v. Nuclear Regulatory Commission* at Seabrook.[2] In 1964, Brazilian women set up the Ação Democrática Feminina Gaucha which soon evolved into an advocacy group for sustainable agriculture. Before long, the question of self-determination had come into focus, as the continuum of eurocentric capitalist patriarchal exploitation of natural resources, of women, and of indigenous peoples was recognised.

Magazine articles on male supremacy and hierarchical structures in the environmental movement appeared, and arguments for collectivity, interdependence and decentralised campaign networks were developed. Parisian writer Françoise d'Eaubonne's *Le féminisme ou la mort* and US democratic socialist Rosemary Ruether's *New Woman, New Earth* gave early intellectual impetus to ecofeminism. Another French contribution along these lines was Anne-Marie de Vilaine's philosophical article 'La femme et/est l'écologie.[3] A conjectural history of the appropriative and self-deforming culture of masculine mastery was drawn. Celebrating the social value of caring, these authors explored the primordial affinity of women to household or *oikos*, habitat, and Earth's timely cycles. Curiously, that Greek word *oikos* is the etymological root for both ecology and economics, but somehow patriarchal economics lost its integral way.

In 1974, the unquiet death occurred of Karen Silkwood, union activist at Kerr-McGee's Oklahoma plutonium processing plant. In 1975, women blockaded the clearing of land for construction of a nuclear reactor at Wyhl in Germany. More than economic loss of vineyards, they said, it was a matter of our human being in nature. By 1976 in Australia, women Friends of the Earth in Brisbane, tired of supplying coffee, minutes and free sex, conferenced on women and ecology; Helen Caldicott, physician and mother, was campaigning vigorously against the mining of uranium; and women were taking a strong coordinating role in the new Movement Against Uranium Mining. Even the mainstream Australian magazine *Woman's Day* carried an article on women and the anti-nuclear issue in 1977, and similar material was coming out in *Ladies Home Journal*, *MS* and *Village Voice* in the USA. That year two groups – Another Mother for Peace and Women's Action for Peace – were formed in the USA and a consciousness-raising group, Women of All Red Nations (WARN), emerged among tribal peoples in South Dakota. These women were especially worried about aborted and deformed babies, leukaemia and involuntary sterilisation among their people.[4]

In Australia a bumper all-women's issue of the Friends of the Earth magazine *Chain Reaction* was produced in 1978, with critical articles on artificial needs and consumerism, the exploitation of animals for cosmetic manufacture, Aboriginal health, recycling and, of course, uranium.[5] Several separatist anti-nuclear groups had become established by now: Women Against Nuclear Energy (WANE) in Sydney, Melbourne, Hobart and Brisbane, Feminist Anti Nuclear Group (FANG) in Perth. Addresses were also circulating for feminist ecology collectives in Paris, Hamburg and Copenhagen; ads for feminist farming communes were popping up everywhere. A serious, scholarly yet magical and poetic text, Susan Griffin's *Woman and Nature: The Roaring inside Her* was published in 1978, as was theologian Mary Daly's compelling trial by words, *Gyn/ecology.* Elizabeth Dodson Gray's incisive little book *Green Paradise Lost* followed in 1979. Each of these women in her own way described the self-alienation of the eurocentric masculine ego; the obsession with control of Otherness, the fascination with militarism and death, and its cognitive counterpart in instrumental logic and calculation. Emphasising cultural change over economic injustices, they urged the need for a new language, reintegrating reason and passion. Wholeness.[6]

Again in 1978, near Niagara Falls, USA, local mothers leading the Love Canal Home Owners Association were fighting the authorities over shocking public health scandals caused by industrial chemical waste dumps in their town. A very mainstream political body, the US League of Women Voters, began lobbying for a moratorium on nuclear plant construction licences; the Young Women's Christian Association (YWCA) initiated an anti-nuclear education campaign; while the National Organisation of Women (NOW) instituted a National Day of Mourning for Karen Silkwood. A further group, Dykes Opposed to Nuclear Technology (DONT), organised a New York conference on the energy crisis as male-generated pseudo-problem, and a vigilant anti-expert Women and Technology Conference was held in Montana the same year.[7]

A trickle of papers on the ecofeminist connection was now arriving in GS feminist journals such as *Off Our Backs* and *Commonwoman.* In the UK *Womenergy* appeared, and nonviolence activists were reading numerous articles from and about women in *Peace News.* Whilst mainstream feminists greeted news of a man on the moon with 'And let him stay there!', Delphine Brox-Brochot of the Bremen Grünen called for an end to high-tech aggrandisement while millions still starve. From Manchester came an anarcha-feminist approach to the ecology question, with poet and painter Monica Sjoo reinforcing the personal-as-political theme and linking the ecofeminist problematic to mythic archetypes of femininity long devalued.[8]

Everywhere in the so-called developed world, women's political lobbies and protests over the effects on workers and children of pesticides and herbicides, of formaldehyde in furniture covers and insulation, of carcinogenic nitrate preservatives in foods, of lead glazes on china, were gaining momentum. But there was a weary road ahead; to quote Joyce Cheney:

> I am annoyed that I feel forced to deal with the mess the boys have made of the earth. It is a hard enough struggle to survive and to build and maintain a lifeaffirming culture ...[9]

Some First Wave feminists, thinking one-dimensionally, turned away from ecofeminism, seeing it as merely a public extension of the housewife role. But the new politics went much deeper than this. Another facet of the focus on pollution was a need, felt by many women demeaned by capitalist patriarchal expectations, to purify and rebuild a sense of self. The consistent linking of personal and political, inner and outer, is a feature of ecofeminist environmental work. Much of women's political activity has gone hand in hand with attention to psychological growth, usually undertaken in consciousness-raising sessions with a re/sisterly support group. This kind of revolutionary strategy entails a profound existential commitment.

Of course, an account of women's unique involvements should not suggest that they were not active in ecology and peace movements generally. Worldwide, over half the membership of such movements is female; women take a keen organisational, if not public leadership, role in them. What impresses is that so many re/sisters have felt this to be not enough. Hence, separatist associations calling themselves Women for Peace were set up in Australia, Switzerland, West Germany, Italy, France, Norway and, by 1980, the UK. A collective called Women Opposed to Nuclear Technology (WONT) organised a Women and Anti-Nuclear Conference in Nottingham that year, and two middle-of-the-road English organisations, the National Assembly of Women and the Cooperative Women's Guild, were rapidly becoming caught up in the peace issue as well. Another manifestation of the woman/peace axis occurred in Argentina between the years 1976 and 1983, with the Mothers of the Disappeared.[10]

In the USA, Women in Solar Energy (WISE) began meeting in Amherst, Massachusetts, and Ynestra King mounted the first Women and Life on Earth Conference there in April 1980. Next, a Mobilisation Against Conscription was staged in Washington, and in November 1981 a 2,000-strong body of women marched on the US capital, symbolically encircling the Pentagon. By now Helen Caldicott was international president of Physicians for Social Responsibility and had started a Women's Party for Survival in the USA, with some fifty state and local chapters. This was subsequently broadened to become Americans for Nuclear Disarmament. Meanwhile, more small journals – *Valley Women's Voice* and *Sojourner* in the USA, *Women* in the UK, *des femmes hebdo* and a special 1980 number of the French magazine *Sorcières* – were pumping ecology. In India, the *Manushi* collective published its influential piece 'Drought: God Sent or Man Made Disaster?'[11]

THE ROARING INSIDE HER

A book by historian of science Carolyn Merchant, entitled *The Death of Nature: Women, Ecology and the Scientific Revolution,* began to make itself felt in academic circles from this time on.[12] By the early 1980s, the following networks were operating in the USA: Lesbians United in Non-nuclear Action (LUNA), against Seabrook Reactor; Church Women United; Feminists To Save the Earth; Feminist Resources on Energy and Ecology; Dykes Opposed to Nuclear Technology (DONT), at Three Mile Island and Columbia's TRIGA reactor; Women for Environmental Health, demonstrating in Wall Street; Mothers and Future

Mothers Against Radiation, taking on Pacific Gas and Electricity; Women Against Nuclear Development (WAND); Spinsters Opposed to Nuclear Genocide (SONG), and Dykes Against Nukes Concerned with Energy (DANCE), against United Technology. More women's environmental conferences were held, at Somona and San Diego State universities.[13]

In Japan, a kamakazi encampment of grandmothers known as the 'Shibokusa women' were running continual guerrilla disruptions against a military arsenal near Mount Fuji, while a further 2,500 women marched on Tokyo in the cause of world peace.[14] Women for Peace in the Netherlands started a series of chain letters which began weaving the globe in 1981, and 3,000 German women demonstrated at the Ramstein NATO base. In the UK, WONT had grown into a string of nonviolent direct action cells around the country – in Manchester, Leeds, Liverpool, Bristol, Brighton, Nottingham, Cambridge and Edinburgh. A more conservative response, the group Oxford Mothers for Nuclear Disarmament, was holding its first protest too. Australian Margaret Morgan drew together a rural anti-nuclear organisation at Albury, New South Wales, and the *Sun Herald* was reporting on the decisive intra-party policy stand by women of the Australian Labor Party (ALP) and Australian Democrats against any lifting of bans on uranium mining.

The US magazines *Heresies* and *Environment*, as well as the UK broadsheet *Sanity*, published by Campaign for Nuclear Disarmament (CND), all ran special numbers on feminism and ecology. Women on editorial boards, in research establishments, hospitals and universities had begun to weave the issue into their work and to use the resources of the workplace in their campaigns. The year 1981 climaxed on Hiroshima Day with a women-led March for Peace: 50,000 people walking from Copenhagen to Paris. A further peace walk followed in 1982, from Stockholm to Vienna via the USSR, and a Syrian women's peace march at Kuneitra attracted 5,000 supporters. On 8 March, International Women's Day (IWD), 15,000 women came out singing and dancing for peace in the streets of Brussels. In the USA, Catholic nuns were arrested on the White House lawns while praying for peace, and 3,000 women reinforced the first Pentagon Action, to the chant of 'take the toys away from the boys'.

The old-established Women's International League for Peace and Freedom (WILPF) and the Union of Australian Women injected heavy emphasis on disarmament into the Australian 1982 IWD celebrations. Other feminists protested outside the Smithfield airforce base in South Australia. In Britain, two more groups – Babies Against the Bomb and Families Against the Bomb – emerged, and by December 1982 there was a vast spontaneous grassroots swell calling itself Women for Life on Earth. Coordinated by Ann Pettitt and Stephanie Leland, 30,000 of these women converged on the Greenham Common missile site, creating a human chain around its nine-mile perimeter fence and decorating it with tokens of life: baby photographs, flowers and teddy bears. Moving accounts of their dissent, models of nonviolent direct action, can be read in *Undercurrents*, in Lynne Jones's edited collection *Keeping the Peace*, and in Alice Cook's and Gwyn Kirk's *Greenham Women Everywhere*, both 1983 publications.[15]

That year, as Ethiopian mothers came on to the streets to reclaim their children from conscription, Britain saw the continuing blockade of Greenham Common. There were repeated attempts by the state to enforce closure of the women's camp set up there; police violence; multiple arrests. Britain's left-wing *Guardian* newspaper would later describe these ecofeminists as 'moles on the dole'. Other women's blockades occurred in the UK at Capenhurst uranium enrichment plant, at the Marconi torpedo factory in Neston, and at bases in Northern Ireland; and in Sicily. Then an East German Women for Peace movement formed. 24 May 1983 was named Women's International Day for Disarmament and it brought synchronised actions from re/sisters all over the world.

In Australia, Women Against Rape in War and Women Against Violence Against Women together represented yet another facet of the insurgent global confrontation with the destructiveness of men in a capitalist patriarchal system. In Sydney a new collective, Women's Action Against Global Violence, staged a demonstration camp outside Lucas Heights Atomic Energy Establishment, and the year culminated with a nationally organised on-site protest in conjunction with Aboriginal men and women over the top-secret US reconnaissance station at Pine Gap in the heart of the Australian desert. In the UK, old-time radical educationalist Dora Russell diagnosed the modern malaise in her *Religion of the Machine Age*, and the first ecofeminist anthology, *Reclaim the Earth* was put out by Leonie Caldecott and Stephanie Leland. Wilmette Brown of the London Collective of Prostitutes now brought out her stinging critique of class and race blindness in the peace movement: 'Already in the women's movement, black and white working class women have been silenced from expressing justifiable rage because of the touchy-feely ethic which dominates.'[16]

A parallel effort to deepen the political agenda of environmentalists, at a 1983 Environment, Ethics and Ecology Conference in Canberra, provoked the perennial debate between ecofeminism and deep ecology.[17] While the 1983 British elections were notable for a combined Women for Life on Earth/Ecology Party ticket, ecofeminist Petra Kelly led the German Grünen into the Bundestag in the 1984 West German elections. Kelly's passionate autobiography, translated into English as *Fighting for Hope*, described how her moral and political drive grew from watching a young sister die of leukaemia. But the lack of gender awareness among many eco-activists would soon mar the experience of women in nascent green parties across the world. In 1984, US Ecology Party organiser and spiritual ecofeminist Charlene Spretnak coauthored *Green Politics*, revealing the sexism encountered by women in the German Green party. Helen Caldicott's *Missile Envy*, a study of the nuclear arms race as psychopathology, delved further into masculinism.[18]

That year, a new Third World network called Development Alternatives for Women in a New Era (DAWN) was launched in Bangalore, and a graduate course on ecofeminism was offered at the University of New South Wales. In Botswana, women formed an NGO known as Thusano Lefatsheng, with a research farm for supposedly inferior veld plant crops such as the morula fruit, morama tubers and beans, and the medicinal Kalahari devil's claw. This work now supports a thriving market trade. Meanwhile, Namibian women tackled corporate dumping of obsolete medicines in their communities and surreptitious use of Depo Provera by the South African government to control their fertility. By July 1985, the World Conference of the United Nations Decade for Women was buzzing in Nairobi. Here, Finland's Hilkka Pietila gave her path-breaking workshop on ecofeminist economics, a thesis circulated in pamphlet form as *Tomorrow Begins Today*. In the months that followed, a Filipino Women's Manifesto, from the GABRIELA coalition, would claim 'women know all about exploitation', because we live as victims of monopolies and false advertising.

Throughout the 1980s, hispanic mothers in Los Angeles, joined by black and some white mothers too, relentlessly opposed a planned incinerator near their homes.[19] The reactor accident at Chernobyl, USSR, in 1986 alerted women to the lack of accountability in capitalism and socialism alike. Across Germany and Eastern Europe, a 'birth strike' expressed outrage, as governments from Turkey to France suppressed vital facts about environmental radiation levels for fear of damaging national economies. Sami peoples to the north of Scandinavia met official lies with a firm resolve for land rights. From the other side of the Earth, Joan Wingfield of the Kokatha tribe flew from the Maralinga site of British nuclear bomb tests in the 1950s to address the International Atomic Energy Authority conference in Vienna.

Meanwhile in Caracas, Venezuelan architect Giovanna Merola was publishing an ecofeminist tract *La mala vida*, and out of Eureka Springs, Arkansas, came a thoroughly researched little handbook called *We All Live Downstream*, spelling out the 'how to' of water conservation. 'No headway till we've toilet trained America,' according to Barbara Harmony, travelling the USA with her Water Centre trading table. In Czechoslovakia and India too, women worked to make the voice of water heard above the rumble of dam builders. In 1986, sociologist and activist Maria Mies produced her *Patriarchy and Accumulation on a World Scale*, the first substantial socialist ecofeminist analysis and critique of high-tech notions of progress.[20]

DEEPENING ECOLOGY

Equally preoccupied with technology, though rather more New Age, was bioregionalist Chellis Glendinning's *Waking Up in the Nuclear Age*. In 1987, Darlene Keju Johnson of the Marshall Islands, Lorena Pedro of Belau, and others from Women

Working for a Nuclear Free and Independent Pacific, went public about the jellyfish babies born to island women and about radiation-induced cancer among ocean communities following US atomic tests. The month of April 1987 saw the First International Ecofeminist Conference held on campus at the University of Southern California. Another woman's love for the green wild tumbled out in poems:

> If ever you have seen a knuckled pine
> grasp a ledge, water tumble
> cold minerals in spring, steelheads
> gum the edge of their galaxy for flies,
> or a long scalp of bending timothy hay
> take a rolling hill to be its own …
> —Emily Hiestand[21]

Ecocentrism was also reflected in passionate animal liberationist statements from ecofeminists such as Connie Salamone, and others like Marti Kheel – who blockaded the US Greens chicken barbecue in 1987. The book *Rape of the Wild* by Andrée Collard and Joyce Contrucci, soon unfolded the horrors of animal experimentation in the scientific laboratory. By 1989, capitalist and communist hegemonies were both to be unsettled by dissident women. Earth First! activist Judi Bari was badly injured when a car bomb exploded under the seat of her car as she was on her way to an anti-logging protest on the US west coast. Later, in cross-examination over a timber machinery torching, Bari defended herself thus: 'I was in bed with five witnesses.' In China, former physicist and children's storyteller Dai Qing, opponent of the Three Gorges Dam, suffered prison and torture after the Tiananmen Square uprising.[22]

Next, Marilyn Waring's *Counting for Nothing* delivered an ecofeminist challenge to Keynesian economics. This New Zealand parliamentarian-turned-goat-farmer highlighted women's role in a global production system whose gross national product (GNP) indicators are tied to military activity. Netherlands development worker Irene Dankelman gave the literature another international turn with *Women and Environment in the Third World.* Co-authored by Joan Davidson, this study analysed women's labour with nature as producers of food, water managers, conservers of energy, and collectors of medicinal plants. Here we learned about our re/sisters in the Pinabetal Women's Organisation, Mexico; Women of Bhopal, India; Green Belt Movement, Kenya; and Ação Democrática Feminina Gaucha, Brazil.

A study of US women activists by Anne Garland, sponsored by the Ralph Nader think-tank, also came out in 1988; it told of the isolation that women activists encounter in their work for life, and the anger that drives them and protects them from threat and ridicule. A year later Rachel Carson, another lonely figure and perhaps the first ecofeminist, was honoured by Pat Hynes in *The Recurring Silent Spring.*[23] Hynes, a civil engineer, was a disaffected staffer at the Environmental Protection Agency (EPA). In 1989 the National Women's Studies Association Conference held its first session on ecofeminism and gave rise to an *Ecofeminist Newsletter* edited by Noel Sturgeon.

By the close of the decade, ecofeminists had strengthened their political critique of the transnational structure of oppression – a New World Order in which so-called advanced societies were rapaciously dependent on the resources and labour of an 'undeveloped' Other. Voices from the periphery were major catalysts in this, notably those of journalist Gail Omvedt and others in *Women and Struggle* and Vandana Shiva in *Staying Alive: Women,*

Ecology and Development, which has run to several reprints. At a 1989 meeting in Bangladesh, the Feminist International Network of Resistance to Reproductive and Genetic Engineering (FINRRAGE) produced its Camilla Declaration castigating the assault on women's reproductive powers in the name of scientific advancement.

Meanwhile, a Czech survey showed that fathers were spending nine minutes a day with children. But given the new liberal climate in the country, a plethora of womanist groups was forming: the Political Party of Women and Mothers, Prague Mothers, Single Mothers, and Gypsy Women.[24] With love and hope in the face of gendered insanity, Serbian women formed a green democratic party called Zenska Stranka in November 1990. The analysis by Hilkka Pietila and Jeanne Vickers of the role of women in development agencies, *Making Women Matter: The Role of the United Nations*, gave encouragement to the globalisation of ecofeminist politics in a world where every day one whole species dies out.[25]

In the USA, Carol Adams's book *The Sexual Politics of Meat* explored the cultural meaning of vegetarianism. Essays on ethics, art, self-realisation, and ritual featured in edited collections like Judith Plant's *Healing the Wounds: The Promise of Ecofeminism* and Irene Diamond's and Gloria Orenstein's *Reweaving the World: The Emergence of Ecofeminism.* In US society, where an entrenched division between mental and manual labour exists, a socialist ecofeminism grounded in day-to-day material questions has been slow to take on. Excellent reports such as *Turning Things Around: A Women's Occupational and Environmental Health Resource Guide* looking into the tintacks of daily survival have not made centre stage.[26]

By 1990, Sydney ecofeminists were lobbying a federal government inquiry into genetically modified organisms; offering a community course on Women, Science and Society; and setting up a small quarterly called *ecofeminist actions*. In Chile, women under the Pinochet regime set up Radio Tierra in order to highlight women's political agency, demystify the feminine stereotype, connect with indigenous ways, and learn again how to relate collectively and in harmony with the natural environment.[27] In New York, a spiritually oriented reading circle, Ecofeminist Visions Emerging (EVE), was meeting in 1991; in Minnesota, academic Karen Warren steered a special issue of *Hypatia: A Journal of Feminist Philosophy*. US ecofeminism was now coming under attack from social ecology, and ideological exchanges between ecofeminism and the gatekeepers of eco-socialism were getting under way in the journal *Capitalism Nature Socialism*.[28] As for the political mainstream, the masculinist fix on Big Oil climaxed as mothers of US children were dispatched to the Gulf; inadequate welfare provision at home gave many single African-American parents no choice but a job in the forces.

These were years when women permaculture farmers spread the word about the one-straw alternative to monoculture, when Green Grannies chained themselves to Forestry Commission barricades to save Chaelundi, and Mary Hutchinson and Marilyn Opperman turned themselves into artists-in-residence at Mugga Lane garbage tip near Canberra. Y's Eyes activist Ruth Lechte was putting out her *Energy and Environment Newsletter* from Fiji, with accounts of re/sister groups in Japan, the Solomon Islands, Uruguay and Denmark. Zimbabwe ecofeminist Sythembiso Nyoni told Sydney audiences about her grassroots community development work, and Julia Martin brought ecofeminism to literature courses at the University of the Western Cape, South Africa. In Canada's Great Lakes area, a new Women and Environments Education and Development Foundation (WEED) was campaigning strenuously on the ecological and health impacts of the chlorine industry.[29]

November 1991 saw the New York Women, Environment and Development Organisation (WEDO), led by former Congresswoman Bella Abzug and Mim Kelber, host a Women's Congress for a Healthy Planet in Miami. Here, a Women's Action Agenda was developed as a guide for the upcoming UN Earth Summit. A response to devastating International Monetary Fund (IMF) structural adjustment provisos (SAPs) came from the Caribbean DAWN, while the costs of the General Agreement on Tariffs and Trade (GATT) were spelled out by lawyer Kristin Dawkins of the Institute for Food and Agriculture Policy. At the UN Earth Summit itself in Rio de Janeiro in June 1992, women from all continents converged on the huge marquee Planeta Femea to renew their vision. In the UK, the *Ecologist* marked 1992 with a special women and ecology issue. But it was also a cruel year. In February, Peruvian women's leader Maria Elena Moyano fell to the death squads. In April in Kenya Wangari Mathai, founder of the Green Belt programme, was beaten unconscious by police at a Nairobi demonstration and forced into exile. Kenyan women who stood in the December elections were punished by ostracism and even rape; nevertheless, among them forty-five civic leaders and six parliamentarians were successful.[30]

BIOCOLONISATION

With Yugoslavia torn in two, an unpublished manuscript circulating between Kosovo and New York described how women were seen as symbolic of the national consciousness. Thus violation was encouraged as a trespass on the enemy's land. The Croatian Women's Party replied with a Centre for Anti-War Action.[31] From

Hungary, Judit Halasz sent news that a green women's group was forming there and that women in Poland were active. In October, Petra Kelly, under constant attack in public and now speaking out about the upsurge in neo-fascist violence in Germany, was mysteriously shot dead at her home in Bonn. Despite such crushing losses, ecofeminism seemed to be coming home: the reflective editorial on Kelly's death by Michael Hammond of the UK journal *Environmental Values* was a strong sign. By now, the mainstream US feminist magazine *Ms* was running a regular ecofeminist column, and Rosemary Ruether had produced *Gaia and God: An Ecofeminist Theology of Earth Healing.*[32]

Connections between socialism, feminism and ecology were revisited by UK sociologist Mary Mellor in her *Breaking the Boundaries*, though socialist-identified Mellor avoided calling her position 'ecofeminist'. Joni Seager's book *Earth Follies: Coming to Feminist Terms with the Global Environmental Crisis* also drew heavily on ecofeminist politics, yet with Second Wave feminist caution about linking women and nature too closely.[33] By now, the Women's Environment Network (WEN) in London, steadily working away on consumer matters, closed in on the chocolate industry. Researcher Cat Cox found women on Malaysian and West African cocoa plantations had menstrual irregularities, nosebleeds, dizziness and rashes caused by Lindane pesticide sprays. A new boycott of Nestlé products was announced.

Post-Rio, the Canadian journal *Women and Environments* put together a special number on 'development', and a spate of new ecopolitical books by women were published in 1993. Australian authors included Val Plumwood, whose *Feminism and the Mastery of Nature* gave a detailed critique of Western dualism, and Corin Bass and Janet Kenny, whose *Beyond Chernobyl* collected the stories of women living through the meltdown. Greta Gaard's

US anthology *Ecofeminism: Women, Animals, Nature* took a new look at animal liberation and in particular the question of political inclusiveness. As she put it, 'the ideology which authorises oppressions such as those based on race, class, gender, sexuality, physical abilities, and species, is the same ideology which sanctions the oppression of nature'.[34] An international volume from Brazil, *Ecologia, Feminismo, Desenvolvimento*, edited by Maria Inacia d'Avila and Naumi de Vasconcelos, also hit the shelves in 1993, along with *Ecofeminism* by Maria Mies and Vandana Shiva. The latter gave a definitive account of bio-colonisation from green revolution to *in vitro* fertilisation and surrogacy. As Shiva summed up the situation, 'liberation is best to begin from the colonised and end with the coloniser'.[35]

In a sense, all women are colonised – by men right and left, Catholic, Muslim, communist. So activists from fifteen European countries went to Zagreb in February 1993 to protest against rape camps in the Balkan War. Outraged by the Archbishop of Sarajevo's direction that raped women 'accept the enemy into them' as 'flesh of their own flesh', they turned to the Geneva Convention to get rape accepted as a war crime. Meanwhile, a capitalist patriarchal press heralded commercial breakthroughs in the use of umbilical cords for cancer treatment. Protesting against the resourcing of women and nature alike, Patsy Hallen's *Habitat* essay 'Ecofeminism: Reawakening the Erotic' was greeted by howls of protest from the Australian science-trained conservation fraternity.[36] But women's momentum was unstoppable.

By 1994, international ecofeminist meetings were proliferating: Women, Politics and Environmental Action organised by Natalia Mirovitskaya at Moscow State University; Women and Agriculture in Melbourne; Science, Students and Sustainability at Sydney's Macquarie University. Also in Sydney, veteran ecofeminists Carol Sherman and Lee Rhiannon called a major gathering of World Bank watchers. At the same time, Indian anti-dam organiser Medha Patkar, of the Narmada Bachao Andolan, collected two thousand NGO signatories for her Manibeli Declaration against World Bank megaprojects on communal farmlands. In July 1994, the Institute for Social Ecology in Vermont found heart and hosted a summer symposium for North American ecofeminists. In September, women at the UN Conference on Population in Cairo argued their rights with frocked citizens of the all-male Vatican state.

In November, Raina Lai-Lin Grigg exhibited ecofeminist paintings and sculptures at the Queen Emma Gallery, Honolulu; mothers marched with photographs of deformed Chernobyl children to halt a fourth nuclear power plant in Taiwan; seventy-year-old Roz Boyd could be found working a stall for New York Greens at Farmers Markets in Union Square; Russian mothers arranged a peaceful exchange of prisoners at Chechnya; and the Liberian Women's Initiative brought warring parties to the table in Monrovia. That year too, the Jewish-Palestinian organisation Women in Black faced down the Israeli army on the road to El-Khader, site of settler land grabs; New Zealand Greenpeace started a Green Women's Network; and Ngarrindjeri women blocked construction of a road bridge to their sacred fertility site at Hindmarsh Island south of Adelaide. Their stand on the veracity of 'secret women's business' would soon turn into a multi-million-dollar witch-hunt through the courts.[37]

The 1995 US National Political Congress of Black Women took Time Warner to task over violent images of women in gangster rap. In Bangladesh, women echoed Taslima Nasrin's call for land redistribution and an end to outrageous fatwas on female factory workers and molested village girls. Australian medical researcher Lynette Dumble campaigned tirelessly on the use of women as pharmaceutical company guinea pigs; hospital workers created a waste watch group called Nursing the Environment; and ecofeminism found itself upstaged by a packaging industry public relations front called Mothers Opposing Pollution (MOP).[38]

In advance of the Fourth World Conference on Women for Equality and Development in China, Helen Hill brought Asia-Pacific activists together in Melbourne – including Hesti Wijaya from rural Indonesia, Vivienne Wee from Singapore's ENGENDER, Philippines community worker Luz Lopez Rodriguez, and Irene Fernandez of Asia-Pacific Pesticide Action Network in Malaysia. September 1995 found delegates to the Fourth World Conference harassed by Beijing police and facing a newfound brotherhood of the Vatican, Sudan, Iran, and Yemen over control of female sexuality. Another aspect of masculine resourcing under the spotlight in Beijing was the Burmese slave trade in 'AIDS-free' twelve-year-old girls.

While historically ecofeminists close to the dominant English-speaking publishing houses got their ideas broadcast first, voices from the periphery are being heard more often now. At the Conference on Equality and Development, Kanaky and Tahitian women had plenty to say about the lot of French colonised peoples. Later, during French nuclear bomb tests in the Pacific, Losena Salabula and friends would march through Suva streets, while WILPF re/sisters mounted embassy vigils from Wellington to London. In Hamburg, a national roundtable of women architects met in November 1995 to prepare for the UN conference Habitat Two; participants were pleased to note that most women already use sustainable modes of transport.[39]

Ecofeminism is about engendering a discourse where not only nature is a subject to be emancipated, but women and men –

as nature – are too. So wise matrilineal tribeswomen from Milne Bay, Papua New Guinea, are resisting World Bank proposals for 'registration' of their communal lands. In Suva, Aroha Te Pareake Mead warns against commodifying traditional knowledge of fish and plants through intellectual property law and patents. Henrietta Fourmile from Cape York urges Aboriginals and Torres Strait Islanders to be wary of the Human Genome Biodiversity Project and prospecting TNCs. Indigenous resistance to capitalist patriarchal folkways is sharpened by bio-colonisation – the latter's *in vitro* technologies pioneered on the compliant bodies of suburban housewives in the North. Meanwhile, a US Indigenous Women's Network has invited Disney Corporation to share its $34 million spoils from *Pocahontas*, the movie.[40] Theft takes many forms.

PART II

AN EMBODIED MATERIALISM

3

BODY LOGIC: 1/0 CULTURE

THE POLITICS OF DIFFERENCE

Women, peace workers, greens, anti-racist and indigenous alliances introduce a form of politics quite distinct from the modernising ambitions of nationalism or labour. The new movements set out to unmake cultural habits that are deeply ingrained in daily life. Alain Touraine describes this activism reaching beyond conventional political institutions as 'a different type of social conflict, whose stake is control of the main social patterns, that is, the patterns through which our relationship[s] with the environment are normatively organised'.[1]

Modernism delivered neither liberty nor equality across the board, though fraternity continues to enjoy the glow of the hearth. Moreover, as we have seen, women's political agency is all but invisible to theorists of socialism and ecology.

The process of tracing systems of ideas to their bedrock in social life is called the sociology of knowledge. When it comes to normatively organised relations, there is no doubt that a complex historical fallout of actions, feelings and ideas has led to the sedimentation of masculine domination over time. By tracing the strains of that hegemony through culture – nature – body – labour – logic – technology – culture – and around again, ecofeminism shows how, in the last analysis, all social movements share a common denominator. This chapter looks at the social construction of libidinal energies in gendered form, and how sublimations of these forms come to be validated as a ubiquitous 'logic' of identity and difference. To steal an innocent phrase from Vaclav Havel: 'The line does not run clearly between Us and Them, but rather through the heart of each man and woman.'

How so? Eurocentric cultures are arranged discursively around what has standing (A) and what does not (notA). Such a logic gives identity to A expressed by the value of 1. NotA is merely defined by relation to A, having no identity of its own, and thus 0 value. While this thought habit is not necessarily universal, it is symptomatic of a phallus-loving society which favours the eye over all other senses. Psychoanalytically, the proposition reads: since only Man has 1, he is one. When you look at Woman, by contrast, you see only 0, a hole, zero. She is thus defined negatively as a lack. Woman is 'inferior', 'different', Other. That notions of logic are informed by conceptions of the body is demonstrated by the classic tragedy of Oedipus, who killed his father and slept with his mother. His transgression was literally unthinkable in terms of an identitarian logic, A = A, for he became son and husband to his mother, father and brother to his children. Nature does not conform to the 1/0 and must be put right by Humanity.

The 1/0 metaphor was implicit in Sherry Ortner's classic anthropological essay 'Is Female to Male as Nature Is to Culture'.[2] However, the same rationale of identity and difference marks the social relations of exploiters and colonisers regardless of historical context. The ancient Judaeo-Christian hierarchy reaching upwards from streams, rocks, forests, beasts, natives, children, women, to Man and his God rested on this crude system of value.[3] The English nursery game Farmer in the Dell sings the rightness of the ontology into each new infant mind. Until the 1960s, the Australian legal system actually classified Aboriginal peoples along with flora and fauna. Conversely, what is impressive about many indigenous ways of seeing is the fact that man is assumed to be the last and lowest form of life to be created: here is a genuine humility about our human dwelling in nature.

To point to Man/Woman=Nature assumptions as an ideological fabrication is not to deny what poet Adrienne Rich calls the amazing generative capacity of women's bodies, nor either to deny men's links with the natural.[4] Rather, it is to examine how a stereotypical gender dualism is imposed over everyday happenings, only to become a highly repressive social apparatus. In too many cultures, girls come to adulthood with assumptions about themselves as essentially Other: as instinct-driven, irrational creatures, as temptress, Earth Mother, dark, evil, damp, passive, moon goddess, and so on. Masculinity, by contrast, elicits associations of rationality, sun, activity, goodness, light and order. Man evokes law, regularity and permanence, while Woman implies chaos and unpredictability.

Fatna Sabbah's account of *Women in the Muslim Unconscious* shows how M/W=N notions pervade the legal, erotic and chivalrous discourses of Islam. As village shrines to the Earth Goddess were desecrated by the centralising messengers of Allah, supposedly masculine principles of reason and control were installed over female desire, disorder and devilry.[5] It is not far to travel from here north to the witch burnings of Scotland; east to the Chinese tradition of yin/yang; or south, where an Eritrean proverb announces, 'Just as there is no donkey with horns, so there is no woman with brains.'[6]

In Khomeini's Iran, the female marriage age was lowered to thirteen, then schools were directed not to accept married girls. Often, androcentric usages of difference are institutionalised through terror: for example, foot binding, suttee, or genital infibulation – actions that inscribe men's law over women's recalcitrant bodies.[7]

But it is up to women scholars to assess their own traditions and prove the cross-cultural validity or otherwise of the M/W=N pattern. The immediate ecofeminist focus is capitalist patriarchal relations, daily exported by metropolitan powers to peoples at 'the periphery'. Domination over nonhuman nature, black devils and white witches has been crucial to Western colonisation, each group facing inclusion yet exclusion from the rational social contract.[8] By conformity to the Great Chain of Being, most women have been reined in, domesticated; the rest have been resourced as 'dirty animal' whores. Tribal Aboriginals would be treated as 'vermin' to be extinguished, for in Australia it was native land for grazing that squatters were after, not cheap labour. Further down the Chain, a Save the Children study of military conflicts in twenty-six countries reports that even in the late-twentieth century, poor and orphaned children as young as six were being used by adult men for frontline soldiering and mine clearing.[9]

To speak of a dominant ideology is to denote a set of concepts convenient to those with power over others. Conservative thinkers invariably perpetuate the mystification of social relations by assuming that inequality reflects 'given' 1/0 capacities of black and white, masculine and feminine. From religious men to sociobiologists, the wisdom has been that women's reproductive process necessarily confines their social, intellectual and emotional functioning to nurture and associated tasks. The social division of labour between men and women is thus considered inevitable and good because it protects women's supposed natural inferiority and vulnerability. Arguments for the slavery of dark-skinned people echo the same logic.

These attitudes have graced the Western political tradition from Aristotle through the Church Fathers to Locke, Hegel and even Marx. As a result, any feminist talk of biology invites the charge of 'essentialism' from re/sisters anxious about capitulation to M/W=N code. The fact is that men are equally creatures of nature and our political theory should begin to take stock of this. There is no need to accept the dualism of either History versus Nature, or of Man versus Woman. In fact, sexualities form a continuum rather than a polarity.[10] The presence of hormonal oestrogens can produce an empathic, receptive orientation in bodies, whether male or female, animal or human. Under certain circumstances, a man also can feed a child at the breast. Currently, environmental pollution from chlorine-based products is causing feminisation of males, from fish to footballers, by stimulating bodily manufacture of oestrogens. Small penises, low sex drives and low sperm counts result. A strict M/W bifurcation cannot be upheld on biological grounds.

Feminists should note that physiological 'inscription' of the body is just as real as the discursive sort. The trouble is that powerful codes like the 1/0 formula become embedded in language and trap people's thinking in a seemingly changeless reality. By contrast, if we reason dialectically, we can open out the multiple potentials contained in our condition. As Theo Adorno would say: the object is never fully contained by the concept. An ecofeminist sociology of knowledge seeks to expose the connection between oppositional thought and sensual repression; in doing so, it lends support to gender, ethnic, and biological diversity. Julia Kristeva demonstrates this approach when she says, 'speaking subjects have within themselves a certain bisexuality which is precisely the possibility to explore all the sources of signification, that which posits meaning as well as that which multiplies, pulverises'.[11] To argue dialectically is like unwinding a chain that has become twisted over time. The first move in deconstructing an ideology is reversal, bringing into view the suppressed potentials of de-valued Others. But the recursive moment is never complete, because as we move with it, new historical forces come into play around us.

REPRODUCTIVE CONSCIOUSNESS

It is one thing to talk about biology with an unreflective positivist certitude, it is another to talk about how humans come to know nature through their bodies and to make sense of that experience. In *Green Paradise Lost*, Elizabeth Dodson Gray shares this view of 'a learning' that goes on somewhere between biology and gender socialisation. Hence she writes:

> Women during puberty come to an awareness of the long-term parameters of their sexual encounters, and if they do not immediately understand, they pay the price for their lack of comprehension. There is no comparable biological occasion for helping men overcome their penchant for taking short-term profit and exporting the long-term costs to others – women, other social groups, the environment.[12]

Midwife and philosopher Mary O'Brien carries this further, developing a gendered phenomenology based on observation of people in the act of reproducing their species selves. O'Brien notes that men encounter a process full of personal disjunctions and dissociations from the life process. In *The Politics of Reproduction*, she explains that the first of these occurs with

> the alienation of the male seed in the copulative act. The unity of the seeds is quite objective, not abstract at all, but it is a unity and development which is experientially present in an immediate way only to female reproductive consciousness.[13]

By contrast, a woman's consciousness of the seed as it grows enters an enduring time. The placenta is not a hard-and-fast boundary, so a mother's relation to the seed is a continuing biological negotiation between self and other. The pleasure of suckling a child is a reciprocal process, the very opposite of the 1/0 fracture.

Then again, a mother's separation from the seed during birth is an experience of hard physical work. The philosopher Hegel suggested that Woman could never attain full consciousness, because she did not risk the self-negation of death through conflict. Masculine-identified feminist Simone de Beauvoir followed his lead, eschewing what she called the 'mammalian function'. In the eurocentric tradition, not 'giving life' but 'risking life' is the event that raises Man above the animal.[14] In reality, reproductive labour is traumatic and highly dangerous. Each time a woman brings a child into the world she puts her life right on the line. The struggle to give birth is just as much moment of truth as the New Guinea shark hunter's ritual catch or the Russian astronaut's heroic display. But birthing is more than this: it is an experience that carves the meaning and value of life into flesh itself.

Now if, as Marx suggested, 'human consciousness develops dialectically because it reflects the primordial experience of people in their productive existence in the world', then it is easy to understand why men's and women's thoughts about life and labour come to be structured differently.[15] Unlike maternity which is practical, concrete and sensuous, men's effort to make sense of the life process is abstract and ideological. As O'Brien suggests, paternity is 'the conceptualisation of a cause and effect relationship'. I think it, therefore I am it: an act of patenting, labelling and appropriating. Against this quintessential idealism, women's epistemological orientation is a very much embodied materialism. Nevertheless it is important to remember that sexual reproduction is not the only source of such learning for women; they engage with the world in other ways too.

Women's involvement here is multisensual, whereas birth and suckling remain merely visual experiences for a man. The masculine reproductive experience is understood as an inclusion yet exclusion, 1/0, from the natural event. An early sociologist, Georg Simmel, acknowledged the sensibility that comes from women's privileged immediacy, describing it as living in a world without the fixed separation of subject and object.[16] This in turn implies a valuation of others that is direct, intrinsic, unmediated by some imposed standard of equivalence.

At childbirth, it is the man who 'lacks'. Why else should the act be so shrouded by secrecy, hushed voices, and now medical mystification. Nevertheless, paternity, basically a property relation, soon reinstates the correct 1/0 order of things. Once Named, the baby becomes 'his' child and the woman is incidental again. Recall the young Farah Diba sent from Paris to provide a son for the Shah of Persia and, more recently, how the body of Princess Di was used in the manufacture of monarchy. The sense of dislocation in masculine reproductive consciousness is very pervasive in the Western tradition, and it goes hand in hand with the suppression of women's actual contribution. Wordsworth even describes children falling from eternity into time by the hand of the first good Father:

> Our birth is but a sleep and a forgetting
> ... not in utter nakedness
> But trailing clouds of glory do we come
> From God, who is our home ...[17]

If men cannot 'produce' life, they can certainly 'appropriate' it, and thus fatherhood becomes formulated as a 'right'. But, O'Brien notes:

> The assertion of a right demands a social support system predicated on forced cooperation ... a patriarchate is, in every sense of the phrase, a triumph over nature. ... Men did not suddenly discover in the sixteenth century that they might make a historical project out of the mastery of nature. *They have understood their separation from nature and their need to mediate this separation ever since that moment in dark prehistory when the idea of paternity took hold.* ... Patriarchy is the power to transcend natural realities with historical, man-made realities. This is the potency principle in its primordial form.[18]

Engels's thesis in *The Origin of the Family, Private Property and the State* substantiates this 'world historic defeat' of women.[19] Nevertheless Engels did not perhaps appreciate the extent to which men would turn their 'right' to ownership of family labour into material measures of their worth through the 'production' of things.

This idea of production seems to have a symptomatic meaning for men, at least in eurocentric cultures, but the compulsion to produce appears to have brought the rest of life-on-earth to the brink of annihilation.[20] O'Brien suggests that in an attempt to bridge its experiential fracture from the life process and 'natural time', the alienative consciousness of men has invented compensatory 'principles of continuity' such as God, the State, History, now Science and Technology. The modern gynaecological profession, *in vitro* fertilisation, surrogacy, and biotechnology research mimic women's generative capacities, carrying men's powers to great heights. Third World people's bodies are invaded and mined in order to expand eurocentric frontiers. On 14 March 1995, the US National Institute for Health patented a gene from a member of the Hagahai people of Papua New Guinea. The contractual agreement promised a percentage of royalties from any vaccine or product containing retro viruses developed from this body tissue. Yet, in effect, the patent means that all Hagahai people become the property of the US government.[21]

Habitat and animal rights are equally disregarded. In Guatemala, for example, without notification to government or locals, the California-based pharmaceutical Asgrow conducts field trials on transgenic tomatoes and squash.[22] Japanese companies raid Africa for monkeys to use in AIDS vaccine research.[23] Sheep semen containing a human gene is exported to New Zealand for mass production of alpha-1-antitrypsin in ewe's milk – a treatment for chronic smokers with emphysema. Transgenic pigs are bred to 'give their hearts' to wealthy humans, and empirical men in white coats steal DNA from spiders' webs to make bulletproof vests.

The one principle of continuity that is missing is that of white men's own continuity with Nature. This marks only Woman's experience, positioned as biological and social mediator of Nature for men. However, 'the assertion of right without responsibility is the hallmark of naked power'.[24] What happens in the fullness of capitalist patriarchal time, is that men retain their 'rights' in a public and legal sense, while social 'responsibility' falls to women. The double standard with regard to ocean pollution is another case in point: the New South Wales government urges housewives not to tip cooking fat into their kitchen drains, but toxic heavy metal discharges to the sewer system by industry are ignored.

BOUNDARIES AND SPILLS

Extending the structural psychoanalysis of Lacan, Kristeva is fascinated by the special exile into Nature that marks women's lives and the insight that this alienation gives them. Whereas Virginia Woolf mourned because Woman has no country, Kristeva celebrates the feminine condition as intrinsically cosmopolitan: 'How can one avoid sinking into the mire of [masculine] common sense, if not by becoming a stranger in one's own country, language, sex and identity?'[25]

Fatherland, subjectivity, narcissism and legal standing belong to the realm of what is publicly signifiable, Lacan's 'symbolic' realm. As individuals mature, consciousness achieves a fixed ego identity by finding a place inside the law and language of the Father. But Kristeva is more interested in the material relations that exist prior to subjectivity. She attends to the bodily drives and discharges that show up in movement, voice timbre, laughter and word play.

This prelinguistic 'semiotic chora' is what gives embodiment and integrity to symbolic expression. Here, rules and categories give way to the memory of maternal *pleasure, jouissance,* where the subject-versus-object dichotomy is unknown. A logic of heterogeneity or diversity replaces the Father's 1/0 system of representation. The differentiation of self from M/Other is not brought about simply through language, according to Kristeva. There are presymbolic moves to break, and these correspond with the anal phase. As social relations stand, the mother's 'semiotic' authority sets up corporeal prohibitions in dealing with food, cleanliness, excrement, which helps the young ego towards unity and independence by marking out the boundaries of the body, 'me and not me', Humanity versus Nature.

In *Powers of Horror*, Kristeva describes how the most terrible phobia is that of imperfect separation from the mother. In the originary self-positing thetic moment, M/Other becomes unconsciously associated with what the drives expel – M/W=N. She is the internalised abject, the other side of the ego, what Narcissus does not want to see when he gazes into the pool. The murk and mud, soft flesh as opposed to the clean precision of anality. For regular guys, a litany of pub jokes armours the 1 from the fear and fascination with oral, anal, genital excretions. Menstrual blood, placenta ... the body may be both human and filth, and of course, it is always potentially a corpse: 'a decaying body, lifeless, completely turned into dejection, blurred between the inanimate and the inorganic, a transitional swarming'.[26] Where the identitarian logic of ego has been established, the corpse is absolute horror. Dissociated from natural time, the alienative consciousness finds death as problematic as birth. For what is death but the other end of lived time where humanity recedes ambiguously back into nature? Mothers, wives and daughters know this well. Greek peasant women wash their loved ones for burial chanting, 'the earth which fed you, now must eat you'. This same awareness is expressed in Rosemary Ruether's reminder:

> The sustaining of an organic community of plant and animal life is a continual cycle of growth and disintegration. The

> Western flight from mortality is a flight from the disintegration side of the life cycle, from accepting ourselves as part of that process. ... In order to learn to recycle our garbage as fertiliser for new life, as matter for new artifacts, we need to accept our selfhood as participating in the same process. Humans are also finite organisms, centres of experience in a life cycle that must disintegrate back into the nexus of life and arise again in new forms.[27]

But as against the spills and smells of birthing and dying which frame women's lives, the abstract principles of continuity – Church, State, and Science – fail to orient masculinity in enduring time. This is why Derrida repeats Hamlet's lament:

> 'The time is out of joint': time is *disarticulated*, dislocated, dislodged, time is run down, on the run and run down (*traque et detraque*), *deranged*, both out of order and mad. Time is off its hinges.[28]

Men's entry into the public realm is only achieved through a contract between brothers, a homosexual contract that must repress the originary *jouissance*. Kristeva notes that in societies where protection by patrilineal power is weak, there is a preoccupation with pollution. But what exactly does this mean? A favourite at the Gay Mardi Gras in Sydney is 'trough man', a public servant who lies naked in a horse trough inviting party-goers to urinate on his body at their pleasure. Is this defiance of corporeal prohibitions a celebration of pollution? And, if so, what are the prospects for a queer ecology?

Perhaps we should reorganise child 'caring' practices, so that fathers also get their hands dirty and mothers cease to become the butt of resistance?[29] Nancy Chodorow's *The Reproduction of Mothering* supports this logic, using object relations theory to account for the construction of gender difference.[30] Looking into the early years of life, she too finds that while a girl experiences her first living relationship empathically as a fusional continuum between self and mother, the boy child's ego identity emerges negatively, by differentiation between self and M/Other. Masculine identity is developed oppositionally in infancy by exclusion of those characteristics that nurturant Woman displays, 1/0. Hence the need for separation from intimacy by flight or fight, which many men go on to show in relations with women right throughout their lives.

At the same time, the father remains a distant figure in too many cultures, often unknown, deserting, gone to war, or simply a nine-to-five man. He is rarely primary carer; rather, he presents a hazy, abstract role – an imaginary ideal. But insecure identification for a son can lead to overcompensating macho posturing. In any event, the skewed process of identity formation appears to leave young boys in touch with only half of their psychological resources. Not surprisingly institutions that bolster the fragile ego have a long history. In this respect, the props of capitalist patriarchal privilege set up a deforming and vicious circle for men as much as for women.

According to Sally Cline and Dale Spender, women's role in the West is to mirror men at twice their size; those who refuse these labours are typically avoided.[31] Aggressive competition in sports, property ownership, administrative control of Others, technological manipulation of nature all are instruments of reassurance. The Man/Woman=Nature complex can thus be read as a collectively contrived compensation for lost wholeness of self. The preoccupation with personal potency in all its social manifestations, the making over of the environment according to masculine will, these things assuage the emptiness of the ungrounded self. Cornelius Castoriadis has this to say of the alienative consciousness:

> Humanity emerges from the Chaos, the Abyss, the Groundless. It emerges therefore as psyche: rupture of the living being's regulated organisation, representational/affective/intentional flux which tends to relate everything to itself and to live everything as constantly sought after meaning. This meaning is essentially solipsistic, monadic ... the human species is radically unfit for life.[32]

The world of 1/0 relations rests on a shocking reversal of material reality. It is the capitalist patriarchal ego that experiences itself as void (0) and must constantly affirm itself by consuming the energy of the Other – native, woman, child (1). Psychiatrist Phyllis Chesler describes the unresolved violence that hovers around the memory of the originary break with nature:

> What, oh what do men want? To forget, to deny, to relive; the rape, the dismemberment, the murder of the original parent. Matricide, not patricide, is the primal and still unacknowledged crime. Father killing comes only later.[33]

The wish for monuments, permanence and identity, is a substitute for the lost knowledge of oneness.

Identitarian logic is reflected in old notions of Man as form or essence, and of Woman as merely matter/mater/inert stuff, like Nature. In the culture of domination, recognition of women's potency is too much threat, annihilating to men. Woman is only 'good' when bound by the Father's law. Nature too must be harnessed.

> The products of necrophilic Apollonian male mating are of course the technological 'offspring' which pollute the heavens and the earth. Since the passion of necrophiliacs is for the destruction of life and since their attraction is to all that is dead, dying, and purely mechanical, the father's fetishized 'fetuses' (re-productions/replicas of themselves), with which they passionately identify, are fatal for the future of this planet.[34]

Mary Daly's conclusion is uncompromising; some might say unkind. Nevertheless, a connection with these subliminal drives must be made if we are to understand why the global political response to ecological disasters is so weakly motivated.

IN THE NAME OF THE FATHER

Among the masters, Freud has come closest to theorising the emotionally loaded Man/Woman=Nature saga with his psychoanalysis of the Oedipus complex. And this theory seems to follow a historical version of the ontogeny-repeats-phylogeny pattern by which a civilisation's perversity is replicated in the developmental saga of each individual bearer. Freud's *Moses and Monotheism* instantiates the beginning of patriarchy at the moment in history when men first sever cognitive from sensuous experience.[35] The Oedipal dynamic represents the power struggle of each man as father, to assert himself as sovereign within the familial cradle of politics. So, a boy child under the father's threat of castration, 1/0, must renounce his sensuous libidinal pleasure in his mother as he grows, and install her person with abstract love and respect in its place.

Further, the desired object, Woman, is herself split in two by this idealisation, the two parts representing the rift in masculine sexuality. On the one hand is the Mother Madonna and God's police, on the other a damned Whore who must be everything that the first is not. The whore, of course, is nothing else than a projection of the boy's own con/fused desire to embrace Mother=Nature. Capitalist patriarchal economies thrive on these sublimations. I once heard a Tasmanian mine manager brag about company brothels near the plant. When industrial strife broke out or worker morale was low, miners made heavy use of the women's bodies. It was an effective win/win model of diversification on the part of the proprietors, with Woman as resource.

The anti-porn campaigner John Stoltenberg summarises a man's first betrayal of the feminine within himself by the following process of objectification.

> The authority of the anger of the father is interpreted by the son as follows: (1) Not-Mother hates Mother and Not-Mother hates me; Not-Mother hates us. (2) It is because I am like Mother that Not-Mother hates me so. (3) I should be different from Mother; the more different I am from Mother, the safer I will be. These are the cardinal principles of logic in male maturation under father right.[36]

By Freud's reasoning the emotional cut or incest taboo establishes the dualism of natural and cultural orders. Woman objectified as idea is made 'manageable'.

Given the asymmetry of M/W=N values, a woman's seduction of her son means defilement, whereas a man taking pleasure in the body of his daughter is an act of guidance. Today, domestic violation by the father is experienced by one daughter in twenty. Paedophilia with coloured youths in sex tourism offers multiple satisfactions for the master of matter.[37] Bondage equipment broadcasts the emotional confusion: chains, cattle prods, nooses, dog collars, and ropes are all items for the control of animals. Emerging from this cycle of 'objectification, fragmentation and consumption', women often talk about being treated like meat.[38]

Given the impoverished capitalist patriarchal heart, is it any surprise to find small children buggered, the body parts of tribal people displayed in museums, women disembowelled in snuff movies, and 'hens … routinely boxed, caged, injected with hormones, forcibly inseminated, denied access to their young, and made to suffer immeasurably in transit to their deaths'?[39] Increasingly, more is known about animal consciousness and its similarities to human physiology, adaptive responses, communication, intentionality, caring, and self-awareness. But methodically

> 60 days after a calf is born, the mother cow is inseminated again. And so it goes – year after year – until the cow falters in her ability to produce either calves or milk at which point she is sent to the slaughterhouse … 80 per cent of ground beef comes from 'spent' dairy cows.[40]

Universally, men are encouraged to bond by feasting together on meat; this feasting affirms the privilege of humanness and maleness. But as Greta Gaard points out, in order to eat the flesh and secretions of other animals, we must disconnect.

Significantly, the break from touch and smell sets up a fetish for visual or specular qualities in the languages and epistemology of the West. Luce Irigaray's *Speculum of the Other Woman* provides ecofeminism with yet another reading of the M/W=N dissociation as denial of primal dependency.[41] When a growing boy breaks with the libidinal flow of inner nature, he is prepared as a man for detachment and 'objectivity' in thought. The Cartesian *cogito*, Newton's scientific method, and Bentham's utilitarian calculus are its familiar forms.

> Anything conceded to nature is immediately taken back and will be found useful only in so far as it ensures more rigorous dominion over her. *Thus, the function of the transcendental schema will be to negate all intrinsic quality of the sensible world*, and this irremediably. Diversity of feeling is set aside in order to build up the concept of the object.[42]

Eventually, 'the role played by the object will be rediscovered … as a gap'.

The specular self manufactures himself by negation as a unity, solid and upright, his libidinal economy homogenised by the number 1. In the illusory world of masculine autonomy, women have no part but as tokens of exchange passed from one man to another. According to anthropologist Claude Lévi-Strauss, it is the exchange of women between men that installs the rule of Fathers marking the ascent from nature to culture. But specular men speculate in women. The Indian dowry system and its abuses are well known. Irigaray writes that whereas virginity is pure exchange value, once a woman is positioned by marriage as reproductive use value, she falls back into the world of biological time, and so out of circulation for exchange. Prostitution stands midway between use value and exchange value, it being both a biological service and a way of affirming fraternal solidarity.[43]

Nevertheless, while eurocentric citizens fatten themselves on the Great Chain of Being, their progress is marked by ambivalence. Polarities like Mother versus Whore, 'nigger slave' versus 'noble savage', replay the psychosexual tensions. For capitalist patriarchal men, wilderness is sacred precisely because it tells their absence: Nature immaculately conceived. Weekend nature is worshipped as intrinsic value, but mostly land is scraped bare and processed, entering the value-added transcendental schema of the bar code. Thus Irigaray concludes that the modern subject

> must resurface the earth with this floor of the ideal. Identify with the law-giving father, with his proper names, his desires for making capital, in every sense of the word, desires that prefer the possession of territory, which includes language ...[44]

It is very apparent that the more such 'development' is celebrated, the more the species creativity of women is denigrated. In fact, in international agency jargon, development and population are two sides of a 1/0 coin. For the compensatory apparatus of science has furnished infallible contraception, so that woman too can experience sexuality without any necessary relation to the other. In the West, a free market in sexual competition operates, a consumption and turnover of human commodities that matches the intentional waste of productivism. But the separation of sex and reproduction typifies the alienative consciousness. By denying time and life process, contraceptive technologies deepen the hold of exchange value in a fundamentally homosexual economy. The liberal feminist movement for equality that is modelled on this masculine instrumentalism has failed to grasp that despite 'sexual revolution' the old trade in women still goes on.[45]

On the gynaecological couch, the mother 'is not able' to give birth without the assistance of professional men, steel stirrups and chains which 'dismember' her legs, steel forceps which 'deny' her abdominal muscles, gas masks, epidurals, episiotomies – the very questioning of which appears to breach a fundamental taboo.[46] Beyond this, medical *in vitro* fertilisation (IVF) programmes now strive to bypass the womb entirely. As Maria Mies explains:

> not only is the symbiosis of Mother and child disrupted. ... More than ever before, the woman is objectified and made passive. Under patriarchy she has always been an object for male subjects, but in the new reproductive technologies she is no longer one whole object but a series of objects which can be isolated, examined, recombined, sold, hired, or simply thrown away, like ova which are not used for [commercial] experimentation.[47]

Reproductive technology involves a condensation of masculine energies around the symbolic M/Other. Dr Alan Trounson, Australian father of IVF research, casually describes the human female as 'capable of substantial litters'. But the slow and painful test-tube love boasts a success rate of only 5 per cent, and multiple birth defects are frequent. Meanwhile, the very term 'surrogate mother' – a myopically specular concept – reveals the libidinal game. The point is that, if a woman has a child in her womb she is, in fact, labouring as a mother. In any event, with so-called advances in capitalist patriarchal science, women are redefined as 'gestational carriers', with babies 'products' subject to commercial contract. The writing was already on the wall for feminists with the arrival of the contraceptive pill. After all, reproductive technologies offer women a kind of 'self-determination' but only in functional terms prescribed by the phallic order.

ATTUNEMENT

The varieties of Otherness are libidinally, phenomenologically, politically and discursively overdetermined.[48] But there is yet another causality. According to the classic functionalism of

Talcott Parsons, gender role conditioning follows the following pattern: women, nurturant and expressive; men, competitive and instrumental. In a study of the Trobriand Islanders, Margaret Mead found that this instrumental/expressive dualism was not universal.[49] But since it shapes the eurocentric development paradigm which now invades all sovereign states, this is what needs attention from environmentalists. A recent US survey of young people's wilderness excursions illustrates the asymmetry clearly: for 60 per cent of boys and 20 per cent of girls, the trip was to conquer fear and expand limits. For 57 per cent of girls and 27 per cent of boys, the trip was to 'come home' to nature.[50]

In the West, girl children are allowed more free play of their feelings whereas boys are encouraged to inhibit emotional display – bar aggressive behaviours, as befits the warrior/breadwinner role. Girls are taught to be supportive of others, caring and protective, to mend hurt feelings and disrupted social situations, to massage egos. It could be said that women produce the libidinal surplus value that keeps the wheels of social exchange turning. Women's own ego gratification is rarely obtained in this process though, socialised for contingency as they are. Hence the usually intermittent achievement pattern of women professionals. Conversely, being able to juggle several tasks at once turns women into very good managers of systemic relations.

Ortner has argued that traditionally women's work always involves the mediation of exchanges between nature and culture: sweeping floors, cooking vegetables, washing small bodies and clothes, in other words, putting the dirt back 'where it should be'. Few women arrive at positions highly rewarded by income or public status. True, prevailing assumptions about women are prejudicial to their acceptance in the public sphere, but objective forces aside, women's training leaves them with mixed feelings about achieving success in masculine terms. And then there is always the fear of threatening those notoriously vulnerable masculinities and thereby inviting social rejection.

Internal conflict, resulting from two contradictory niches, the valued 1 and a demeaned 0, is a very real inhibitor of women's success – at least in conventional masculine terms. Women who opt for the double shift have less chance to compete as equals with men, but this may result in their having a more flexible attitude to their work, and fewer vested interests. Further, women who work alongside men are often disillusioned by what they see. For many reasons then, even liberated women remain relatively detached from the capitalist patriarchal opportunity structure and its alienative consciousness. This leaves them free to question what goes on.[51] The climate of self-interested speculation, the rapid exploitation of natural resources for profit, or technological advance for its own sake – these things are not particularly impressive to women, educated or otherwise.

North and South, women's ecological sense is often sharpened by the fact that they are both mothers and intellectually trained workers. Their political consciousness thus resists the split between private and public spheres of responsibility – M/W = N – and the lack of caring that derails conventional politics. These women have composite identities able to use their emancipation to preserve what they see as valuable in the 'feminine' role. But because most can meet the structurally opposed demands of public and private spheres only partially, the prevailing social system is not a very gratifying one for them. The marginality experienced by such women is often painful; they find themselves living right inside the kernel of a double bind. Lorraine Mortimer, for example, describes one 'stay-at-home Mother who is lonely and depressed without adult companionship ... who swears that having the child is the best thing that she has done'.[52] Mortimer argues that political analysis must take hold of ambiguities like this and examine them.

Third World re/sisters and indigenous minorities are also innovative in dealing with insider/outsider positions. Patricia Hill Collins maintains that 'Black women's lives are a series of negotiations that aim to reconcile the contradictions separating our own internally defined images of self as African-American women with our objectification as the Other.[53] Disjunctions in daily experience sharpen women's critical awareness. Such disjunctions may throw women into the creative chora that Kristeva writes about, subjective moments of free-wheeling drives and dissolving meanings. But there is no doubt that social contradiction and marginalisation help women to see right through the hollow instrumentalism of the Father's law. The 1/0 regime contradicts a woman's internal sense of becoming; and the energy released by this contradiction is what impels an ecofeminist politics to move beyond the static Woman=Nature dualism.

If nature's devastation is the inevitable outcome of success in masculine role attainment, the penny soon drops that the less women are 'liberated' in that way, the better for all life-on-earth. For as Carol Gilligan's famous judgement reads, 'in the different voice of women lies the truth of an ethic of care, the tie between relationship and responsibility, and the origins of aggression in the failure to connect'.[54] A keen sense of how complex systems work, identification with living processes, an eye to the future, responsiveness to surrounds, a protective attitude, and collaborative style – all these add up to feminine ecological attunement. But how can one 'fight' for a nurturant world? Can the voice of those whose daily labour is to nourish and to bond actually be heard as a 'political' voice?

Have concepts of politics, socialism and ecology perhaps become so masculinised as to make this impossible? Certainly Irigaray, O'Brien, Kristeva, and Chodorow, regard the sovereign state as a fetishisation of the paternal function. While a woman activist may lack a fully articulated theory of the why, who, what, and how of social change, most ecofeminists come to activism with a clear and practised ethical vision and a sophisticated understanding of group dynamics. One thing is sure: women across the globe are refusing to play the 1/0 game anymore. Irigaray exhorts us to '[o]*verthrow* [patriarchal] *syntax* by suspending its eternally teleological order, by snipping the wires, cutting the current, breaking the circuits'.[55] At the same time, women and men, socialists, postcolonial activists, deep ecologists or others need to be in agreement over just which capitalist patriarchal wires to snip.

4

MAN/WOMAN=NATURE

HEAD, HAND AND WOMB

Just as 'wilderness' has contradictory meanings, so does the word 'woman' – that other projection of self-loathing. But if a 'virgin' is the 'reserved object' of masculine desire, in the original and ecofeminist sense the virgin is a woman of strong and self-reliant spirit. It is no surprise that the global push for resource management is matched by a parallel imperative to appropriate women's reproductive processes, as if real live women were *terra nullius*, 'not really there'. Again, consider the so-called 'autonomy' of a young white woman whose sexuality is effectively leased to a contraceptive pharmaceutical company. Consider also the young Gungalidda woman as described by Aboriginal elder Wadjularbinna. She chooses her moon, meditates on the land with her man, goes deep into herself to see if it is right for her to conceive. Who is really free here? Who is really civilised?[1]

An ecofeminist response to ecological breakdown means finding ways of meeting human needs that do not further the domination of instrumental rationality. There are many inspirational possibilities for this cultural reinvention. For one, an anthropological reading of the north Mekeo in Papua New Guinea shows a people who are able to know themselves and their habitat in a metabolic sense, beyond the corporeal prohibitions of the Western Humanity/Nature divide. The relational sensibility of the Mekeo is one where

> bodily experiences are not hidden away ... which does not hypostatise 'the body'. ... Where indeed, every body is a composite of different identities; where bodies do not belong to persons but are composed of the relations of which a person is composed.[2]

This dialectic is most apparent during early marriage, when a Mekeo bride's body is considered to be 'open' or '*aiskupu*'. She is fattened for the imminent reproductive event and produces the gift of copious wastes for nature in return. This opening phase climaxes with her giving birth.

Conversely, the groom's body is most 'open' during sexual courting, and the tribe ensures that he too eats abundantly at this time. With recognition of the young wife's pregnancy, he starts to close with a 'ritual tightening', involving complex patterns of oral and genital fasting. Marilyn Strathern observes here a life-affirming homology of body, clan and wider nature. An anticipation of the holographic paradigm, perhaps?

> [T]he basic issue is that the Mekeo do not imagine space as infinitely receding. ... The outside village has at its centre its own inside space (an inverted outside), 'abdomen' is also used of bowels and of the womb ... transfers include gathering food and disposal of leavings and wastes.[3]

In related vein, Fiji scholar Asesela Ravuvu explains how the South Pacific island word *vanua* means 'tribe', as well as 'land', 'animals', and 'trees of the land'; each being as important as human interests are.[4] After all, death and compost are merely other forms of life, but under the 1/0 regime, high technology deals only with the expansionist side of the equation, 1, omitting its side effects in entropy and decay. These are conveniently called 'unanticipated' effects or 'externalities'.

Eurocentric constructions of social/natural relations around a logic of identity and difference could not be further from the materially embodied epistemology of the Mekeo. In the West, feminine and other abject bodies are split off and positioned as dirt, Nature, resource, colonised by masculine energies and sublimated through Economics, Science and the Law. Within the ecofeminist literature, there are several sources of conjecture about the repression of life process entailed in this Man/Woman=Nature equation.[5] Among them, socialist ecofeminist Maria Mies focuses on the arbitrary privileging of body parts and the pivotal role that the notion of 'labour' plays in an emerging capitalist patriarchy. Mies observes that talk of 'labour' is usually

> reserved for men's productive work under capitalist conditions, which means work for the production of surplus value. ... The instruments of this labour – or the bodily means of production ... are the hand and the head, but never the womb or the breasts of a woman .... [since] the human body itself is divided into truly 'human' parts [head and hand] and 'natural' or purely 'animal' parts.[6]

Men's tacit presumption of women's animality, then, has served to rationalise the exclusion of women from economic production. Because of their fertility and what follows from it, women particularly are said to spend their lives in the natural sphere, their reasoning faculty poorly endowed.

As we have already seen however, the humanist hierarchy of Man over Nature is a psychosexual fuse. For the truth of the matter is that in economic production, the appropriation of nature is equally a metabolic consumption of human bodies through labour. A continuum of energy exchanges is involved, though this is something that middle-class urban dwellers, whose needs are met by industrial production, find very difficult to imagine. Working-class men certainly deal with the material world, but women may labour with the uterus as well as with the organs of brain and hand. There is also a qualitative difference between men's and women's work, for feminine labours are organised around a logic of reciprocity with nature rather than mastery and control: 'They are not owners of their own bodies or of the earth, but they cooperate with their bodies and with the earth in order "to let grow and to make grow".'[7]

In *Patriarchy and Accumulation on a World Scale*, Mies sees reciprocity as basic to the first productive economy, one invented by women. It was a subsistence economy and it is still the mainstay of life for the majority of people on Earth today, despite the introduction of supposedly more efficient mass-scale, high-tech modes of production. During prehistory, men's practice as hunter-gatherers meant their notion of productivity was closely tied to the use of tools. Modern instrumentalism still reflects this assumption but, according to Mies, it is women's labour that most often produces something new, whereas tools used primarily in hunting and warfare are not strictly speaking productive. In fact, Mies claims that men's relation to nature has most often been one of destroying life. Moreover, tooled men have held the power not only to appropriate 'the abundance of nature' but also to coerce the complex productive capacities of women and other colonised peoples.

It is probable that the first 'private property' was productive women and children brought back from adventure raids into neighbouring territories. M/W=N institutions such as marriage still free men to go on expeditions together, since women's work maintains a reliable subsistence backup for them, not to mention minding their children. The accumulation of wives, especially by 'big men' of older status, is still condoned in polygamous Third World societies, and the pattern exists in residual form in the North, where men at midlife buy a new car and put aside their first wife for a younger model. Mies's analysis of economic processes is complemented by Rosemary Ruether's conjectural history of gender from biblical times and classical Greece to twentieth century capitalist patriarchal forms. Her fundamental thesis is that 'self-deception about the origin of consciousness ends logically in the destruction of the earth'.[8]

Ruether's *New Woman, New Earth* traces three moments in this false consciousness: Conquest of the Mother, Negation of the Mother, and Sublimation of the Maternal Principle. Early in civilisation, Woman was equated with Nature as 'life force' and fertility symbol. Judaism initially respected feminine creativity, the kabbala term *sophia,* denoting intellectual production as female. But misogyny set in with the discovery of biological paternity: hence Conquest of the Mother by new strictures, with women now treated as chattels. By the time of the Psalms, femininity was truly subordinate, though hostility to Nature was not yet evident – lending weight to the ecofeminist argument that psychosexual domination is prior to the abuse of nature. In the early Judaeo-Christian tradition, men defined themselves as part of a harmonious scheme where Man in covenant with God acted to protect Nature. Disaster and pollution would happen if the covenant were broken – social and ecological justice being interwoven.

Ruether's second stage – the Negation of the Mother – is a move from objectification of reproductive woman to paranoid rejection. Like O'Brien, Kristeva, Chodorow and Irigaray,

Ruether speculates that the awareness of infantile dependency is unspeakable. Judaism projected a transcendent Father deity as source and provider. Classical Greek philosophy introduced a technical split between body and mind, subject and object. But an 'ideology of the transcendent dualism cannot enter into reciprocity with the "other".'[9] After the fourth century BC, Platonic idealism and Aristotelian entelechy, both celebrations of mind, set the parameters for modern capitalist patriarchal culture. A phallic masculine identity became embodied in laws of logic using the 1/0 model. Pauline Christianity, Judaic and Greek misogyny combined to produce ascetic, life-rejecting creeds. Woman, the material source, was not only unclean but also, by literal translation from the Latin, *fe/minus*, lacking faith: naturally, she would be unfit for priesthood or other public duties.

THE PURITY OF SCIENCE

The Church would soon build on these libidinal foundations, adopting Aristotle's argument that the male seed provided the 'form' of a child, the female egg being merely its sustenance. In the drive to rise up over mater/matter, the English physician William Harvey, would go one better. For him, semen had its 'transcendent' impact on the egg by means of magnetic vibrations. The 'scientific revolutions' ushered in a further episode in the M/W=N saga, one recounted in Carolyn Merchant's historical study *The Death of Nature*.[10] By the seventeenth century, tools had evolved into technologies, 'productive forces' to further men's emancipation from Nature and its grubby subtext Woman. Thence to the purity of science. But just as it does today, the new ideology of scientific progress meant subjection of all Others to white middle-class masculine will. So, each year, US industrial laboratories slaughter an average of 63 million animals – primates, dogs, rabbits, pigs, frogs and birds.[11]

Merchant describes the rise of science as characterised by an elective affinity with several interlocking processes: an optimistic mood of commercially driven progress; a predilection for mechanism as instrument of expansion; and an ideology of individualism, at least for men of the North. Each secured men's attentions from bodily *jouissance* and disorder. A mythology of feminine lustfulness was put about; like wild Nature, She would need to be tamed. Independent women were pursued in witch hunts, drawn and quartered like animals. Conveniently, fines for sorcery and funds collected through confiscation of witches' property went to the coffers of what would become the bourgeois state. Prosecuting army officers claimed their 'rounding up' expenses – travel, meat and wine – out of these funds, constituting a crude bureaucracy. Vagabond priests too made a living from the public hysteria by selling holy relics to protect the innocent from women's sorcery. More than one social grouping had an interest in the first European holocaust.

The nascent state and science walked hand in hand to achieve the elimination of knowledgeable women as witches. For an emerging medical profession also, the removal of herbalists and midwives was essential. Bacon's role in shaping 'modern' scientific methods by the M/W=N regimen is telling. An ambitious careerist at the court of King James I, Bacon took as his credo an ingratiating play on His Majesty's instructions for the witch hunt.

> For you have but to follow and as it were hound nature in her wanderings ... for the further disclosing of the secrets of nature. Neither ought a man make scruple of entering and penetrating into these holes and corners, when the

> inquisition of truth is his whole object – as your majesty has shown in your own example.[12]

Bacon's *New Atlantis* would even anticipate the twentieth-century craze for reassembling nature according to Man's design through genetic engineering.

Meanwhile, Descartes's *Discourse on Method* and its disembodied *cogito* smoothed out the imaginary mechanical order of nature: each part predictable under a rationally determined system of law. Based on the Platonic 1/0, Cartesian mathematics functioned on the assumption of a dead corpuscular world, moved only by the efficient causation of God. Newton's *Principia* brought a parallel formalism to physics. The vitalist philosophy of Leibniz and his friend Anne Conway, drawing on the kabbala and the dialectical theology of Böhme, remained a minority tradition. Scientist Margaret Cavendish also stood against the tide, holding to a belief that nature is self-perceptive. Merchant notes that several images of nature coexisted before the European masculinist hegemony was consolidated under science. Each has social and political implications: Nature as 'order' implies a logic of social hierarchy fitting to feudalism and nazism; Nature as 'dialectic' accords with a sociology of conflict and change, Whig or proletarian struggle; Nature as 'arcadia', upholds a communitarian ethic.

The principle of mechanism found its way into liberal political theory with Hobbes's *Leviathan.* This tract emerged in reaction to both hierarchical feudalism and communalism. In Hobbes's hypothetical world, secular men governed by egoistical drives would agree to relinquish their own interests in return for a greater social gain under the sovereign eye of the Leviathan. The sovereign state was symbolised as a man dispensing rules, rather than, say, a caring mother with semiotic authority and corporeal prohibitions. Merchant's text makes plain that in Hobbes's writing, the line between an alienated masculine identity and the machine was already becoming very blurred.

> For seeing life is but a motion of limbs, the beginning whereof is in some principal part within; why may we not say that all automata (engines that move themselves by springs and wheels as doth a watch) have an artificial life: For what is the heart, but a spring; and the nerves, but so many strings; and the joints, but so many wheels, giving motion to the whole body, such as was intended by the artificer?[13]

My own ecofeminist understanding of instrumental reason crystallised while reading the neo-marxist analysis of the Frankfurt School.[14] The 'perpetual internal conquest of the lower faculties' which had marked eurocentric culture since classical Greece was a preoccupation of Max Horkheimer, Theo Adorno, and Herbert Marcuse. They saw the Enlightenment image of science as command of disenchanted nature paving the way for detached rational manipulation of matter. The Industrial Revolution, by providing a sophisticated machinery for the exploitation of natural and human resources, soon propelled the dream of mastery forward under the banner of 'development'. An early sociologist, Comte, translated the positivist hegemony into 'social engineering' or 'policy'. Non-Western scholar Tariq Banuri would name this 'the impersonality postulate of modernism'.[15]

But, as Marcuse observed, the self-estranged functional rationality of science would yield only knowledge of 'a dead world', apprehended in terms of fungible atomic units, to be reduced and reassembled according to human will.[16] The ideal form for presentation of this knowledge was the neutral algebraic formula, it being poor science, delusion, lies, to intrude value considerations into the generation of pure positive knowledge. For physicists, matter thus faded into mathematical and topographical relations: a vocabulary of events, projections and abstract possibilities was ushered in. The entire methodological trend implied a suspension of inquiry into the nature of reality or 'the reality of nature', replacing it with an emphasis on the specific operations to be used in its transformation. As Marcuse lamented, 'technological man [becomes] a uniform measure of the worth of classes, cultures and genders. Dominant modes of perception based on reductionism, duality and linearity are unable to cope with equality in diversity.'[17] It is hard to imagine anything further from an ecological sensibility.

Gendered resources would be dealt with like the rest of physical nature: air, streams, minerals and forests being tantamount to free goods. European discourses on produced wealth, nature and labour also began to take their distinctively modern shape from the seventeenth century. The entire world was available to men in common as a gift of Divine Providence.[18] But wealth as such was humanly made. Every man, Locke wrote, 'has a *property* in his own *person'*, and so 'the *labour* of his body and the *work* of his hands, we may say, are properly his'. If, in the providential sense, Nature is 'the common mother of all', conversely it is through labour that an individual appropriates the fruits of Nature to himself, 'so they became his private right'.[19] Labour was a man's world; women's domestic and reproductive labours were furnished as gifts – 1/0. Unfortunately, Marx would inherit these prejudices.

In Ruether's view, the Eurocentric Sublimation of the Maternal Principle was complete once industrial civilisation got under way.

> The nineteenth-century concept of 'progress' materialised the Judaeo-Christian god concept. Males, identifying their egos with transcendent 'spirit', made technology the project of progressive incarnation of transcendent 'spirit' into 'nature'. The eschatological god became a historical project. Now one attempted to realize infinite demand through infinite material 'progress', impelling nature forward to infinite expansion of productive power.[20]

The word 'infinite' in her text reiterates the blind linearity of specular instrumentalism. A social consequence of this sublimation was that women's economic marginalisation was deepened by the relocation of production from cottage to factory floor. With this change, women lost both the work companionship of spouses, and autonomy as part owners of their means of production. Both women and men were forced to contract into wage slavery with a capitalist entrepreneur. In the competition over wages that followed, the new brotherhood of trade unions pushed women back into the home. By the twentieth century, the 'feminine' domestic arena had come to be thought of simply as a site of economic consumption.

SILVER AND SPICE

With mothers correctly 'incarcerated' in the home, a mood of romanticism reversed earlier images of Woman as vampire. Victorian femininity was projected as innocent, delicate, and self-effacing. The ideological bifurcation of Madonna versus Whore kept Freud's consulting room busy; child abuse and hypocrisy thrived. In most European cities, an underclass of industrially displaced women had no option but to prostitute themselves to waged men – often the same upstanding citizens who gave public adherence to prolonged courtship and idealised Protestant marriage. According to Ruether, black women slaves served a similar biological function in the USA. Since morality was now lodged in the private sphere, feminine participation in business and politics was precluded. Women were said to be not tough enough, or should not be sullied by the world of wheeling and dealing.

It was industrialisation that constructed Western men as 'breadwinners'. Although, in the early stages, women and children worked alongside husbands and fathers on the shop floor, this was soon halted by union men and bourgeois reformers with their Factory Acts. Trade unions have continued to consolidate masculine privilege over women, historically stripped of their independence by the change from land to factory economies. A few might become wives of successful entrepreneurs, but many more slipped into the capitalist patriarchal pool of reserve labour. The feminisation of poverty has a long history. Early in the day, celebration of domestic monogamy foreclosed women's options. In the early 1920s, a 'scientific' approach to homemaking reinforced the importance of unpaid housework as women's proper role. The household became the colony of the little white man, while big white men would appropriate continents. Before long, it would be planets they wanted.

Black men, on the other hand, remained labouring bodies, energy resources for the taking – like women and nature. Extending Rosa Luxemburg's marxist analysis, Mies argues that housewifery and colonisation were joined by the discourse of 'naturalisation'.[21] Both colonisations extend 'rights' of white middle-class men and rest 'responsibilities' on women and coloured peoples. The European nation-state was consolidated with gold from witch hunts, piracy and colonial raids – primitive accumulation of capital. But new manufacturing technologies and cheap urban labour from a displaced peasantry soon made the extended reproduction of capital possible. The Christian missionary rationale of 'civilising' savages would console the white man's nascent guilt.

Black women's gentle nurture of German men, even intermarriage, was encouraged because many West African women held local economic power. Such liaisons stabilised the colonial presence.

> Regarding the free intercourse with the daughters of the land – this has to be seen as advantageous rather than as damaging to health. Even under the dark skin the 'Eternal Female' is an excellent fetish against emotional deprivation which so easily occurs in the African loneliness.[22]

Nevertheless, Mies observes, colonising men were encouraged to keep sexual unions sterile, since white purity was essential to social dominance over 'natives not yet evolved to the level of the master race'. In 1908, however, a German edict excluded mixed-race children from European citizenship and inheritance. Meanwhile, the German Women's League kindly sent Christmas gifts to the colonies, binding hegemony with obligation.

Mies observes that initially only a German aristocracy could afford the spices, exotic foods, silverware, ceramics and jewellery plundered from Africa. But gradually this affluence filtered down to a *nouveau riche* bourgeois class whose household would become an arena of display under housewifely direction. Such conspicuous consumption gave a new dimension to the meaningless metropolitan existence of housewives in the North. The lack of political independence of European women stood in sharp contrast to that of their re/sisters in Burma or Senegal. The latter even orchestrated a birth strike in response to colonial policies. After World War Two, women in the developed world, having been temporarily emancipated for the military effort, would be pushed back into home-based reproductive activities. The new domesticity boosted a failing population. Gratis, the mothering class now provided the capitalist patriarchal North not only with a labour force but with consumers for the anticipated boom from commercial adaptation of war technologies, electronics and pharmaceuticals especially.

After World War Two, Christianity was eclipsed by Cold War anticommunism as *raison d'être* of colonial penetration, and entrepreneurs went off in search of Third World markets. Soon the success of union wage bargaining would drive factories offshore as well and into cheap labour havens in Mexico or Southeast Asia. By the 1970s, transnational companies in Korea and Brazil were marshalling a labour force of teenage girls for a fifteen-hour day. Their North American sisters were kept in line by the drone of advertising, and soon by MTV. Not just manufacture but sex too would go offshore, prostitutes being cheaper in the South and nonverbal intercourse less emotionally costly for men conflicted about women as equals. More recent colonial penetration by the USA has turned into gun-running for local warlords and narcotics traders. These visitations from the North pulverise local indigenous communities, creating a vacuum for further tele-pharmo-nuclear expansion in the name of 'aid'.

International agencies like the United Nations (UN) treat 'development' as postcolonial and emancipatory: progress without subjugation. But import of the technological *a priori* through 'transfer' and 'capacity building' merely carries colonisation to a new phase. These days, Ruether's transcendent dualism takes the form of a pact between local elite men in the South and entrepreneurs from the North. The exclusion of women as partners in social decision making is sealed yet again. From her Research Foundation for Science, Technology and Natural Resource Policy in the hills of north India, ecofeminist Vandana Shiva finds that indigenous women pick up the costs of development and see few benefits. Further, the more responsibilities they are asked to carry, the more these women are themselves 'victimised' as 'burdens' on society. The same applies in the 'developed' world, where abandoned mothers are blamed for causing the feminisation of poverty, and black youth in ghettos are targeted as genetically criminal by a US National Institute for Health research programme.[23]

Shiva's *Staying Alive: Women, Ecology and Development* offers a paradigmatic analysis of the plight of Third World women everywhere. The erosion of traditional land-use rights by the introduction of cash cropping strips these women of control of their means of production. For centuries, women engaged hands-on with habitat to provide food and shelter. But technologically transferred development ruptures this re/productive nature–woman–labour nexus, leaving starvation and ecological destruction in its place. Shiva writes that eurocentric science and economics in their arrogance pit a linear, reductionist, managerial logic against nature's cyclical flows – a pseudo science quite inappropriate to its task. The Green Revolution was a case in point and desertification its result.[24]

But the capitalist patriarchal response to the ecological crisis becomes a further assault on life and the disposable mother. Perhaps nothing shows up the difference between M/W=N attitudes and life-affirming attitudes as does the issue of population control. Whilst the average US citizen uses some three hundred times as much energy as a Bangladeshi, the North rejects calls for a new international economic order based on fair distribution. Instead, in hotel bars from Costa Rica to Cairo, a jet-setting brotherhood in suits coordinates efforts to reduce population, merrily pushing greenhouse emissions higher as they go. The affluent lobby for genocide includes the Agency for International Development (AID), the UN Fund for Population Activities, the International Planned Parenthood Federation, the Population Council, consultants from Johns Hopkins, Columbia, the University of Michigan, and Northwestern University, and various parliamentary associations.[25]

The US establishment argues that poverty is a cause of population growth, that it produces environmental degradation and threatens the security of nations. The issue has been driven by figures such as former UN Secretary-General Kurt Waldheim, John D. Rockefeller III, former US Secretary for Health Caspar Weinberger, and former World Bank chair Robert McNamara. The anti-abortion President Reagan's rhetoric even pushed population control as 'reproductive rights'. Unfortunately, many liberal feminists also enter the debate on this wrongheaded assumption. What is not recognised is that a woman in the South may lack the means of feeding her family precisely because of measures such as land enclosures for ranching or dam construction, initiated by the World Bank or IMF. The capitalist patriarchal assault on her rights is doubled when she is given food in exchange for an agreed sterilisation. A larger economic blackmail is played out on local communities when the IMF demands implementation of population control programmes as prerequisite for development loans.

ORBITAL DEBRIS

By what passes for common sense, the things that men do – called 'production' – are valued, while the things that women do – and especially re/production – are not valued. An extract from the Kenya *Standard* illustrates this well:

> As more and more land will be required for food production in order to meet the demand from the population ... cash crop expansion may stagnate. Given the costs involved in adopting more modern farming *techniques to raise productivity* ... population growth, if allowed to continue, can only result in more encroachment on vital forest reserves.[26]

The causality pursued here deflects responsibility away from men's privileges; it is women who must change, who must stop having families since that is detrimental to 'economic growth'.

Investigations by the magazine *New Internationalist* substantiate the reverse case. The reason for Africa's falling food production is not scarcity of land or lack of technology, but village men's seduction by the 'formal' economy which takes both land and men's labour time away from domestic food growing.[27] Where children now become supplementary farm labour for their mothers, it is inappropriate to demand population control according to the Western trend. Third World children are producers as much as consumers. That is, they are what we all should be: autonomous 'prosumers' who know how to meet our own needs. The focus on population in development debates is symptomatic of deeply unresolved psychosexual energies in the alienative consciousness. And so are the compensatory preoccupations with status in an international economic pecking order or with expertise in destructive technologies. Consider this piece of fraternal deference from the Kenya *Sunday Nation:*

> Only sound social, economic and political policies that favour or promote indigenous scientific and technological

> potential will help the continent meet its *basic human needs* ... the minimum target of 1,000 scientists and engineers per million inhabitants.[28]

The iniquitous financial transfers from South to North that World Bank-IMF programmes for imported 'development' involve, the predatory consumption of food and energy resources by an industrialised North; the lessons from the Green Revolution – all are very good arguments for disconnecting from the transnational corporate order and concentrating on one's own back yard. So why not? The reason is the elective affinity that exists between science, commerce and masculine aggrandisement. This is the real meaning of 'development'. I once shared a taxi to Nairobi airport with a Dutch engineer who had been giving workshops on irrigation. Mindful that African women cultivate 80 per cent of the continent's food, I asked: 'And how many women come to your workshops?' 'Only men', came the reply. Apparently, the Kenya authorities are anxious to be seen playing by white brother's rules. This was their ego investment. Western aid programmers have their own status needs.

Making her critique of capitalist patriarchal development in terms the coloniser can accept as valid, Shiva has tabled an array of indicators on the nutritional status of male versus female children; soil loss from monoculture; fertiliser application by sex; corporate funding of biotech research; salinity following irrigation; male versus female shares of agricultural work. She concludes:

> The dispossession of the poorer sections of rural society through the green revolution strategy and their reduced access to food resources is, in part, responsible for the *appearance* of surpluses at the macro-level. The surplus,

> according to prominent economist V. K. R. V. Rao, is a myth because it is created by lack of purchasing power.[29]

A review of the 'unanticipated' costs to farm ecosystems of soil degradation, waterlogging and salinity shows that the Green Revolution actually reduced productivity. Nonetheless, Food and Agriculture Organisation (FAO) experts again gave transnational engineering companies the go-ahead for more irrigation works at the October 1996 World Food Summit in Rome.

Meanwhile, in Australia the coal industry has captured government aid money for coal-fired projects in Southeast Asia.[30] The peacetime nuclear industry is a further concern. Ecofeminist physicist Rosalie Bertell estimated that by the year 2000 this would have resulted in 90,000 cancers and over 10 million children with genetic defects.

> We don't 'see' these damages where they are concentrated, in the Marshall Islands, among the aboriginal people of Australia, the Navajo and Dene people of North America, the circumpolar people or the Congolese and Namibians of Africa, because these people are powerless and voiceless within the dominant western patriarchal culture. Where the health problems are less concentrated, people are left wondering where or how their cancer or their damaged child originated ... governments spend their time trying to discount independent studies demonstrating the problems. Science by non-investigation is fraudulent.[31]

Every space shuttle pumps 37 tonnes of chlorine into the ozone layer; a Russian Mars probe crashes to Earth off the Pacific coast of Chile dispersing 200 grams of carcinogenic plutonium-238 from its battery cannisters; US Space Command at Colorado Springs currently monitors 8,000 items of space junk.[32]

Shiva addresses the epidemic of violence on Indian women which ensued from men's frustration after the failure of the promised Green Revolution. It was no surprise that the development failed: many imported pesticides are just old war technologies such as nerve gas. Now, introduced genetically engineered seeds threaten to become a further ecosystemic pest. The irony is that Indian women farmers already know how to nurture resistance within plants themselves as opposed to attacking pests from the outside.[33] Shiva describes the sell-out of academic scientists to the corporate sector as a privatisation of 'intellectual commons', made necessary because science has become habituated to expensive high-tech equipment in order to research. But laboratory-based investigations, which shuffle 'mythical constructs' around on computers, have lost touch with the founding canon of empiricism as hands-on knowledge.

Rather than acknowledge women's work, either by including it in labour statistics or according it the status of scientific observation, governing elites in South America, Africa, India publish annual trajectories of 'manpower' needs – engineers, accountants, sanitary chemists, biologists, electricians ...[34] In the expressive drive for 'masculinisation' and control, scientists and politicians fail to register that

> the 'Dust Bowl' technology for the manufacture of deserts from fertile soils was first mastered in the colonization of native Indian lands in North America ... western patriarchy's highly energy-intensive, chemical-intensive, water-intensive and capital-intensive agricultural techniques for creating deserts out of fertile soils in less than one or two decades

> has spread rapidly across the Third World financed by international development and aid agencies.[35]

And what else does progress offer? Bubonic plague bacteria are now available by mail order from commercial labs in the USA. Consider also the Super Rambo Electro Shock Baton made by British Aerospace and exported to Saudi Arabia under a 20-million-dollar deal signed by Defence Minister Heseltine in 1985. One third of all US and British engineers work for the tele-pharmo-nuclear complex. Bertell thinks that we are dealing with a collective behaviour problem. Ivan Illich adds that capitalist patriarchal 'growth' certainly seems to leave men more unhappy: 'in every country discrimination and violence spread at the rate of economic development: the more money earned, the more women earn less, and are raped'. By Louis Arnoux's perceptive diagnosis, 'the physical flows of energy can be used as a measurement of the anguish.'[36] Economics as a planning discourse generates the very problems it is supposed to solve, for in the 1/0 treadmill, business failure is quietly experienced as a virility issue and a loss of standing.

Brian Swimme, himself a former physicist, is well qualified to discuss the 1/0 regime. He claims that the dominant masculine mind-set is utterly helpless when it comes to knowing what to make of the world. On the other hand, Swimme adds, 'there is one thing men really can do, and that's count'.[37] Perhaps poet Susan Griffin was the inspiration here, for *Woman and Nature* reminds us:

> He says that through numbers 1 2 3 4 5 6 7 we find the ultimate reality of things. ... *He tells us how big he is.* He measures his height. He demonstrates his strength. ... He numbers his

> genes. ... He is counting his possessions. ... *Counting. We count each second. No moment do we forget. ... We are counting the number he has killed, the number he has bound to servitude, the number he has maimed, stolen from, left to starve.*[38]

By counting, the specular subject swells to unitary subjecthood. What is manufactured by the instrumental hand is properly human. It is the sight that counts.

Geared up to the visual sense, the alienative consciousness makes a sharp separation between the person 'inside' who thinks and acts, and things 'outside' that are acted upon. This dichotomous mode of thinking is basic to the exercise of power including industrial *machismo.* Disconnected from the primal body, capitalist patriarchal reason deflects the life-force and floats in a void. It copes by ordering, planning, managing, manufacturing, so 'mastering' the world. The global consequences of this transcendent project are plain to see, to quote one Australian mother:

> There is nothing to eat anymore! Beef has *e coli*; lamb has scrapie; rabbits have calici virus; chicken is full of synthetic hormone; fish carry heavy metals; soy beans are genetically engineered; vegetables and fruit are covered with pesticide; seaweeds are radioactive. What can I give the children tonight?[39]

5

FOR AND AGAINST MARX

NATURE, HIS REAL BODY

A number of ecofeminists such as Ruether, Merchant, Mies, and Shiva have been influenced by the generous spirit of Marx's work. He too was writing at a time when land enclosures by powerful interests were displacing self-sufficient communities. Then, enclosures took place for sheep grazing; today they are done for agro-industry, cash cropping, dams, and golf courses. So North and South, country folk still straggle into cities looking for other ways to survive, soon forced to sell their bodies as a labour or sexual commodity for capitalist patriarchal men. This nascent proletariat leaves behind a habitus organised by kinetic values for an artificial reality split off from the implicate circuitry of ecological processes. As opposed to active land-based ways of life, which ground the senses, industrial production disconnects people from the pulse of their material being. The 1/0 civilisation of the metropolis is geared to an abstract idol called profit, but when humans become ignorant of the complex web of internal relations that nurtures them, they enter a world of mystifying symbolic exchange which disguises real energy exchange.

Alienative consciousness now reaches new depths. Thus, Marx describes how by selling his own bodily powers, a worker's well-being and identity are impoverished by removal from his own self-directed capacity to work creatively with nature. The thoughtful fashioning of useful things, which once absorbed head and hand in understanding nature's potential, is replaced by an unthinking machine to which the worker's body is a mere appendage. Rather than identifying with what he has fashioned with his own skills, the worker faces objects made in factory production, numbly, as if somehow they were alienated powers directing him. As a human creature, one of a species, the worker becomes alienated from what his own species is or might be. Ensnared in somebody else's idea of production, the worker is reduced to accepting daily survival itself as 'the meaning of life'. Internal to all these things is a working man's status as mere commodity in a labour market, estranged from nature both inside and out of himself. He comes to feel separate, even competitive.

Marx and Engels were very much ahead of their time in seeing a dialectical interplay of Humanity and Nature. Marx expressed concern over soil depletion by capitalist farming methods and argued for protection of flora and fauna. He suggested sewerage be recycled as agricultural fertiliser instead of polluting the River Thames. Engels's naturalistic tract *Anti-Dühring* was published shortly after the word *Ökologie* (ecology) was coined in Germany by the biologist Ernst Haeckel.[1] Even so, with hindsight, we can see that the ecological understanding of Marx and Engels was undermined by their own Enlightenment conviction that reason with technology might shape the 'forward march' of History. Marx's vision of human dominion over the natural world spoke a linear notion of progress – an idea reinforced by his contemporary Darwin's evolutionary schema.

In this latter respect, Marx's position reflected the transcendent ego and its ideology criticised by Ruether and other ecofeminists. For human instrumental mastery rested on Man's objectification of Others as matter and resource, cancelling

Nature's subjectivity and potential partnership in History. The traditional identification of Woman along with Nature in turn, crippled her equal exchange with Man. But it is inappropriate to expect Marx's work to do full justice to emerging twentieth-century preoccupations. His passion – and immediate focus – was to be rid of the suffering that he witnessed in the nineteenth century factory system. Had he been writing in another era, he might well have developed different vantage points – this is certainly implied by his dialectic of internal relations. This question of historical context needs to be born in mind when Alfred Schmidt observes that there is 'no systematic Marxist theory of nature of such a kind as to be conscious of its own speculative implications'.[2]

Similarly, gender equity was not the prime undertaking of Marx and Engels, though Engels's provocative study of patriarchy in *The Origin of the Family, Private Property and the State* broke new ground in joining personal and political, becoming a catalyst for feminist studies one hundred years later.[3] However, their combined opus does not rest very long at a level of generality that would throw light on the Man/Woman=Nature dynamic in Western societies. Accordingly, just as men of Reason have continued to situate women's activities in the realm of Nature, socialists too, bar some valiant efforts to assimilate feminist insights in the 1970s, have continued to use gender-blind analytical categories and values.[4] From an ecofeminist perspective, the traces of the M/W=N formula in marxist theory appear to set up a profound contradiction within its emancipatory project, one that flaws attempts to formulate a self-consistent eco-socialist programme.[5]

On the other hand, the dialectical method of Marx and Engels fortifies our thinking about 'the Nature question' and, indirectly, the Man/Woman problematic as well. And, lest we forget it, the very idea of postmodern deconstruction owes much to Marx's urging us to go beyond mere appearances and find what is not seen. In a diagnostic reading of Marx's own thought, Bertell Ollman's *Dialectical Investigations* argues that Marx's level of analysis is constantly changing with his political design in any given essay.[6] This many-levered methodology offers new conceptual possibilities for ecopolitical analysis, and we shall return to it later. But first, it is worth spelling out how the M/W=N theme fares in Marx's preferred vantage point. For it is this work, albeit reified over several generations of uncritically masculinist and positivist readings, that remains influential in new movement politics.

As early as the *Grundrisse* Marx can be found commenting on how humans evolve within nature and so are an intrinsic part of it. In fact, he writes that Man must grasp 'his own history as a process ... and the recognition of nature as his real body'.[7] Human identity exists relationally with nature in another sense as well, for Man labours on nature and transforms it; while this work activity, in turn, has a transformative effect back on him. Humanity learns from practical interactions with the objective world, developing its 'slumbering powers'. So far so good. However, Marx goes on to say: 'Neither nature objectively nor nature subjectively is given in a form adequate to the human being'.[8] In other words, it is imperative that he remake what he finds in nature. Thus:

> man of his own accord starts, regulates and controls the material reactions between himself and Nature. He opposes himself to Nature as one of her own forces ... in order to appropriate Nature's productions in a form adapted to his own wants.[9]

The human producer is contrasted with the animal, whom Marx claims works only by instinct without any capacity to conceptualise. Now, from an ecofeminist perspective, some potent ideological themes are fused in this passage and it is riddled with ontological assumptions derived from the Great Chain of Being.

This ancient theological rationale established a value structure based on God's domination over Man, and men's dominion over women, the darker races, children, animals, and wilderness.[10] The hierarchy was not abandoned during the secular Enlightenment but reinforced by it, hand in hand with the scientific revolution. Hence, Marx's typical anthropocentrism, or 'human chauvinism' to borrow Val Routley's phrase, and an overconfident estimate of the degree to which men can interfere with and control complex, partially understood phenomena.[11] The anthropocentric motive behind this human urge to control is especially worrying to environmental ethicists who attribute equal intrinsic value to all life forms. Note also, however, the *andro*centric fashion in which nature is identified as feminine.[12]

Marx himself speaks of '*Monsieur le Capital and Madame la Terre*'. Again, he describes labour as 'the father' and nature as the 'mother' in the act of production, echoing Aristotle's dictum that the male parent 'forms' the 'sub/stance' provided by a passive female ovum. Finally, despite the monistic naturalism of the original dialectical idea, the old dualism of Humanity versus Nature creeps back with Marx's oppressive evolutionist distinction between human and Other species. This is not a hard-and-fast divide, any more than sex is a clear-cut polarisation. Indeed, the silent cooperation of animals has been indispensable to men in building civilisation. Animals, like humans, can use tools, behave purposively and co-operatively. Bees communicate by dance until a humming consensus is reached and the swarm moves off; apes are capable of learning deaf-and-dumb symbolism; beavers plug holes with debris to stop up water levels in a pond.[13] Women, like men and other animals, can use tools and behave purposefully as well.

THE CHAIN OF APPROPRIATION

Productive labour is the pivot of Marx's materialism. In fact, Marx stated that History itself began with the first act of production. One might well ask, Why not an act of reproduction, since empirically this is more likely? There may well be a plethora of masculine rationalisations for evading the above thesis, as feminists from O'Brien to Irigaray propose.[14] In Marx's words, the historical moment is a 'conscious self-transcending act of origin'. Human beings realise themselves through work. It is an objectification of human subjectivity, whose expression is true freedom. On the other side of Marx's M/W=N equation, Nature is described both as the material conditions that have created Man and as the material resources to be transformed by labour power. Nature is both active and passive in relation to human beings: but also, vice versa.

Clearly, this is not merely a 'crude domination ethic'. Man's unity with nature does not exist only as a result of his making it over, as Routley argues. Howard Parsons adds that Engels's *Dialectics of Nature*, like Marx's later 'scientific' writings, did not depart from this eco-logic, though the vocabulary describing transactions with objective nature changed.[15] Marx believed that human self-understanding of this dialectic emerged only over time; with socialism representing Man's full consciousness of his place in the chain of 'appropriation'. By contrast Marx noted, somewhat ethnocentrically, that the primitive mystifies nature as awesome and regards it passively. But wherever men must struggle to survive, where resources are scarce and conditions harsh, nature is then objectified as Other and seen as an unpredictable and enslaving force.

Now it is precisely this attempt to gain dominion and control over nature that gives rise to class society, as men harness the labour power of Others to help subdue the wild. With time, and the move to a capitalist patriarchal mode of production, work on nature for the satisfaction of needs becomes production for the sake of profit, appropriated from workers by a ruling class. For Marx and Engels, the very existence of private property equalled an estrangement of human life. Yet, critical as Marx was of the inhumane effects of capitalism, and especially of the four-faceted phenomenon of alienation, he did not settle on the conclusion that the ensuing ecological dissociation was a human alienation from nature. Instead, he endorsed the capitalist stage as a way station towards a world of infinite possibility in the growth of human needs, provided for gratuitously by Mother=Nature. He even endorsed the British colonisation of India as a necessary motor of modernisation.

Caught up in the optimistic rationalism of his time, Marx in his emphasis favoured human will and creativity over nature's presence. But in fairness to his overall conceptualisation, it is probably worth assuring ecological critics that his anthropocentrism was in part strategic. In a very dialectical way, Marx used his writing as an instrument to stir up historical action. Schmidt conveys this rhetorical mode when he describes Marx's 'critical judgment on previous history, to the effect that men have allowed themselves to be degraded into objects of the blind mechanical process of its historical dynamic'. In analysing these repressive human institutions – ones that Frankfurt School neo-marxists would later call 'second nature', Marx insists that we are still really dealing with 'first nature': 'All the contrived machinery of modern industrial society is merely nature tearing itself to pieces.'[16] By saying that we are still within 'first nature', Marx dramatises the human predicament: what has been set in motion remains outside of conscious control.

Conversely, the vantage point adopted in the *Economic and Philosophic Manuscripts* underlines the fact that Nature is crucial to Man's well-being. That

> man lives on nature – means that nature is his body, with which he must remain in continuous interchange if he is not to die. That man's physical and spiritual life is linked to nature means simply that nature is linked to itself, for man is part of nature.[17]

Routley interprets this in the sense that humanity has a proprietary interest in nature, which indeed, under capitalist patriarchal relations, it does have. Taking cue from Irigaray, my own hunch about this passage is that there is something libidinal agitating Marx as he reflects. And along these lines, it is instructive to compare the master's account of Man's relation to Woman. Marx and Engels do after all name women and children in the patriarchal family as the world's first slaves. But Marx's description of gender relations here is distinctly uncritical. Rather it is infused with spiritual notions, essences and such. Hence

> man's relation to woman is the most natural relation of human being to human being. It therefore reveals the extent to which man's natural behaviour has become human, or, the extent to which the human essence in him has become a natural essence – the extent to which his human nature has come to be nature to him.

The last turn of phrase seems to anticipate the social constructionist analysis of gender: but changing tack, the philosopher adds: 'In this relationship is revealed too, the extent to which the other person as a person has become for him a need ...'. Does he mean that the Other – mother, prostitute, waitress, wife, secretary – is objectified? Marx's text fudges this protofeminist breakthrough with a conclusion that it demonstrates 'the extent to which he, in his individual existence, is at the same time a social being'.[18] In other words, he passes over the objectification of women's subjectivity by man in the service of his daily needs as simply a 'social fact'. The asymmetry of women's specific material condition and her own 'needs' are not envisaged using Marx's theoretical vantage point here. Beyond the level of mere appearance, which is where his preferred mode of abstraction leaves 'the Woman question', Woman's relation to Man is, in fact, less than social: it is a 'condition of economic production' just as external nature is. Thus, to make an ecofeminist adaptation of a famous passage from Marx: women 'make their own history but they do not make it just as they please; they do not make it under circumstances chosen by themselves, but under circumstances directly encountered, given [by men] and transmitted from the past'.[19]

Now for Marx it is only the human factor which gives value to what is made or manufactured from nature: 'The purely natural material in which no human labour is objectified ... has no value; as little value as is possessed by the common elements as such'.[20] Land in itself, for instance, has no value by this reasoning. Consistent with this view too is the suggestion that plants and animals are supplied by evolution as a means of human subsistence – Nature is Man's 'inorganic body', the 'instrument' of his needs. There is a clear parallel here with how women are regarded. Thus it follows that in the famous labour theory of value, labour, as variable capital, is treated as the source of all profit or, more strictly, surplus value, while natural resources, being constant capital, are a less significant factor of the productive matrix. A M/W=N formula through and through, Marx's labour theory of value implicitly places women's reproductive and restorative activities on the unproductive resource side of the equation.

As we have seen in our discussion of the libidinal economy, a woman has value and identity, 1/0, only in as much as this is given by a man – as when she is the daughter, girlfriend or spouse of a man. In many cultures, a woman is valued only once she has produced a son. Psychoanalytically speaking, this gives her a vicarious right to hold the phallus, universal emblem of patriarchal power.[21] Sadly, mainstream feminism remains phallic in orientation, merely shifting the focus of a woman's evaluation from the private to the public sphere. Feminine status now depends on affiliation to masculinist institutions such as top-flight enterprises, academia, and so on. While state bureaucracies serve as 'protector' and very jealous husband to women on welfare, the majority of wives in the private sphere continue to be treated as Man's inorganic body and instrument. In ecofeminist terms: despite decades spent in struggle for self-determination women, like nature, still have little subjectivity to speak of.

It is interesting, as well, to compare Marx's assumption that class society grows out of men's efforts to objectify and subdue nature, as against feminist recognitions by Dinnerstein or Chodorow that 'mastery' is a reaction to 'dependency' on the originary M/Other.[22] This hypothesis is applicable both at the level of primal species consciousness and to each newborn man. Certainly Engels's analysis in *The Origin of the Family, Private Property and the State* intimates a connection between masculine insecurity and the putting into place of institutions based on monogamy and 'the name of the Father'. By these hegemonic manoeuvres, women's productive and reproductive powers are thereby appropriated and safely contained.

NECESSITY VERSUS FREEDOM

Symptomatically, while Marx's text cascades with imagery of the powers of Man and even technology, the powers and 'labours' of women rest unspoken in his interpretation of human existence. Now a crucial aspect of marxism as far as any future eco-socialism goes is the duality between necessity and freedom. This undialectical separation on Marx's part appears to derive from the bourgeois construct of material scarcity – nub of liberal economics. But there is also something Oedipal, or perhaps pre-Oedipal, about the desire to escape one's grounding in the primal stuff of Mother=Nature. Not surprisingly, this unconscious association is reinforced by the compulsory location of women's labours (cooking, cleaning, childcare – chores that 'mediate' nature for men) in the sphere of necessity.[23]

The humdrum, repetitive, personal servicing that is domestic work, despite its substantial contribution to GNP, goes unacknowledged as 'labour' and unrecognised by a wage, even under late capitalism – with all its transcendent promise. Marx endorses a qualitative difference between these unvalued pre-capitalist labours and properly productive labours:

> there are always certain parts of the productive process that are carried out in a way typical of earlier modes of production, in which the relationship of capital and wage labour did not yet exist, and where in consequence, the capitalist concepts of productive and unproductive labour are quite inapplicable.[24]

Women's lot – and socialism in practice failed to remedy it – is to 'reproduce the conditions of production': something like setting the stage? Not seen as an actor herself, nor as a producer, the mothering labourer gives life to, and attends the material needs and emotional support of those who do 'produce'. This 'reproductive sector', as marxists call it, is the realm of necessity *par excellence* and despised as such. But it is poorly understood by male theorists whose lack of activity in that sphere has given them odd notions about what women do. So much so that left scholars have never been able to agree on whether or not housework generating use value can be deemed productive, since the category of 'surplus value' does not readily fit. And marxist feminists have opposed wages-for-housework campaigns, for fear of legitimising women's singular entrapment by the hearth.[25]

Engels quotes Hegel to the effect that 'freedom is the appreciation of necessity'. If this is true, then women's consciousness must indeed be way out front, as ecofeminists suggest it is. But Marx and Engels did not look to the household for rational guidance on the question of human needs. Nor to the peasant in order to gain understanding of Nature's needs. Consider the traditional farmer, whose intimate, many-sided knowledge of local species, water holes, drought-resistant seeds, and fuels allows her or him to produce while still caring for the land. Rather, Marx and Engels, like many socialists, capitalists and managerial environmentalists today, put their faith in scientific knowledge as means of turning external necessity to human ends.

Marx's typically masculinist technological optimism heralds a future society of material abundance, little labour output, and minimum disruption of nature. Modern science is said to 'order' Nature, which now opens up into a field of infinite exploitable potential. Socialist revolution will release working men, allowing them to take the reins of production and the determination of needs into their own hands. The limits imposed by the green wild will finally be broken. Arriving at his utopia by a road paved with abstractions – meaningful to urban men though not necessarily to women – the philosopher and his project for human emancipation lose touch with the messy, viscous dialectic of life process. The fact that nature is our ground and sustenance is superseded by the freedom fetish inherent in the timeless logic of bourgeois masculinity. Even so, Marx writes: 'The development of human energy which is an end in itself, the true realms of freedom ... can only blossom forth with this realm of necessity as its basis ... the shortening of the working day is its basic pre-requisite.'[26]

What has quietly taken place under this banner – in capitalist and socialist, 'advanced' and 'developing' societies alike – is the partial liberation of women from the private realm of necessity to enter the public one, so achieving a double shift of necessary labour: half of it unpaid, the other half receiving a fraction of a man's wage. Ecofeminists note that it is not, in fact, women's experience that technological advance has brought a diminution of working hours. African women farmers now complete a sixteen-hour day because the lure of industrial growth takes men away to the cities; girls in Asian 'free trade zones' likewise work a fifteen-hour factory day. Further, as domestic consumerism expands in the affluent West, household working time grows with it.[27]

And here we arrive at the cleft stick of modern scientific productivism. The promise of technology somehow captivates men, North and South, resonating for them in a deep, structural way. At the same time, the invisible but dependable work of women keeps even high-tech economies afloat. Women, 50 per cent of the world's population, put in 65 per cent of productive labour time for less that 10 per cent of its wage.[28] Marx claimed that under a socialist revolution, a world of alienation and mystifying appearances would be thrown off. But what guarantee? The model of progress he outlines shares too much in common with the paradigm of transcendent ego. Marx himself was entranced by the qualitative shift from tools to production by machine technology, and he impatiently waited on the large-scale industrialisation of agriculture.

Recall Marx's disdain for the peasant and the so-called 'idiocy' of village life. Nor is women's domestic work far removed from the pre-industrial character of rural subsistence labour, with its hands-on skill and worker autonomy. Yet right here is demonstrated an 'appropriate' one-to-one relation between worker and tools – an integration of job planning and carry-through – essential to Marx's notion of humanity developing its 'slumbering powers' through sensuous interaction with Nature. Machine technology, by contrast, operates independently of the worker, stands over her or him as an external force with its own rhythm and direction. Marx perceived this, writing, 'the machine accommodates itself to the weakness of the human being in order to make the human being into a machine'.[29] For a tool is much more than a technology. Thanks to Marx we are now in a position to recognise that the latter carries an oppressive complex of social relations along with it. But he remains ambivalent, even assuming an ontological voice in the *Grundrisse* when he speaks about the locomotive, telegraph, etc. 'They are organs of the human brain, created by the human hand, the power of knowledge objectified'.[30] And, one might add, the power of very imperfect knowledge. Some of Marx's technological enthusiasm comes from his vision of automated production as capitalism's eventual undoing. The objectified labour congealed in the machine is believed to be more efficient than the traditional exploitation of workers' time.

> The greater the productive power of the machinery compared to that of the tool, the greater is the extent of its gratuitous service. ... In Modern Industry man succeeded for the first time in making the product of his past labour work on a large scale gratuitously, like the forces of Nature.[31]

Through this development, he argues, exchange value will eventually cease to be the basis of production.

THE TRANSCENDENT TOOL

But what of the degree to which the exchange society and its commodity fetish have already taken hold of human relations, becoming identical with human second nature itself? How will this unwind? And beyond this, what of the gendered violence, harassment and discrimination – which are functionally prerequisite to keeping a female workforce intimidated and pliable, regulating its supply, and ensuring the international accumulation of benefits in men's hands? Again, Marx's ideological position on technology overlooks the environmental dialectic of the machine's existence. The ecosystem is ravaged as its resources are mined, smelted, turned by other workers, transported, assembled, operated, repaired, and finally dumped.

There are big environmental and community costs in all this, even before the question of worker health and safety comes up. Even so, like the entrepreneur, Marx is prepared to take this natural infrastructure for granted; such things are 'externalities' omitted from the calculation. From an ecofeminist viewpoint, he also overestimates the human capacity to predict and cope with longer-term effects of scientific and industrial innovation. For example, in *Capital* Vol. III, he persuades the reader:

> Physical necessity actually expands as a result of his wants, but at the same time, the forces of production which satisfy these wants also increase. ... Freedom in this field can only consist in ... rationally regulating their interchange with Nature, bringing it under their common control, instead of being ruled by the blind forces of Nature.[32]

So Nature's utility must be tapped for the benefit of all humans, not just a select few. As for the rest, it is a matter of more human reason, systematically applied; better 'management'. This is a very shallow ecology, for as the engineered trauma of chemical pesticides, VDUs, biotech, nuclear weapons, the greenhouse effect, and garbage suffocation suggest, that perfect Reason is all but an elusive dream. Engels saw it coming: his astute, almost biocentric grasp of internal relations, fired by a love of nature, anticipated the consequences of intervention in the ecosystem once or twice removed down the line from human action. He also intuited what we know today, that 'scientists who have learned to think dialectically are still few and far between'.[33]

One hundred years later, things have not changed, despite methodological challenges to science by women like Carson, McClintock, Bertell.[34] Marx too, was well aware that:

> In nature, nothing takes place in isolation. Everything affects every other thing, and vice versa, and it is mostly because this all-sided motion and interaction is forgotten that our natural scientists are clearly prevented from seeing the simplest things.[35]

Why then did Marx himself succumb to the model of linear thinking, byproduct of both the masculine denial of embodiment and the modern division of labour that capitalism promotes? Marx wrote that:

> The more the worker by his labour appropriates the external world, sensuous nature, the more he deprives himself of the means of life in the double respect: first, that the sensuous external world more and more ceases to be an object belonging to his labour – to be his labour's means of life; and secondly, that it more and more ceases to be the means of life in the immediate sense, means for the physical subsistence of the worker.[36]

Marx understood well that like working men, nature needs time to heal. Yet his case for technology was argued largely outside any ecological or gendered context, quite undialectically. As I have already suggested, a large part of this stemmed from his desire to enable human autonomy for people exploited and oppressed by social forces seemingly beyond their control. His was wishful thinking, in the very best sense. But it was not only that.

Marx has provided twentieth-century thinkers with an imposing collection of conceptual tools, and whatever shortcomings his prognosis of capitalism may have, the application of his epistemology serves as an exemplar in many problem areas. Nevertheless, the Woman=Nature sphere is peripheral to the socialist vision. Why did Marx and Engels choose to specialise their theoretical focus in the way they did? Perhaps the answer lies in *The German Ideology*, where they admit that 'the restricted relation of men to nature determines their restricted relation to one another'.[37] Similarly, as ecofeminists we deduce by triangulation that men's restricted relation to women would determine their restricted relation to each other, and to nature, though differently: M/W=N.

From empirical observation of the adverse impact of technology on both other species and gendered lives, men's awareness of these two 'peripheries' appears to become even more deeply 'restricted' by the preoccupation with technological control. To argue so is to turn upside down Marx's argument for the emancipatory character of technology, while retaining the logic of his method. Marx taught that 'technology discloses man's mode of dealing with Nature, the process of production by which he sustains his life, and therefore also lays bare the mode of formation of his social relations, and the mental conceptions that flow from them'.[38] Using an ecofeminist lens, it can be seen that history has called up the opposite effect. Technology certainly discloses men's mode of dealing with nature, but even where the machine may elaborate raw goods, the emblem of technology is not what 'produces' our sustenance in the first place.

Man's self-projection in technology merely provides the 'forms' to nature's 'sub/stance'. Colonisation and tech-transfer notwithstanding, the bulk of the world's daily needs continue to be supplied by Third World women food growers outside the cash nexus, working independently and with little damage to their land. Again, looking at the North and women's role in domestic 'reproduction' of the 'conditions of production', it is they who pick up the tab for abortions, home nursing of leukaemias, etc., after men's technologically designed blunders such as Chernobyl. The examination of technology does indeed lay bare how 'social relations' are organised hierarchically between Men and Women and Nature. Also true is Marx's insight that prevailing 'ideas' reflect what is called 'the mode of production'. Men's fantastical identification with the spectral power of the machine colonises everyday language: most recently with computer jargon – 1/0 the postmodern face of capitalist patriarchalism.

PRODUCTION/REPRODUCTION

So far though, none of this accounts for why, since the Enlightenment, both capitalist and socialist thought should have been driven along such a perverse course. Feminist analysis, and indeed the critical theory of Horkheimer and Adorno, suggests that the tendency was seeded in ancient times. But building on Bacon's misogyny, Descartes's mirror phase, and Newton's mechanism, the secular theology of the capitalist patriarchal era is spoken by science and economics.[39] Control and efficiency, its sanctified themes, bring new impetus to the marginalisation of women and nature lower down along the Great Chain of Being. Socialist collaboration with this agenda was given with the exclusion of women's 'pre-industrial' work from what came to be called 'production'.

Allocated a backstage role along with Nature, Woman would gratuitously furnish 'the conditions of production'. Her main task area is 'social reproduction', which term has uncritically lumped together a variety of economic functions. Marx's thinking was genuinely troubled by the potential economic emancipation of women. He endorsed the liberatory role of universal wage-labour in the demise of the family hierarchy. But his ponderings over the health of working mothers, not to speak of the moral depravity of factory girls, only served an ego-defensive patriarchalism among working-class men. As for sexual reproduction – the implications of Engels's writing on gender relations were never integrated into the marxist analysis as a whole; for had this happened the entire theoretical edifice might have crumbled. Engels wrote:

> the determining factor in history is, in the final instance, the production and reproduction of immediate life ... on the

> one side, the production of the means of existence, of food, clothing and shelter and the tools necessary for that production; on the other side, the production of human beings themselves, the propagation of the species.[40]

Engels considered the patriarchal family a microcosm of capitalist relations of production, the wife playing proletariat to the husband as master. Domestic monogamy and prostitution were two faces of the one coin. However, whereas a wife sold her body once and for all in a marriage contract, the prostitute sold it after the manner of piecework. These days, *de facto* arrangements between politically correct couples equally lack a declared 'work contract' and, to women's cost, are even less explicit about the gendered division of domestic labour.

This gendered plane of comprehension could have nudged Marx and Engels towards a transhistorical formulation of 'production' and 'value', but it did not. Since global indicators show women are in fact the productive sex, in addition to their sexual generativity, why are they universally assigned a position outside production?[41] It would seem that the term 'production' has a very special significance for men in the West, one that they are reluctant to share. Postcolonial theorists such as Ashis Nandy observe the same, and note the disqualification of women, children, and the aged that follows.[42] Ecofeminists conjecture that the identification of 'production' and 'masculinity' may arise because at some deeply unconscious level men are mystified and alienated by women's unique potency in species reproduction.[43] Indeed, Marx's comment that 'man produces even when free of human need' supports an interpretation of productivism as somehow compulsive.[44] In true compensatory fashion, production is claimed by men as their own arena of competence, and language, philosophy and political institutions are designed to bolster this reality.

So we arrive at an 'advanced' society whose public institutions and values are anti-life; whose science, economics, and even radical thought leave Woman and Nature out of the equation. Without reviewing Marx's personal politics among the 'fairer sex' and 'weaker vessel', it is plain that when he came close to analysis of what we call the M/W=N complex, his focus slipped back to his proper theo-economic concern. However, Marx's own exquisitely naturalist exploration of the role of consumption in the labour process can actually support a notion of species reproduction as human labour. He clearly sees how 'The labourer consumes in a twofold way. While producing he consumes by his labour the means of production, and converts them into products with higher value.'[45] This consumption describes the body's bioenergetic metabolism with nature during the exertion of work. Similarly, in carrying, bearing and breast-feeding a child, a woman consumes her own body while converting nature into a 'higher' form. Feminists would prefer to say 'another' form here. But in any event, there is no reason in the world why one exertion should be canonised as a labour creating 'value' and the other not.

Mies has remarked on the strange persuasion that thinks some body organs are properly Human and productive, namely hand and brain, while other body organs such as breasts and womb are seen to belong to Nature. The common objection that sexual production is not a 'conscious self-transcending act' simply speaks many men's appropriation of women's sexual power to the service of their own irrational, that is ungrounded, desires. Women who are in a position to control their fertility do so in a way that does take rational account of their own habitat. Women well know that the uterus is a productive organ, whose labours do have economic outcomes. Predictably, now that men are beginning to move into this field with scientific *in vitro* fertilisation techniques, the economic dimension is being made socially explicit. Now life comes to have value through having a price.

But none of this should be read to imply an argument for biologism, on the one hand, or economics, on the other. Rather, the argument is about cultural politics. The question is how to reconnect men with ecological time – materially and discursively – as opposed to taking women away from it, which liberal, socialist and postmodern feminisms have done. Ecofeminism challenges the discourse of false consciousness that has polarised gender in this way (just as necessity and freedom were split apart, where in a sustainable society they would be joyfully experienced as one). The 'identity' of humanity and nature may well rest on our constantly working with the latter to provide for our needs – just as Marx prescribed. But this transformative process does not have to be conceived in the linear, exponential sense of capitalism or socialism.

Degradation of the environment as an unanticipated effect of positivist physics, chemistry, engineering, together with corrosion of the human body through iatrogenic disease, all amplify how the West's instrumental reason is poorly equipped to imitate sustainable flows. Just as there are Other kinds of 'labour' overlooked by Marx, so the human metabolism with nature can be based on a logic of reciprocity and nurture, rather than exploitation and control. This more dialectical logic is contained in the sensuous praxis of women workers, from Third World subsistence farmers to urban mothers.

Some sociologists have argued that Marx's theory of class struggle has been made obsolete by the emergence of joint stock companies, or new subclasses such as managers and professionals.

But the major criticism levelled at socialism has concerned failure of the working class to mobilise politically and carry off the revolution that Marx predicted back in the nineteenth century. Could it be that the relative advantages of masculinity have sabotaged Marx's vision by drawing even disparate men together under capitalist patriarchal privilege? This is where ecofeminist insights may help remodel the left agenda and tactics. For it is clear from the spontaneous global initiatives of women that knowledge steered by one unique vantage point has been overlooked by existing political theory.

Consider a nonalienating way of objectifying human energies: the kinetic exchanges that are women's lot. When a woman labours to produce a child of her own, she is not usually alienated from that physical activity or its material result, the infant itself. When the child is brought to the wider community, the mother is acknowledged and her joy is shared. At the same time, the child basks and grows in this affirmation. In objectifying her reproductive powers, the mother's mind and body mediate the child's being as well as her own, as one species, in the wider web of nature. Despite our jungles of concrete and steel, this historical experience of species powers continues still, inside industrialised societies. Now this is not to give a 'sociobiological account' of gender, or to argue that women are 'closer to nature', or 'better than men'; nor is it to celebrate 'the essential feminine' as naive readers might conclude. Rather, it is to highlight the relational character of a particular human sensibility that has been marginalised, censored, repressed.

6

THE DEEPEST CONTRADICTION

THE INCONSEQUENTIAL SOCIETY

The alienative consciousness and its 1/0 abstractions have achieved new heights in the past two decades through an elective affinity of five kinds of disembodiment. (1) A US President delinked the dollar from the gold standard, so floating global currency exchanges. (2) In Paris, structuralist philosophers delinked the linguistic signifier from its material referent, allowing the signifier to serve as its own referent. (3) A contraceptive pill for women and a gay scene for men delinked human sexual exchanges from generational outcomes. (4) Human communication was delinked from speech, processed numerically and telegraphed across space as electronic digits. (5) Also inspired by information theory, genetic engineers delinked reproductive DNA from the ecosystem, and began circulating it freely under the dollar sign.

The dissociative economic practices that accompany these overdetermined tele-pharmo-nuclear moves are of deep concern to financial analysts like Joel Kurtzman and David Korten. As the latter writes:

> Each day, half a million to a million people … turn on their computers, and leave the real world of people, things and nature to … enter a world of cyberspace constructed of

> numbers that represent money and complex rules by which the money can be converted into a seemingly infinite variety of forms, each with its own distinctive risks ... the players engage in competitive transactions aimed at acquiring for their own accounts the money that other players hold. Players can also pyramid the amount of money in play by borrowing from one another and bidding up prices. They can also purchase a great variety of exotic financial instruments that allow them to leverage their own funds without actually borrowing. It is played like a game. But the consequences are real.[1]

The speculative money markets create an illusion of social prosperity in the same way that discourse disconnected from action in the world creates an illusion of knowledge and free sex creates an illusion of love. The outcome is economic instability for farmers and manufacturers, as speculators control public policy by insisting on downsizing and pushing ethical businesses off the map as inefficient. The buzz word – 'flexibility' – obscures new class divisions and legitimises ever more brutality in the pursuit of profit. The capital accumulation is phenomenal, with the top 10 per cent of Americans owning more assets than the other 90 per cent.[2] Yet the $1 trillion lost in the October 1987 stock exchange crash could have fed the total world population for two years.

Kurtzman labels the emergent speculative class 'stratos dwellers', a term reminiscent of Susan Griffin's 'space cases'.[3] Neither is too far off the mark:

> Eighteen years ago we had DOS, Lotus 1-2-3 and Word Perfect running on a 286. Have we really improved plan-

> etary productivity now with a Pentium Pro and Microsoft Office Suite? Now look at all the innovation on the Net in the past two years. *If you stand on the moon and look down, that perspective is stunning.*[4]

Meanwhile, some 500 transnational corporations (TNCs) account for two thirds of all trade. Of the world's 24 largest companies 9 are in electronics, 5 are in oil, 5 are in motor vehicles, 2 are in food, 1 is in building materials, 1 is in chemicals, 1 is in tobacco – hardly life-affirming activities.[5] The great TNCs emulate the military in both structure and strategy. In the words of Phil Knight, chief executive officer (CEO) of Nike gym shoes: 'business is war without bullets'.[6] TNCs are powerful enough to manipulate elected governments; nearly all directors, managers, politicians and bureaucrats are men. This is what it means to speak of a capitalist patriarchy.

The corporate push for free trade leaves behind it ecosystemic and human stress.[7] Greenhouse polluting practices such as trucking carrots from Italy to Belgium for washing and peeling, then back to Italy for packaging and distribution are called rational.[8] Regional trade organisations such as the Asia Pacific Economic Cooperation organisation (APEC) lobby Asia Pacific governments to remove health and environmental protections – 'non trade tariff barriers' – as a favour to investors.[9] But the costs to working people are high. The North American Free Trade Agreement (NAFTA) abolished overtime, compensation, and occupational health and safety standards. In Mexico, deregulation has served International Monetary Fund (IMF) debt collectors well, the unanticipated effect being job losses, peasant displacement, 50 per cent inflation, and increased birth defects among women living near the *macquiladoras.*[10]

While economic 'growth' appears to bring material benefits to some men and women in the North, in another sense it can be said that almost all women inhabit the South. The annexation of women's work is reinforced with industrialisation and consumerism, whether by computers, labour-saving gadgets, or new reproductive technologies. Meanwhile, in 'developing' regions, expropriation of farmlands for commodity markets, technocratic green revolutions, and now gene patenting undercut the very means of women's labour for subsistence. Continued capital accumulation, the expanding hegemony of transnational operations, and the rise of 'phantom-states' like international drug cartels all add up to deepen nature's and women's subjection.

The globalising Man/Woman=Nature programme reincarnates ancient gender relations, in which most women experience a social reality very different from that of their brothers in capital or labour. Relatively few women possess assets in their own right, and the majority of women are 'not quite labour' either. Even United Nations figures cannot hide the universal scandal of feminine marginalisation, where women own less than 1 per cent of all property and do two thirds of the world's work for 5 per cent of all wages paid.[11] A 1995 United Nations Development Programme (UNDP) study shows no change in the pattern. Of a $23 trillion global output, women were responsible for producing $16 trillion, or two thirds.

However, the UN System of National Accounts, the IMF, the Organisation for Economic Co-operation and Development (OECD) and the World Bank still have difficulty in counting household services. In fact, even for some socialist thinkers, women's place in this predatory economic system falls notionally somewhere between a 'natural resource' and a 'condition of production'.[12] Either way, women are treated as an economic 'externality', just as they are a historical externality in bourgeois liberal political institutions, and sometimes new green ones.[13] Typically, a Greenpeace tour of California showing how tapa cloth is made in Papua New Guinea took only men in the promotional party, even though they did not know how to make tapa because at home it is women's work.[14]

In her classic statement *The Global Kitchen*, published in 1985, activist Selma James provided this assessment:

> In the United States in 1979, only 51% of adult women were 'in the (paid) labour force', 48% in China and France; in Latin America only 14% of the total female population was counted as workers in 1975. In Britain, 40% of women are in the paid labour force now.[15]

Marilyn Waring updated the indicators in *Counting for Nothing*, amending these again in her study *Three Masquerades*.[16] But while a burgeoning service sector in the North and explosion of free trade zones in the South shift the statistics around a little, the basic character of this female exploitation remains unchanged by globalisation and the workplace restructuring that comes with it. Women swell the ranks of part-time, contract, and seasonal positions, without security, advancement opportunities or retirement benefits. Maternity leave and work-based childcare programmes are rare.

CAPITAL INCARNATE

The entrenched gender division of labour is so fundamental to the modern social fabric that, two decades after a 'sexual revolution' and installation of affirmative employment schemes, even salaried women in the industrialised nations typically receive only two-thirds of an average man's wage. More significant, the greater portion of women's labour is altogether left out of gross national product (GNP) calculations. Yet a housewife in the 'developed' world often puts in at least seventy unsalaried hours a week – that is, twice the standard Australian working week of thirty-five hours. Using subsistence skills, she produces 'use value' in cooking, sewing clothes, cleaning, house maintenance and gardening. A 1994 estimate by the Australian insurance company National Mutual put a wife's economic value at

> Full Time Housekeeping $380–$450 per week or $19,760–$23,400 per year Childminding $300–$380 per week or $15,600–$19,760 per year.[17]

That is a total housewifely wage of A$43,160. Non-metropolitan women in the South grow the bulk of community food needs as well. But, it seems, women must wear the veil – to save men's eyes from seeing what they cannot bring themselves to see. A substantial part of women's social function under the 1/0 regime is to provide for men an inverted mirror image of reality.[18]

Then there are the intangible obligations of women's open-ended labour roles: tending children, comforting the aged and sick, ego repairs and sexual relief for the man in her life, and possibly the labour of child-bearing consequent to that. As pregnant bodies, a bridge between self and other, women become very aware of links with nature through the food chain. Mary Mellor, in the UK, describes all this as putting in 'biological time'.[19] But under the symbolic M/W=N order, that time cannot be represented in the alienative consciousness. Hilkka Pietila observes that 'the invisible economy "produces things that are not available on the market and cannot be purchased for money, such as the feeling of being somebody, closeness, encouragement, recognition and meaning in life".'[20] Many middle-class women take on a heavy round of voluntary commitments such as parent-teacher association (PTA), Amnesty work, or residents' action campaigning. Migrant and refugee women use extra energy absorbing new strains on the family and rebuilding community, often after a full day on the assembly line.

The unpaid services that women give under capitalism can, in principle, be abstracted as 'labour time' and remunerated: examples are prostitution, fast lunch counters, professional laundry. This shows that there is no natural necessity for organising the economic system in this way – only capitalist patriarchal convenience. As James notes, 'the woman who cleans a house is not "working", but the military man who bombs it, is. Further ... the work of the same woman, if hired by her husband ... would pop into GNP'.[21] The paternalism of capitalist economic arrangements is such that even when women's domestic labours are recompensed as supporting mothers' pensions or benefits for elderly care, these payments are perceived as a 'gift' of the state, charity or welfare: never as an 'economic exchange' transacted between free citizens, 1:1, as in the contract between 'labour' as such and capital.

Using capitalist patriarchal economic criteria, the significance of women's contribution to the global economy is easy to demonstrate. James, Waring, Pietila and others all substantiate that if we were to allocate domestic hours to standard job categories, apply the going wage, and then total everything up, we would find housework constitutes a large portion of GNP.[22] Pietila estimates that for Finland in 1992, women's domestic labour in 'the free economy' constituted between 42 and 49 per cent of GNP.

This compares more than favourably with turnover in the public family or 'protected state sector' now deregulating everywhere under IMF advice. It also compares more than favourably with overseas trade, a 'fettered sector' tied to the whim of global free markets. However, Pietila may soon choose to revise her tripartite model of the capitalist patriarchal economy, adding a fourth or 'stratas' sphere, representing the vast disembodied sums that circulate as pure speculation.

Giovanna Dalla Costa writes that development agencies operating in Latin America and the Caribbean have quietly come to recognise the economic function of the family in the containment of poverty, and thus its essential part in the market mechanism. According to an International Labour Organisation (ILO) report:

> The recession reveals in all their amplitude housework's importance and strategic nature. … [Housework] consists in enabling the 'active' members to adjust the price of their labour … downwards as a means of reducing in monetary terms the gap in physical productivity that separates them from formal firms, giving them a competitive capability that would otherwise be very difficult to obtain.[23]

If domestic labour were given a place in the formal economy, with the massive redistribution of income and opportunity this would entail, would women themselves be more highly valued by society? Most feminists doubt it, for women's oppression is not simply economic. In any case, to advocate such reform is to presume that the capitalist system at large, and the patriarchal family as a microcosm of it, are institutions worth preserving.

Women's work makes accumulation possible for all kinds of men, and the economic surplus women generate is crucial to the operation of capitalist patriarchal relations. During the 1970s and 1980s, an extended debate was carried on among socialist feminists on how capitalist and patriarchal systems interact.[24] Scholars still disagree over how to formulate women's subordination in marxist terms, and the overlap of female exploitation with ethnicity and the North-South axis was barely touched on. It has remained for ecofeminists to broach 'the Nature question', so reframing the entire debate. By proposing that the nature–woman–labour nexus be treated as a fundamental contradiction of capitalist patriarchal relations, ecofeminism affirms the primacy of an exploitative gender-based division of labour, and simultaneously shifts the economic analysis towards an ecological problematic.

While many feminists may be content with nothing more than equality alongside men in the existing system, ecofeminists are concerned about global sustainability as much as gender justice: in fact, they see the two as intrinsically interlinked. For example, Berit As from Norway argues that economic growth in a masculinist economy only adds new burdens to women's lives.[25] Money that might sustain women breadwinners goes instead into armaments. US dollars spent on military and space research and development is double the billions invested in civilian production or public utilities.[26] The rest is a whirlwind of electronic speculation, for to quote Korten:

> the financial markets have largely abandoned productive investment in favour of extractive investment and are operating on autopilot without regard to human consequences .... Since humans cannot make the calculations and decisions with the optimal speed required by the new portfolio management strategies, trading in the world's financial markets is

> being done directly by computers, based on abstractions that have nothing to do with the business itself.[27]

Under the 1/0 regime, the presence of a few women in high places has little impact so long as such practices remain unchallenged. Consider also the uncritical contributions of women economic advisers to national governments or the OECD in promoting the latest round of the General Agreement on Tariffs and Trade (GATT).

From a global capitalist patriarchal vantage point, the Third World debt crisis generated by World Bank and IMF policies has provided an excellent opportunity to restructure class and gender relations across continents, integrating new proletariats into the global economy and simultaneously cheapening the international price of labour. Silvia Federici points out that during the 1980s, the IMF offered African nations standby loans in exchange for privatisation, retrenchments, wage freezes, currency devaluation, and structural adjustment of health, welfare and education spending.[28] The economic rationalist idea is to allow everything to reach its 'market value' so that incentives will operate again, drawing foreign investment in and allowing exports to earn hard currency.

NATURAL AND GENDERED RESOURCES

The problem is that the erratic speculative economy interlocks with materially productive activities, so that reliable economic judgements simply cannot be made. The toll can be seen in Ghana, for example, where the salary of a middle-level public servant will barely pay one third of the family food bill. Globalisation means that many broken communities rely on remittances from transient loved ones in Italy or Iceland:

> hunger is spreading in places like Nigeria, traditionally the yam basket of Africa. … Not only is meat disappearing, gari (cassava flour), the cheapest and most basic staple, is also becoming very expensive, particularly in the urban centres, where it must be transported by trucks and vans fueled with gasoline now costing what whisky cost in the past.[29]

Federici concludes that economic liberalism and social fascism can be friendly partners.

The structural intertwine of women's exploitation with predation on nature, is illustrated at so-called development's every turn. Ethiopia suffers desertification and famine as land is taken out of women's hands by men who would 'render it profitable'. In the USA, women in electronics corporations exposed to toxic contaminants of skin, lungs and nervous system suffer foetal damage. The import of tractors to Sri Lanka degrades soil and water, and forces women to pick cotton twice as fast, in order to keep their wages at the same level. Sex tourism, a male-organised and male-oriented skin trade, balances 'foreign exchange' in the South, as debt accumulates from the rush for ecologically disastrous masculinist status symbols such as weapons, hydro dams and oil.[30] Living things are expendable for a capitalist patriarchy, which does not value what it does not itself produce.

Sisters North and South have more in common than many think, and that commonality increases as globalisation expands. Ecofeminists do not separate women by stratifications of class, race, age and so forth, since the nature–woman–labour nexus as a fundamental contradiction defies these conceptual boundaries. The 1/0 rule applies cross-culturally and for women it reads thus: maximum responsibilities, minimum rights. Hence, while technology transfer from the industrial core – the USA, Germany and Japan – introduces an era of neocolonialism to the periphery, development also heightens the subsumption of women's work. Village girls become silicon slaves, while the erosion of traditional land-use rights with cash-cropping strips their mothers of cultural autonomy and economic control over their means of production.

Vandana Shiva points to an implicit pact between advisers from the North and local elite men, the upshot being 'modernisation' projects and structural adjustment programmes passing the costs of 'economic' growth down the line to women, and then nature.[31] In India, a culturally sustainable woman-nature metabolism has been undermined by imported scientific techniques.[32] Indigenous women's expertise developed over thousands of years – knowledge of seed stocks, the water-conserving properties of root systems, transfer of fertility from herds to forests, home-grown medicines and methods of contraception – is lost. Ecological and human needs go unfulfilled; societies and cultures disintegrate as rural men leave families for the city lights and promise of a wage. Meanwhile, men of the *comprador* class and their World Bank role models publish annual trajectories of 'manpower' requirements – for engineers, accountants, chemists, whose very skills exacerbate the entropy.

Ecofeminists have long argued that an identification of women with nature defines women's work in the North as well as South. Take the complex of tasks that housewives perform under capitalist patriarchy: sexual satisfaction, birthing and suckling children, carrying the young about, protecting their bodies and socialising them, growing and cooking food, maintaining shelter, sweeping floors, washing and mending clothes, dealing with garbage – and these days recycling it. The common denominator of these activities is a labour of 'mediation of nature' on behalf of men, which function continues despite legal recognition of 'female equality' by nation-states. Such legalities are incidental to the underlying accord between governments, capital and labour, guaranteeing each man his own piece of 'the second sex'.

Women's traditional positioning between men and nature is a primary contradiction of capitalism, and may well be the deepest, most fundamental contradiction of all. In anthropological terms – shaped by androcentric interests – women's bodies are treated first as *if* they were a 'natural resource', the uterus as organ of birthing labour being the material origin of 'formal labour' as such. The time-honoured eurocentric imagery of Mother=Nature and the ancient Indian notion of *Prakriti* are certainly more than 'mere' metaphor. But under the scientific hegemony, their celebration of women's potency is greatly diminished before the celebration of men's technological production. Under the capitalist patriarchal version of the 1/0 regime, women's bodies have never come to obtain a rent as land does, but they are none the less 'resourced' for free by capital to provide ever-new generations of exploitable labour.

Consequently, given that women are really human beings, a profound antagonism is set up between Woman as objectified reproductive matrix and women as subjects of history in-their-own-right. This tension is expressed in the form of a reproductive rights debate: new arguments around the issue of paid surrogacy and the possibility of an 'industrial contract' for child-bearing in a 'value-added' world. How the ideological line may be drawn between woman as 'natural resource' and woman as 'not quite labour' appears to be infinitely flexible. In addition to being a 'natural resource', women using hands and brain in caring labour become subsumed by capitalist patriarchal economics as 'conditions' of existence, in the sense of *oikos* or habitat, necessary for creative human productivity to take place. Women's bodies are utilised by working men to build a taken-for-granted daily infrastructure, enabling performance of the male work role.

At the same time, since women are 'not quite labour', they find themselves existing in contradiction with 'labour as such', and this is so even when they become paid workers themselves. The tensions between women and 'formal labour' erupt in the family and workplace, with formal labour backed up by a masculinist trade union movement. Women are doubly objectified by the structural violence of M/W=N lore. Like nature, they are readily available and disposable; and like nature they have no subjectivity to speak of. Meantime, as Naomi Scheman observes, men are free to imagine themselves as self-defining – but only because women hold the intimate social world together.[33]

Women, really objects in a so-called 'division of labour', have customarily been exchanged between men, father to husband, pimp to client, from one entrepreneur to another. This exchange of female 'resources' may well have constituted the earliest form of 'commodity' trade. Likewise, the children women produce are appropriated and named by men. Yet, even as women begin to take back control of their fertility, so men use new reproductive technologies to wrest control of that 'resource' back from them. The latest move on this front is corporate patenting of DNA, whereby the basic building blocks of life itself are formulated as 'property rights'. And this fantastical hubris will cover not just 'genetic' interventions in human reproduction such as remedies for inherited ailments, but transgenic combinations between human, animal and plant life as well.

Women also 'make goods', for use in domestic shadow labour, and for exchange in peasant agriculture, or as commodities in piecework or factories. Yet these commodities too are usually taken away by men – husbands, middlemen, or transnational management. Maria Mies recounts this process of dispossession, and observes that violence pervades every facet of male/female interaction under capitalism. By this means, men are simultaneously agents for capital and for themselves as workers, keeping women intimidated and pliable.[34]

INCLUSION/EXCLUSION

Although the oppression of men by men along class and racial lines is well documented, the extraction from nature and from women's complex of productive capacities long predates the theft of value from a working class. Moreover, nature and gender exploitation subsists through and beneath the abuse of wage-workers. Socialism, until now, has tended to place too much emphasis on a theory of the proletariat, and has dulled people's awareness of different forms of social exploitation.[35] Ecofeminists assert that the enclosure and privatisation of women, the subsumption of women's time, energies and powers through patriarchal family and public employment alike, parallel or more accurately underwrite the class exploitation of labour by capital.

Women's position as 'mediator of nature' constitutes a prior condition for the transaction that takes place between capitalist and labouring men – big men and small. In the androcentric discourse of economics, the material contribution of women remains largely unspoken in the same way that the material contribution of nature is attributed 0 value. Women's labour is 'freely given' behind the curtains of domestic decorum. What women do 'gratis', whether birthing labour or sustaining labour, is called 'reproduction' as opposed to production. Yet, the word 'reproduce' here connotes a secondary or diminutive activity, as distinct from Marx's 'primary historical act' of production itself. And since re/production is not recognised as primary, it cannot be seen to generate 'value'. By a symbolic sleight of hand sometimes called Reason, women's work is cheated of a place in a system of accumulation resting on the libidinal and economic surplus value they create.

To underscore how the Man/Woman=Nature grid works, an ecofeminist analysis of the classic capitalist patriarchal ontology is useful. The domain assumptions of this discursive armoury are as follows:

- an artificial distinction between History and Nature;
- an assumption that Men are active historical Subjects and Women passive Objects;
- an assumption that historical action is necessarily Progressive and activities grounded in nature necessarily Regressive;
- an association of Masculinity with the historical order through Production and association of Femininity with the order of nature through Reproduction;
- Valued production and De-valorised reproduction.[36]

Hanging on the eurocentric logic of dualism that penetrates philosophy just as much as everyday talk, the symbolism of these time-honoured pairs reiterates the 1/0 morphology of sex, erases women's humanity, and functions to keep men superordinate to women and to nature, so-called.[37]

Yet, obviously, it makes no sense to speak as if nature is somehow prior to history, for time is a condition of all existents. What is also missing in these formulations is any reflexivity in understanding the libidinal grounding of these constructed categories. In epistemological terms, capitalist patriarchal thinking simply floats on thin air. The 'natural order' can be known only through history, that is, by subjects living within a medium of socially generated languages and practices. Capital manages to obscure this historical dimension by the sheer force of its ideological machine – such that people actually do come to believe that reality is striated in this way, and universally so. Religion, ethics, economics and even sociobiology hang on these essentialist dualisms. Some left critical thought, and even varieties of feminism, are infected by them too, taking the content of each paired assumption as given.

While a careful deconstruction of conventional essentialist thought categories is needed, what is undeniably given is the fact that women and men do have existentially different relationships to nature because they have different kinds of body organs. But to say this is not to say that women are any *closer* to nature than men in some ontological sense. Rather, it is to recall Marx's teaching that human consciousness develops in a dialectical way through sensuous bodily interaction with the material environment. Just as someone who has no organ of sight may develop a unique awareness, so men and women, differently-abled, come to think and feel differently about being in the world as a result of how they can act on it, and how they experience it acting on them in turn. Biology can inscribe cognitive structures just as much as discourse does.

At the same time, it is a postmodern truism that bodily activities, including labour, are mediated by language and the ideological assumptions embedded in it. Accordingly, women's sensuous interchange with habitat gets to be shaped in a second-order sense, by assigned roles which force them to 'mediate nature for men'. Historically trapped within masculinist logic, women's sensual enjoyment and creative reciprocity with their environment are denigrated as regressive by an artificial and compulsory association with Nature. In such labours, women give up the substance of their bodies, experiencing entropy like that which nature suffers in the process of accumulation. Curiously, while the value of their work does not register in national accounts, their deterioration does. So the capitalist patriarchal state provides a plethora of clean-up programmes – battered women's refuges, addiction counselling – which parallel environmental efforts at resource recycling and restoration of toxic lands.

In the discursive construction of gendered labour, mining or engineering by men is also a hands-on transaction with the environment. But such work is typified by the conventionally positive side of the symbolic grid, endorsing masculine identity as separate from Nature, productive and progressive. By contrast, the language that typifies women's work – reproduction – degrades her along with nature itself. This ontology is legitimated by M/W=N institutions – Church and State, Market and Trade Union, Science and Technology. When women challenge this status quo for a share of male privilege as 'labour', they meet ideological weapons such as harassment and rough handling in order to reinstate their properly feminine status as part of Nature.[38] This dynamic is inevitable, since men themselves, or 'formal labour', can purchase progress under capitalism only by trading off further exploitation on to women and thence nature, down the line.

Plainly, male workers are abused under capitalism, but this is not sufficient reason to neglect the distinctive constellation of women's exploitation. What ecofeminism demands is a fully amplified critique of capital's degradation of 'conditions of production', based on a recognition of the nature–woman–labour nexus as a fundamental contradiction. Socialist treatment of women becomes abusive when, in the analysis of capitalism, the complex of feminine labours is seen as somehow auxiliary and sidelined in favour of an historically privileged proletariat. As trade union activist Giovanna Ricoveri expresses it, only by being open to 'difference' can one hope for 'the creation of a new politics that would contain strong elements of the Green, the red, feminism, and so on, but would look like none of these well-established tendencies'.[39] Until the problem of gender blindness in contemporary politics is overcome, however, women need to be on constant guard against premature closure in any new theoretical totalisation. This is part of why it makes 'strategic' sense to prioritise ecofeminist voices at this point in time.

PART III

MAKING POSTCOLONIAL SENSE

7
WHEN FEMINISM FAILS

THE MOTHERING CLASS

Bringing ecology, feminism, socialism and indigenous politics together means giving up the eurocentric lens for a genuinely global one. Thus

> If we could at this time shrink the world's population to a village of precisely 100 with all existing human ratios remaining the same, it would look like this:
>
> - There would be 57 Asians, 21 Europeans, 14 from North and South America, and 8 Africans.
> - 30 would be white; 70 would be coloured.
> - 30 would be Christian; 70 would be of other religions.
> - Half of the wealth would be in the hands of only 6 people, and all 6 would be from the United States.
> - 70 would be unable to read, 50 would suffer from malnutrition, and 80 would live in sub-standard housing.
> - Only 1 would have a tertiary education.[1]

Most social movement activists and political theorists are yet to take these realities on board, but this chapter will focus specifically on how feminism in the North needs to become more sensitive to ethnic and class difference. The discussion may also be useful for environmentalist men, who are not always clear about the political implications of various feminisms.

The twentieth-century women's movement has passed through several stages. Beginning with a rather uncritical adulation of the 1/0 domain, First Wave feminists, broadly equality or liberal feminists, set out to secure constitutional basics for women such as the vote and right to property ownership. Feminism's Second Wave deepened the agenda, grappling with injustices such as illiteracy, domestic violence, reproductive rights, and equal pay. Eighty years after the birth of liberal feminism, these struggles still go on. Second Wave activists used two kinds of theory: radical or cultural feminism which saw the psychology of patriarchal masculinity as the root problem, and socialist feminism which stressed economic exploitation. Ecofeminism is a third and international wave which draws on all three approaches. Women now shed the victim role, going on the offensive against the entire capitalist patriarchal assault to life-on-earth.

While ecofeminism builds on existing feminist theories, these in turn are challenged by the need to make sense of ecological crisis and biocolonisation. With ecofeminism, inputs by women from nonmetropolitan cultures become salient to political critique; increasingly, ecofeminism expresses a 'womanist' sensibility overlapping with Third World and indigenous knowledges. Practical gains won through liberal, socialist and radical feminist activities continue to support ecofeminist politics. But when it comes to a choice between either older-style reforms for equality or a sustainable future, only the latter, ecofeminist option makes global democratic sense.

What characterises a womanist politics? African-American writer Alice Walker has claimed that 'Womanist is to feminist as purple is to lavender'. A 'womanist' woman is responsible, flexible, courageous, wilful, preferring feminine culture yet committed to the whole community's well-being.[2] The key here is a transvaluation of 'feminine' experiences and, in particular, the relational sensibility often gained in mothering labours. The almost adolescent character of much Second Wave feminist politics became apparent as early as the 1970s in discussions between black and white women. If white students massed on the streets of Sydney demanding abortion rights, Koori sisters living in car bodies on the outskirts of country towns wanted the right to keep their children alive. Black priorities were womanist rather than feminist: health, housing, and survival.

The same race/class divide still occurs in the 1990s, among women at international forums such as the Cairo conference on population. In fact, the eurocentric feminist answer to global crisis often coincides with the view of most middle-class white men that population control in the Third World is the answer to women's equality and environmental stress.[3] The unexamined masculinist assumptions behind much liberal feminism also show up in bell hooks's comment that 'Often feminists talk about male abuse of women as if it is an exercise of privilege rather than an expression of moral bankruptcy, and dehumanisation.'[4] For too many equality feminists, the link between their own emancipated urban affluence and unequal appropriation of global resources goes unexamined.

Capitalist patriarchal institutions are comfortable with this kind of feminism and encourage it. But the new Women's European Interdisciplinary Scientific Network for risk management studies instantiates its limits. Funded by the European Union and involving women from the Ukraine, Armenia, Kazakhstan, Belarus, and Siberia, the idea grew from a symposium called 'Women's Realities' – taking account of gender in emergency situations. In other words, what this cross-national programme is actually about is 'women's responses' to realities designed by men. The programme provides legitimation for industry and government but is a retroactive move for feminism – though some environmental consciousness-raising may come out of it.[5]

As the 1970s turned into the 1980s, young women with banners were quickly offered opportunities to teach Women's Studies, funded to run rape crisis centres, or enticed into government watchdog jobs as femocrats. Were these successes a form of repressive tolerance by the establishment letting feminism close in on itself? And what happened to the intergenerational womanism that still sustains working-class and indigenous communities? As if to carve out a political identity distinct from the entrapment of their mothers' era, many Second Wave feminists rejected everything to do with 'womanliness' as sharply as growing boys do in their search for masculine identity. Much of the energy that went into abortion campaigning was clearly a sublimation of this hostility toward the problematic mother.

The unreality of mothering experiences to many feminists did not help theorisation. One outcome was a single-minded obsession with exposing the oppressive shadow of biology. Given that women's embodied difference had been the historical pivot of M/W=N oppression, this was an important focus. However, it may prove to be the case that irreducible sex-linked potentials do exist. Equality feminists would then have to assimilate and respond politically to that information. Wise feminists have suggested that given feminist sensitivity to being dubbed 'closer to nature', women might do better to defer brawls over biology until the movement is stronger. On the other hand, Hilary Rose makes a plea for understanding the relation between biology and social forces as dialectically interrelated. My own view is that feminism already entails a sophisticated epistemology critique of identitarian logic (1/0) and should be making use of it in internal debates like this one.

To suggest that mothering is important is not to question sexual self-determination as a fundamental right of women, but rather to prise open deeper layers of political meaning within our movement. For there is no doubt that the cultural stigmatisation of mothers has bound and gagged feminist theory at patriarchal convenience. As Giovanna Dalla Costa has noted: 'In the barrios (proletarian neighbourhoods) of the metropolises, the key figure in the family is the mother, who was the only real reference point, while the father was an inconstant and unpredictable figure.'[6] Middle-class Anglo feminists, fresh from the post-World-War-Two nuclear family, dismissed the grassroots politics of Hispanic peasant women, for example, as not real consciousness but 'marianismo'. In the North, workplace equal opportunity programmes advanced a handful of child-free middle-class girls, but did little for the majority. The hope is that feminism's ideological immaturity will be remedied as this generation of career women take up mothering themselves, and draw that learning into feminist thought.[7]

But while ecofeminist actions break new ground and seek wider alliances, a postmodern academic retreatism has weakened feminism from within.[8] The separation of head from hand, theory from practice, is what gave rise to destructive dualisms such as Humanity versus Nature, masculine versus feminine, in the first place. It is no surprise, then, that salaried discourse theorists claim there is 'nothing natural' about the body. While prioritising the theorised 'body', a good deal of 1990s feminism is itself entirely disembodied. Removed from everyday life problems, it confuses its own epistemological exercise with ontology. Post-structural feminism reduces reality to one dimension – linguistic representation – then reifies it.

A CULTURE OF NARCISSISM?

It is true that ways of knowing are many and relative, but whatever is 'out there' is at least relatively autonomous. To treat women as always already culturally 'inscribed' by language, as postmodernism does, is to accept a functionalist closure that plays right into the hands of the status quo. Paradoxically, in the name of freedom the totalising play of signifiers can end up privileging differences between people to such an extent that shared experiences of oppression are all but cancelled. This undermines efforts to build a global ecofeminist politics based on multicultural alliances among women. As our marxist colleagues would say, postmodern feminism becomes quietistic bourgeois idealism by default. Its scholasticism pacifies an emerging generation of women just as economic rationalism fixes the ambitions of their brothers.

Feminist politics has also been hijacked by the debate over pornography very much as 1960s radicalism was subverted by the drug scene. The controversy also reveals a great deal of narcissism within middle-class Western feminism and an obsession with the sexed body that is incomprehensible to working-class and land-based people. While anti-porn campaigners argue that pornography is the propaganda and rape the practice, the postmodern reply is that this judgement confounds 'representations' of violence with actual atrocities. Yet the dismembering of women – and nature – is everywhere to see. In the USA, a woman is raped every 3 minutes; a woman is battered every 15 minutes; two out of three reported violence cases occur in the home; eighteen out of twenty women are psychologically harassed on the job. So much for development.

Other capitalist patriarchal choices are daily extinction of rare insects and birds, mass slaughter of beef cattle, decimated forests, and poisoned streams. It is healthy that feminists want free expression and sex in abundance, but even in so-called advanced societies the cost of commercial porn is sexualised public terror for women. As with ecological exploitation, so here too the enjoyment of a protected few is displaced as violence on to Other lives.[9] This is not to argue against the 'free speech' of some; it is to reclaim the survival of Others. In a desensitising mechanical culture, porn may indeed revive jaded energies, but can free expression exist at all in a society where sex is a consumer item and performance is mistaken for self-realisation?

There is too little feminist self-interrogation over complicity with the tele-pharmo-nuclear complex. And this shows up in the typical movement jargon of the 1990s. Even the feminist analysis of domination is a matter of 'boundaries', 'contested sites', 'strategy' and 'manoeuvres'. Playful irony? Or booster shot for masculine power and its aura of instrumental rationality? The woman of the cybernetic era remakes herself as cyborg – half organism, half machine. Western feminism 'generates' its own tech 'heads' among those affluent enough to access international computer bulletins and surf the net with the boys. While ostensibly creating a new 'social space' for women, this virtual activity defuses and institutionalises the radical impulse. The other side of these depoliticised electronic adventures is an ongoing privatised hell known as 'getting my shit together'. Two decades after the Second Wave, pop psychology and self-help manuals are the biggest sellers in feminist bookshops.

Professional metropolitan feminism has its own priorities, and international sisterhood – passed off as naive – is not one of them. But ecofeminism has a history of its own, shaped by the day-to-day efforts of ordinary women to survive with their children in an era of excess. Drawing on the grassroots experience of women in both industrialised and indigenous communities, ecofeminism opens feminism up to a new cluster of problems. It is an implicit challenge to the urban-based theoretical models – liberal, marxist, radical, poststructuralist – that have held sway in women's politics. Activists continue to draw insights from these analytical strands from time to time – one is more helpful in policy work, another in intimate life – but by bringing ecology to established feminisms, ecofeminism encourages a new orientation and synthesis. Through deconstruction of the Man/Woman=Nature equation, ecofeminism 're-inscribes' those oppressive links.

The structure of this book reflects that dialectic between multiple levels of discourse. As Ashis Nandy has written in the context of postcolonial politics: 'I like to believe that each such concept in this work is a *double entendre*: on the one hand, it is part of an oppressive structure; on the other, it is in league with its victims.'[10] In reviewing Man's relation to Nature, ecofeminism addresses the same project as environmental ethics and politics. As a feminism, however, ecofeminist theory takes on this project in a compound sense. In its ecological advocacy of Woman's relation to Nature, it must simultaneously call for a review of the socialist project, Man's relation to Man, and the feminist project, Man's relation to Woman, as it goes.

Being always triangulated between socialism, feminism and ecology, ecofeminism cannot go after its political object in a simple, linear way. Rather, ecofeminism moves back and forth dialectically between (1) the liberal–socialist feminist task of arguing its equal right to a political voice; (2) a radical–poststructural feminist task of deconstructing the masculinist basis of that same political validation; and (3) pursuit of its ecological aims by narrating how women have been able to live an alternative relation to nature from men and how men might now join them in this way of being.

The struggle over women factory workers' exposure to lead models the learning that ecofeminism brings to politics. Initially, women labour activists assumed that to argue for special work conditions because of their reproductive role would emphasise their difference from men. This would weaken their voice (1) and encourage employer discrimination against them. Determined to reject the standard patriarchal M/W=N lore that female equals body (2), liberal and socialist feminist negotiators were in a double bind. But by reframing their industrial dispute in ecofeminist terms (3), men were included as 'part of nature' and of social reproduction outside the workplace. Turning attention to how 'men's bodies' are also affected by lead, the women now invited male-dominated unions into the fray. With augmented bargaining power, new work conditions were won. However, the ultimate question – Can we do without lead based products? – was not posed. So the opportunity for industrial conversion, creating healthy and sustainable alternative work in community gardens, was missed.

As to the question of who is an ecofeminist, there are two ways of answering it. One sense is subjective and weak; the other is objective or structural. By the weak meaning, an ecofeminist is someone who calls her- or himself 'ecofeminist'. This subjective criterion is known by sociologists as meaning adequacy: a label being judged accurate if accepted by those named. Given the transcultural context of ecofeminism, the subjective self-definition runs up against linguistic diversity. More important is the fact that people's political consciousness exists along a continuum from action and tacit knowledge to sophisticated theorised justification. Actions often precede ideological awareness.

Since it is ultimately actions that count in making history, not words, labels and self-concepts, an objective structural definition makes better sense as far as social change movements go. By the structural criterion, an ecofeminist is anybody who carries out ecofeminist activities. That is, the term applies to a man or woman whose political actions support the premise that the domination of nature and domination of women are interconnected. To repeat: ecofeminism is neither an essentialising standpoint nor an identity politics.

GLOBAL STRUCTURES: CRITICAL MASS

Critics of ecofeminism as 'essentialist' especially need to grasp these things. For instance, use of the subjective criterion leads Barbara J. Epstein to speculate that the ground swell of women opposing militarism and toxics has little to do with ecofeminism. Her claim depends on a perception that identifies ecofeminist politics with a collection of largely idealist writing published entirely in the USA; a literature less connected to practical grassroots politics than most global ecofeminism is. In any event, she makes the following observation:

> In spite of large numbers of women in the environmental movement, and their increasingly prominent roles in leadership, women in the movement have not made issues of gender central to their political practice in the way that people of colour have made issues of race. ... Women who join the movement may be influenced by feminism but they are not likely to define themselves primarily in relation to it.[11]

This text reduces feminism and ecology to single-issue movements. But women eco-activists may not identify primarily as 'feminist', because ecofeminism is a holistic approach to all forms of domination – sex, race, species – not just a particularistic campaign for women's own advancement.

An ecofeminist standpoint may make little sense to the international minority whose minds and bodies are alienated from reproductive and sustaining labours by years spent in offices or factories, and by a high-tech lifestyle at home. This is why unassuming manual workers such as housewives have been the rank and file of the environmental movement. Women's liberation as such is not their aim, but there is no doubt that when such women are pushed aside by paid ecocrats or technical experts, an outraged sense of fair play stirs them. At this point a class in-itself, with little selfconsciousness, begins to grow into a politicised class for-itself, with a practical perception of just how feminist and ecological struggles are complementary. Besides the thousands of grassroots women volunteers in local nature groups, other ecofeminists network internationally, and others again theorise and write about the movement. But the impulse behind this political work almost always gets back to women's objective relation to social reproduction.

The shared materiality of this structural position persists globally despite differences of region, class, religion or language. Moreover, the fact that ecofeminisms appear simultaneously, from Venezuela, Kenya, or Canada, for example, is surely strong argument against poststructural assertions that discourse precedes/inscribes intention. Epstein seems unclear about the emerging paradigm that is quietly revolutionising the women's movement. Like many socialists and Second Wave feminists, she appears unconvinced by the line that women's life-affirming values attract them to ecopolitics. However, the fact that ecofeminism addresses a historically constituted and not 'essential' relation is demonstrated by those men who increasingly choose to advocate and participate in nurturant activities. At the same time though, we need to ask, Why is it usually women, not men, who so readily labour unpaid in environmental protest organisations?

Perhaps the statement from Love Canal toxics fighter Lois Gibbs helps bring to light the underlying structural logic of ecofeminist actions: 'I was a housewife, a mother, but all of a sudden it was my family, my children, and my neighbours. I believed in democracy, but then I discovered that it was government and industry that abused my rights.'[12] Epstein's subjectivist case that ecofeminism is irrelevant to ecopolitics is a little like claiming that politically active members of the industrial working class are not socialists because they do not read *Capital* and call themselves marxist. Even in socialism, there is always a continuum of subject positions, from a weaker subjective to stronger structural identification. Hence the objective social interests of a left academic and a coal miner will differ at times, despite dedication to the same cause.

Besides commitment, a political movement needs critical mass: a shared understanding of why something is wrong, who is ready to change it, what solutions there are, and how they can be made real. Our glance across ecofeminist history shows each of these prerequisites to be there, though with differing degrees of articulation. Without doubt, ecofeminism qualifies as a new social movement, but it is unique, both in its transcultural sensibility and in being far more than a single-issue identity politics. Can it be argued that ecofeminist women and men constitute a revolutionary social class? They might qualify in Weber's classic sociological sense of shared interests and ideas, though economic opportunities, status and political influence vary a great deal among individual activists North and South. Conversely, marxists determine class membership by relation to the means of production. Women and some men's life-affirming activities come close to what Marx called social reproduction, but ecofeminist emphasis on the ecocentric context of these structural relations extends that paradigm.

In the last analysis, the question of ecofeminism and class depends on the gendered critique of how and why eurocentric political concepts, including socialist concepts, have been constructed as they are. A woman activist from Salvador in Brazil puts her finger on part of the problem:

> My husband sometimes tries to stop me from going to the meetings. But I always try to show him that this is part of a woman's duty. After all, we are the ones who see the major problems in the neighbourhood. Not all men are aware that there are not sufficient schools, nor decent water, or that there are kids playing in the middle of the garbage. So, it is up to women to fight for improvements in the neighbourhood. ... When we had a meeting of all the members in Mar Grande, we took turns in doing the domestic chores. Some men did not want to take their turn, some complained they did not know how to do them ... they all had to learn. ... It is not because of their jobs. Many of them are unemployed. But they prefer to play dominoes instead.[13]

And what of men in/with ecofeminism? In the 1970s, most political writing dealing with socialist, ecological or postcolonial themes was genderblind. With the 1980s, words like 'woman', 'feminism' or 'ecofeminism' began to turn up in indexes of male-authored texts – a token one-sentence observation among 250 pages being the norm. There were also attempts by unreflexive masculinist writers to rebut ecofeminism at this time. Moving to the 1990s, simplified expositions of ecofeminist ideas started to find a place in general treatments of ecopolitical thought. Internationally, a handful of men have taken ecofeminism seriously enough to expound it accurately or make sympathetic contributions, among them Patrick Murphy in English literature, Jim Cheney in ethics, and economist Martin O'Connor.[14] Among grassroots activists we should honour Viktor Kaisiepo, who has embarked on setting up Men Against Violence groups throughout Pacific island nations.[15]

Ecofeminism loves and needs its radical brothers. For despite our socially constructed and other differences, one thing we all want is a new intersubjectivity between men, women, nature – hitherto divided by old and arbitrary labels. Many years ago, one of the grandmothers of Second Wave feminism, Audre Lorde, commented thus:

> Women of today are still being called upon to stretch across the gap of male ignorance, and to educate men as to our existence and our needs. This is an old and primary tool of all oppressors to keep the oppressed occupied with the master's concerns. Now we fear it is the task of black and third world women to educate white women.[16]

There is still truth in Lorde's observation, but the tide is turning. Ecofeminism especially enjoins this task, with women North and South, and some men, beginning to work together for global change.

For the point is that the ecofeminist renaming of 'poverty' has thrown down a material challenge that many green activists, socialists and feminists are yet to hear. Ultimately, for the sake of global justice and sustainability, the North will have to review its high-tech consumption in favour of more species-egalitarian models by which the South provisions itself. Kate Soper contends that

> it will depend on the extent to which those which have been most privileged in the access they have had to the earth's resources come to feel obligated to constrain their own consumption and to provide for those who have hitherto been seriously deprived.[17]

People in the West need to be more critical of how their lives are embedded in destructive technologies such as electricity, house paint, batteries, and insecticide. But addressing the liberal constituency, perhaps, Soper also believes that

> the appeal to altruism has to be complemented by an appeal to self-interest ... it is only if sufficient numbers come to experience the enticement of the gratifications promised by less materially fixed life-styles that they will seriously consider mandating policies to constrain resource-hungry and exploitative modes of production.[18]

The reified social relations that make up the 'industrial juggernaut' run very deep, fed as they are by the divisions of labour and prohibitions between hand, heart, head, and womb. The outcome of this 1/0 mindset is an inconsequential politics. An earth-healing calls for deeply attuned and practical wisdoms. I doubt that Soper's 'enticement' or even 'resensitisation' will be enough. Deep ecologists have already tried spiritual communion with the wild to little political effect – not to mention the profound misogyny which still mars much of their writing. Equally, the efforts of ecocrats and femocrats to fraternise with corporations and governments are neither life-affirming nor liberating. If the eurocentric ideal of masculinity is constructed by dissociation from its material substrate in Mother=Nature, then its objectification in political economy is just as likely to fail feminism and ecology for psychosexual reasons.

Besides, the tele-pharmo-nuclear complex offers ample rewards for those with 'knowhow' to help it expand. Accordingly, the 'capitalisation of feminism' was under way even as early as the 1970s. Governments soon pacified a generation of unruly women by admitting a token few to the ranks of authority, though always to administer capitalist patriarchal goals. These remunerated opportunities deflected the energies of vibrant grassroots radical protest. In addition, the economic independence of women produced visible spinoffs for GNP, with increasing transactions around individual vehicle use, laundry services, law courts, child care. Left sociologists, government statisticians and international agencies had a field day with this data, yet after two decades of campaigning, women's representation in elected decision-making bodies still averaged a mere 10 per cent. This 10 to 1 male/female ratio is the same North or South, and regardless of whether or not there is a local 'feminist' movement.

SHAME AND ASSIMILATION

While ecofeminists argue that the liberation of nature and of women go hand in hand, governments and UN agencies arrange for the 'sustainable management' of feminine outrage. Ecofeminist politics is under pressure of being subsumed by a pragmatic and reformist sisterhood in heels, carried along by the expansionist transnational corporate agenda. Large sums are spent to bring women together at conferences like Copenhagen or Istanbul, but official delegates are handpicked by national bureaucracies so as not to embarrass governments. Given that liberal feminism seeks equality of women inside eurocentric institutions, many on the intercontinental circuit read this as a sign of success. But the NGO procedure divides women between an accredited elite, 1, and rank-and-file participants, 0, so weakening women's movement solidarity. Is a new international class of women 'decision makers' being groomed to provide legitimacy for global business interests?[19]

In 1994, Australian ecofeminists proposed that women set up an international boycott of life-destroying products manufactured by tele-pharmo-nuclear corporations.

> For too long, women's environmental activism has been about 'mopping up operations in our own back yards'. Yet as workers and consumers constituting over 50% of the world's population, women hold a fantastic power – the capacity to bring economic pressure to bear on corporate interests whose activities endanger environments and human health. Ecofeminists question the consumption lifestyle of the North and corresponding transfer of dangerous jobs and wastes into the communities of their sisters of the South. We need to get proactive, by breaking this unsustainable cycle of North/South exploitations which all women are locked into by the new economic order.[20]

In the lead-up to the UN's Fourth Decade Conference on Women at Beijing, a resolution on boycotts was overwhelmingly supported by a grassroots Sydney meeting of the NGO umbrella group Coalition of Participating Organisations (CAPOW). It read as follows:

> Australian women invite international sisters in Beijing to join us in calling for the following 3 strategies: an internationally coordinated 'education campaign' among women on human/environmental costs of nuclear, genetic engineering, and pharmaceutical industries; a 'consumer boycott' of their dangerous products; governments to place a 'moratorium' on such products until they can be demonstrated harmless in our living environment.

The initiative was soon lost from sight, however. Environment was defined as a 'separate issue' by liberal feminists in the upper echelons of the conference planning bureaucracy. Their rearguard objectives would be health, family, and getting more women into decision-making positions.

Following the international meeting at Beijing, the Australian federal government's Office of the Status of Women hailed the resultant Plan of Action as a first-rate set of 'non-legally binding' benchmarks for change. These capitalist patriarchal offerings included training more women in communications technologies and 'a model of best practice' for stopping violence on women; colonial assistance for Pacific island women's projects; and better bureaucratic monitoring of Aboriginal health, cervical testing and mammography. The *coup de grâce* was the formation of an Australian Council of Business Women using Department of Industry, Science, and Technology funds, in 'partnership' with the Institute of Company Directors, the Business Council, and the Chamber of Commerce and Industry. The push would be for a 'Women Mean Business' initiative to increase female appointments on company boards. It also turned out that the conference newsletter *Womenspeak* produced by CAPOW was sponsored by the Westpac Bank.[21]

In effect, supra-democratic events such as Beijing use the ambitions of liberal feminists in pre-emptive strikes against ecofeminism and its exposure of the ultimate game. Further, agency-sponsored programmes handed down to grassroots women are demeaning and cause disorientation and passivity. Ecofeminists and liberal feminists could work together – if femocrats would agree to broaden their virtual political horizons beyond maximising choice in the jungles of concrete, dioxin and steel. Many liberal feminists are well connected and able to find spaces for indigenous, Third World and ecofeminist activists to be heard in the political mainstream. The New York WEDO group, with its status quo legitimacy and ability to attract aid agency funds, has generously catalysed grassroots women's participation in UN-sponsored events. The outcome of this re/sistering has been a useful crosscultural reality-testing all round. For as a recent survey of NGO opinion reports, men and women, developed and developing nationals alike, think 'patriarchal attitudes' are the single greatest obstacle to real communication within UN-organised forums; after this comes the intransigence of national officials and government delegations – the masculine collective subject.[22]

Another tendency that plays into the hands of power are the economic-growth-oriented gender-and-development academics. Despite all indications to the contrary, they refuse to acknowledge that women are the leading protagonists in neighbourhood politics, ecology, and peace.[23] Differences of class, age, race, religion and nation among women dissolve when it comes to social reproduction, and this hybridisation gives ecofeminist historical agency political strength. Thus an international cohort of re/sisters is now preoccupied with food security, militarism and pollution, reproductive rights, land distribution and structural adjustment. As things stand, the liberal feminist lifestyle is uncritically dependent on unsustainable levels of industrial consumerism: the average Australian, for example, wears down the environment twenty times more than her Indonesian sister.

Globalised free trade alone exacts an appalling ecological cost. The Australian Academy of Science lists animal disease arriving through air travel; bulk grain and nursery seedling imports; discharged ship ballast; scientific germplasm imports; and cut flowers.[24] At the Rio Earth Summit, Third World elites lobbied the North to fund ecological repair or, rather, to fund their new urban middle classes to administer the requisite system of licences and compensations. But increasingly the fabric of rural and indigenous communities is neglected. Wolfgang Sachs observes that politics continues to be caught up in the 'internal rivalries' of a relatively small global middle class, condemning the rest to silence.[25] This 'class' is about equivalent in number to the 8 per cent of people in the world who own a car. Needless to say, most women are found travelling by bus.

Among other things, ecofeminism is a kind of reflexive anthropology for women and men in so-called developed societies. If it aims to bring a feminist consciousness to the environmental movement, it also aims to bring an environmental consciousness to feminism. In particular, much of its political activity is to help equality feminists see how their emancipatory dreams assist capitalist patriarchal colonisation and environmental degradation. Victoria Davion typifies the liberal moment in feminism when she claims that the feminine role 'fails to provide a genuine grounding for anything other than the continued oppression of women'.[26] She speaks for women who have been so shamed by the Man/Woman=Nature hegemony that they taboo discussion of links between women and nature. By default, these assimilationists opt for 1/0 formula, thereby suppressing the dialectical potential inherent in that unstable order.

Ecofeminists ask whether what is signified by the 1/0 economy and its privileged term is really worth preserving at all? For example, the so-called liberated woman must adopt an instrumental, rational attitude in dealings with others, including her children. She must be supremely conscious that her time means money. Oddly enough, even liberal feminists maintain that women's entry into the public sphere alongside men will 'humanise' organisations – bring revolution from within. This is a tacit admission of the very feminine 'difference' that they want to deny. Yet what most often happens when women enter the workforce is the crushing exploitation of the 'relational self'. The alternative is to become supremely tough, calculating and manipulative, outsmarting the boys at their own game.

A recent article in the business pages of an Australian daily newspaper described the corporate ethic as one of jobs for the boys, hiding information, decision-making cliques, stealing work and ideas, lack of connectedness to the client, blaming underdogs for errors, and finding the solution before the problem.[27] The US army's secret use of shells tipped with depleted uranium during the Gulf War would exemplify 'finding the solution before the problem'. It scattered 300 tons of radioactive material across the desert, leaving a generation of Iraqi and US veteran families to deal with the consequences of cancer. Again, across the globe, residual military land mines continue to kill or maim five hundred people every week.

Perhaps it takes the experience of Two Thirds World marginalisation to fully grasp the politically incoherent and colonising aspect of the assimilationist strategy.[28] Consider African-American bell hooks's question: 'Since men are not equals in a white supremacist, capitalist, patriarchal class structure, which men do [feminist] women want to be equal to?'[29] The Caribbean action group DAWN also dissociates itself from 'equality-oriented development thinking'. For the problem is that accommodation of women's bodily difference to the androcentric format of human rights legislation, softens the masculine face of state oppression without ever opening up dialogue over its first premise. Critical marxists use the term 'repressive tolerance' for these small concessions. Joni Seager aptly sums up the shortcomings of 'being on line' in the tele-pharmo-nuclear club:

> 'the problem' with masculinist institutions is not primarily that men are in charge, but that structures can be so rooted in masculinist presumptions that even were women in charge of these structures, they would retain the core characteristics that many feminists and progressive men find troubling.[30]

It is a case of free choice, as long as the choice is 1.

8

TERRA NULLIUS

ECOLOGICAL ECONOMICS

Bodies and narratives are nurtured in symbiotic comings and goings of earth, air, fire and water. In nature's coinless economy, solar energy comes to us as light and moves on as heat in the ground – heat that stirs winds and ocean currents that carry fish roe. Energy is held in water, wood, and petrified plant mass. Volcanoes and lightning start wind-driven fires exposing grassland buds. Trees in sunlight make sugars stored in fruits, and nesting birds keep them from insect predators. Oxygen from leaves is used by humans to metabolise grains for warmth. Human breath is used, in turn, by plants. Phosphorus leaches from rocks to soil to streams, is fixed in living bones, then comes back to the earth in the detritus of death. Nitrogen washed from the air by rain is bonded in soil by root bacteria, mammals take the enriched grass and humans take their flesh. Lichens and moulds are eaten by frogs, whose eggs are taken by snakes. And on it goes, a pulsating web of exchange.

Nature's holograph is invisible to capitalist patriarchal reason. The latter's science and economics annul the links that they should preserve and satisfy. The ozone hole, algal blooms, species loss leave eurocentric culture up against a wall of its own making, and that is its domain construct: Mother=Nature. The ongoing marginality of gendered relations and unconscious

Man/Woman=Nature assumptions prolong the dilemma. Life process is readily masked as product. The mystique of the masculine-birthed commodity dusts every variety of thought, from conservative to liberal and from socialist to postmodern conjectures. But needs are not met. In the 1/0 system, an idealised supply takes priority over material demand.[1] So-called growth is driven by a spiral of debt that sucks out the placenta behind it. The bodies of gendered, ethnic and species populations are colonised, and common lands are turned over for a quick buck.

At the same time, the amount of international finance invested in pure speculation is some thirty times more than what goes toward the production of goods.[2] In this ephemeral market, the money itself comes to be treated as a package for sale. Stock is not stock. A bond is not a bond. Originating in the murky regime of 1/0 denial, capitalist patriarchal maximisation continually collapses back into its own self-created vacuum. This is no surprise, since the very idea of money came into being as symbolic debt. Even before a mercantile class was established, a libidinal foundation for this was laid in the originary cut from the maternal body. But there are other ways. Humans joined by reciprocal trust do not have to shore up the moment of lack with a dollar sign. In an ecological economy, a bond means an internal relation.

In the developed world, people talk and shop, numb to the ground that nurtures them. The shame of that first erotic link is sealed off with asphalt. A postmodern intelligentsia tilts at the lost referent, selling pastiche as style, but celebration of 'what is' deflects responsibility away from the brotherhood in suits. Some men and even feminists reach out for pornography to affirm themselves in the broken body of nature. A World Trade Organization (WTO) votes child labour off its agenda, and democracy whimpers in a man's right to bear arms. Under pressure of privatisation and downsizing, bullied white workers find outlet by scapegoating coloured Others. Community is reduced to an electronic image, where ever more lines of exclusion substitute for social structure.[3]

In the ongoing colonisation of the Australian continent, the 1/0 has operated as a legal fiction called *terra nullius*.[4] And as historian Marcia Langton has observed, those who use it 'treat our land as if our people were not there'. Unfortunately, some ecologists re-enact the moment of racial appropriation. Rather than respect the integral connection between Aboriginal survival and biodiversity, wilderness politics creates 'natural objects' to be viewed for entertainment. Just as often, 'protected areas' are hived off as resource banks for capital. Sensing the plot, some indigenous people now want the word 'wilderness' outlawed altogether, in favour of 'country', or 'cultural landscapes'.[5]

Langton draws a parallel between today's push for national parks and earlier forms of genocide. She describes the administered reserves set up to soothe the pillow of a dying Aboriginal race while entrepreneurs ransacked native land for motifs, from Drysdale's paintings to composer Antill's *Corroborree* suite. Blacks and koalas got to be displayed as nice evolutionary oddities on postcards and tea towels and the storybook *Picaninny Walkabout* sold over 100,000 copies. By 1992, Oz high-culture interior decor was showing off with dot-painted textiles in New York galleries, while Mick Dundee took the lone white male outback hero to Hollywood.

If popular Western notions of 'the wild' go back to the Judaeo-Christian tradition, they were reinforced by Enlightenment rationalism with its dualism of civilised versus savage. However, as we have seen, this dissociation and its sublimated M/W=N energies are what compels the capitalist patriarchal project of remaking nature according to human design. In the fractured alienative consciousness, to recall O'Brien's term, nature may be resourced as Man's whore or treated as sacred and virginal, when it represents His absence. By contrast, for most indigenous peoples wilderness or country is always alive with cultural *presence.*

In the European imaginary, Nature, like the arms of Woman, is a salve. In an aggressive and war-obsessed culture, wilderness carries the dream of gentleness and peace. To a materialistic, corrupt and polluted society, it brings purification and spiritual transcendence. In a callous, life-aborting society, a river tells the phases of a human life. For a sexually repressed culture, wilderness recharges the senses; and where emotion is denied, it speaks what is unfelt.[6] Such heartfelt strivings were very apparent in the late 1980s among protesters at the Franklin River blockade in Tasmania. Yet if the 'no dams' struggle promised to liberate nature, the social construction of wilderness as 'out there' also revealed how reactionary its politics was. For the idea of the marginalised wild serves to protect the everyday capitalist patriarchal world from encroachment by the unknown Other.

Tasmanian Wilderness Society (TWS) stalwarts still under the shadow of Van Diemen's Land and its shameful past were not yet ready to reunite Man and Nature or to think about country as indigenous livelihood. Nor were they ready to focus on their own taken-for-granted levels of resource use. For conserved wilderness is simply the other side of rampant urban industrial growth. Thus bearded boys in knitted beanies and fatigues ran heavy-fuel-consumption four-wheel-drives from inner-city terrace homes to TWS strategy meetings. Their compensatory preservationism sidelined the global injustice of a high-consumption lifestyle where forests in the South are 'carbon sinks' for the

North and where indigenous fishing grounds are closed off at the behest of a leisure class.

CORPORATE HARMONISATION

Capital's latest wave of economic colonisation hangs on genetic engineering, and hence bio-prospecting the rich diversity of indigenous lands and bodies. This takes place in four steps – resource assessment, regional agreements, conflict resolution, and intellectual property rights. Preparation for all this was made at the 1992 UN Earth Summit in Rio de Janeiro, sponsored by the Business Council for Sustainable Development, who ensured that its interests were built into Agenda 21, the Global Warming and Biodiversity Conventions. These in turn would be tied into international free trade provisions under a new World Trade Organization.[7]

But there is no doubt that ostensibly democratic regional associations also facilitate the penetration of local communities by TNCs. In Australia, a new Municipal Conservation Association, bristling with rhetoric from the UN Conference on Environment and Development (UNCED) and the principles of Environmentally Sustainable Development (ESD), could readily lend itself to that. At the World Bank and IMF, the language of 'development aid' has been superseded by 'economic cooperation'; where stronger inducement to play ball with big brother is wanted, 'structural adjustment' is the phrase.

The ideology of green business disperses itself through right-wing think-tanks, phoney environmental front groups, and appropriate cultural activities. Thus, Hydro Quebec, which displaced thousands of Canadian indigenes from the Hudson Bay area, set up a university chair of Environmental Ethics – then filled it with a specialist in Leonardo da Vinci! In Australia's

Northern Territory, Ranger Uranium funds Aboriginal Studies at the university – a piece of public relations that is highly divisive of indigenous loyalties, given the company's links to France's environmentally racist nuclear programme in the South Pacific.[8]

One enthusiastic apologist for capital has proposed to solve the environmental crisis by maximising the production of synthetics and 'thereby decoupling' the productive apparatus from nature:

> Perhaps the creation of an environmentally benign economic order calls for ... a truly capitalistic ethos. Capital itself must be regarded as virtually sacred – it represents nothing less than the savings necessary to construct a more prosperous and less environmentally destructive future economy. Capital is deferred gratification writ large.[9]

Today, in Alice Springs, the federal government LandCare programme and the indigenous Central Land Council co-sponsor a computerised catalogue of indigenous mineral, biological and cultural resources. Local leaders anticipate that resource assessment based on geographic information systems (GIS) will enhance Aboriginal livelihood by enabling management of resources in such a way that genetic and mineral items can be extracted while 'ecological balance' is maintained. Men and women elders lead resource assessment researchers to special sites which are mapped after extensive consultation and cross-checking. In this process the necessity for cars and electronic equipment to penetrate 'uncharted' areas is taken for granted.

Paradoxically, the use of GIS for resource assessment comes full circle back to *terra nullius* through the push to assimilate indigenous knowledges to Western technocratic discourse. While the mapping process is said to overlay and 'marry' two information bases, 'cultural data' is supposed to remain with local people. That claim is plainly questionable, as are other aspects of the programme from the point of view of cultural autonomy and survival. If LandCare requires open access to all GIS data gathered, and if the same information can be 'presented' either in bush tucker or scientific terms, there is in fact no way of protecting local intellectual property.

The debate over environmental racism is beginning to focus on problems like these. But many people expect resource assessment to help 'identify' regions suitable for politico-legal negotiation between government, corporate, and indigenous interests. Others wonder if regional agreements, in turn, might then be a way towards sovereignty? Few have asked what role transnational firms might have in steering the new 'regionalism'. Political economist Greg Crough from the Northern Australia Research Unit has been frank about his doubts: basically a resource assessment gets done, then native title on inalienable freehold land is traded away for royalties. That view has been contested by Les Carpenter, a veteran negotiator from the Inuvialuit Final Agreement in Canada, now a roving ambassador advocate for indigenous regional corporations.

The capitalisation of indigenous struggle is now taking place very rapidly in Australia. One advocate of regional agreements is former Northern Land Council director Daryl Pearce, whose advice to Aboriginal communities has been to 'get hold of a lawyer and negotiate a deal'. Straight to the bottom line, Pearce says 'make use of contract law, it's purely about business'. But how can indigenous people negotiate 'fair deals' with mining companies that are 40 per cent offshore-owned? Should self-determination hang on 'economic growth' and the return from involvement in such enterprises? Have white small-business people ever got themselves any political muscle? Would a new class of black small-business entrepreneurs really 'get a go' in an economic system dominated by TNCs? Aboriginal pastoralists think so, as does Phyllis Williams, who runs an indigenous tourist operation under licence from the Northern Land Council.

Regional agreements seem attractive against the profusion of legal remedies applicable to indigenous freedoms in Australia. At the 1995 Ecopolitics IX gathering in Darwin, Michael Mansell of the Tasmania-based Aboriginal Provisional Government pointed to the fact that the Native Title Act of 1993 covers only 3 per cent of all Aboriginal people on the continent. Aboriginal and Torres Strait Islander Social Justice Commissioner Mick Dodson observed that regional agreements could possibly undermine Mabo – the historic High Court decision on indigenous land ownership.[10] And he warned his people not to give up 'native title' rights to get basic 'citizenship rights' such as health and education: 'keep on about human rights so as to access the force of international conventions' signed by the federal government, he advises.

Of course, the very concept of 'rights' is corrupted by its origins in the individualistic and adversarial ideology of bourgeois rationalism. By contrast, indigenous ethics are communitarian, emphasising mutual support and exchange rather than possession. Besides, granting 'equal rights' to another typifies the self-congratulatory delusion of the liberal political tradition. The very act of giving rights, confirms the colonial moment of loss and so takes away as much autonomy as it bestows. Is there a better way towards sovereignty than trading in cultural meanings for white men's rights? If there is, eco-activists can move closer to it by exposing and destabilising the underlying premises of eurocentric culture. One encouraging sign is the multilateral grassroots regionalism growing between groups such as the Melanesian Environment Network and the Australian Conservation Foundation. Women are very active in this particular struggle for survival.[11]

CAPACITY BUILDING

The interplay of race, class and gender politics is complex. The new global business agenda creates enticing economic opportunities for indigenous elites, thereby weakening solidarity among oppressed communities. The new agenda also brings generous career opportunities for middle-class white consultants, including feminists. International treaties and conventions need data collection, analysis and reporting, legislation and compliance monitoring. The healthiest growth industry of all is dispute resolution. This is the latest weapon in the armoury of government and industry to 'contain and manage conflict' while creating an appearance of reasonableness and open consultation. These new psychological techniques, applied to key tribal 'players', include mediation and assisted negotiation, but they are no help to people if the sociological power and privilege of 'partners in dialogue' are not made explicit.

The corporate lingo of 'harmonisation' and 'partnership' thinly veils a greedy and patronising ethos. Martie Sibasado from the Kimberleys summed up the frustration of one such mediation session: – 'Why do you have to leave at 3 o'clock to catch a plane, when I've had to walk all my life?'[12] So-called 'capacity building' activities – assessment, monitoring, management, and dispute resolution 'techniques' – stud the discourse of the Business Roundtable and agencies like the UN and Environmental Protection Agency (EPA). Capacity building, also called 'enhancement', is the export of 'universal' – read white masculine – skills needed to help with 'technology transfer'. Thus a capitalist patriarchal high-tech straitjacket nullifies other ways of life across the globe.

In this wave of neocolonialism, indigenous people are captured by the West, being made to think they cannot live properly without its skills and products. But women in what is called the developed world are also colonised by the 1/0 mentality, liberal feminism being a clear manifestation of this. It is not only politics at the periphery that is being manipulated by globalising forces: women in the North are increasingly divided by class, age, ethnicity and ableness, as transnational business creates opportunities for an articulate few. After two decades, the Second Wave of feminism is conflicted in the same way that postcolonial struggles are. On the one side, a self-actualising politics of affluent women chases institutional acceptance by the privileged 1. On the other, women concerned with the reproduction of life conditions, 0, struggle for community survival.

The feminism of 1 has access to the master's technologies: instrumental reason in practice, and idealism in theory. The cause of this urban, industrial temper is easy to find. No longer autonomous producers, women have been reconstructed as passive consumers and supervised workers, their subversive wisdoms tamed by a productivist accord in which they had little say. If feminists seek justice through a revision of the UN System of National Accounts, they give in to the masculinist logic of accumulation. Meanwhile, the separation of production and consumption fragments and mystifies women's awareness of the consequential loops between labour, resources, time, and so-called ecological waste.

Identification with middle-class eurocentric norms leaves liberal feminism with a number of misbegotten political manoeuvres. In theory, liberal feminism combines conceptual one-dimensionality and ideological pluralism. In practice, it combines ideological separatism with a curious anti-life but pro-choice ethic. In a capitalist patriarchal society, the way forward for women is thought to exist in keeping their options open as men's are. Fertility control is thus essential to personal achievement and postmodern metropolitan amusements. Many liberal women consider time spent on environmental problems as a cost to their own advancement as individuals. When liberal feminists do support environmentalism, they often join the establishment North in advocacy of population control for the Third World. Yet already 40 per cent of Brazilian women are sterilised and an Indian National Family Health survey records the average age of female sterilisation in that country at twenty-six years.

In terms of global justice, when 20 per cent of the world's people need 80 per cent of global resources to get by, something is very wrong. Ecofeminist Pat Hynes argues that the time is long overdue for taking a hard look at global resource distribution in a transnational corporate productivist system and for 'taking population out of the equation' altogether.[13] But at the 1994 UN International Conference on Population and Development in Cairo, the colonial causes of land degradation and poverty were again put to one side and another twenty-year 'consensus' on population control was forged by the brotherhood in suits and their emancipated helpers in pearls.

At the Beijing conference, however, liberal feminists were shocked by what they saw and heard. Lynette Dumble, an expert on Depo Provera, Norplant, and RU486, exposed the misogynist and genocidal medical paradigm that drives the debate over population control:

> long-acting contraceptives that at one extreme may blind women by increasing the pressure within their brain cavities

> … vaccines that render women infertile by creating auto-immune disease; mass sterilisation camps where women die on a regular basis; medical experiments with hormones and an array of other chemicals that disrupt women's fertility or terminate their pregnancies with little or no concern for the acute ill-effects, let alone the chronic future morbidity.[14]

Typifying the interlock of a profitable corporate sector and an ostensibly independent international body such as the Population Council, Upjohn Pharmaceuticals donates US patent rights for Depo Provera to the council, whose bureaucrats in return will ensure an ongoing market for the product.

Dumble concludes that the pharmaceutical industry is assembling an 'impressive armour of pesticidal, or more specifically femicidal weapons. … I have [even] seen an Internet suggestion that population expansion could be more rapidly halted from the use of a genetically engineered virus.'[15] The contraceptive toxin Depo Provera is surreptitiously being used on disabled, black and Hispanic women in the USA and on Aboriginal and immigrant women in Australia. Once again, women and natives are targeted as 'vermin' by white middle-class men. Yet the simple fact is that if we all enjoyed a vegetarian diet and roads to cycle on, a population of 6 billion would not cost the Earth.

VERY PRIMITIVE ACCUMULATION

Women's bodies, traditionally 0, *terra nullius*, are undeveloped, wild, unless the 'protected' private property of husbands. But with new reproductive technologies, feminine bodies that stray by hospitals become cleverly resourced enclosures. Even childbirth is negotiable for a fee, and pre-fertilised ova are stocked under refrigeration on the basis of supply-side planning. The Western connotation of earth, nature, colour, feminine sex, animality, as less than fully human continues to be the capitalist patriarchal rationale for keeping most women and other colonised subjects under. It is understandable that liberal and some socialist feminists should want to be valued like the 1. These assimilationists are especially uncomfortable with 'difference' as a political marker, whether it be discursively constructed or biological variation. Other strands within the women's movement – radical, cultural, poststructural, and ecofeminist – are less fearful of social diversity.

The assault on nature, land, and animal and human bodies has a much longer history in Africa than in Australia and the South Pacific, and is less sophisticated than current PR-designed approaches through partnership, capacity building, and harmonisation. But in each region, resolution of the 'land question' is the cutting edge of World Bank and IMF activities whereby colonising men of the North unravel uniquely communal relations of social reproduction. The pattern is now appearing in New Guinea and in Vanuatu, with registration of custom lands being a first step toward privatisation and thus negotiation with outside investors. As happened in Europe centuries before, once land is valued, a rising urban middle class transforms itself into gentry with an eye for a well-paying operation. Dislocated families are left with nothing but the labour or, less, the organs of their bodies to sell for a livelihood.

In Africa, Asia, and South America, bank loans are followed by cash crop programmes to meet debt repayments, setting up a destructive cycle of poverty. The strife that follows is blamed on 'religious wars' by the international press. George Caffentzis describes the early stages of this capitalisation:

> starvation, mass forced migrations, wars of extirpation and plagues are, of course, the violent symptoms of the most fundamental *liberation of labour power* which is known as primitive accumulation … [this] involves also the expropriation of the body, of sexual and reproductive powers, in so far as they are a means for the accumulation of labour.[16]

The social disruption caused by World-Bank-enforced enclosures has been especially hard on women; African infant mortality has risen and life expectancy has declined. The advent of AIDS has swelled the reserves of cheap labour, pushing down its price to desperate levels.

In Nigeria, harsh structural adjustment measures (SAPs), designed to assist national debt repayments, cancel health and welfare, leaving women dependent on relatives. Female genital mutilation, a cause of sterility, remains a low priority. Caffentzis's judgement is that

> The second success of the debt crisis is in [mastering] the African body, a male/female body of mythic dimensions in the imagination of economic analysts. For the economic consequences activated by the debt crisis and SAPs have given legitimacy to their attempt to control African fertility … by 1984 A.W. Clausen (then president of the WB) … called for a 'social contract' between African governments and African parents.[17]

Silvia Federici notes that under the influence of encouragement from the World Bank, the Nigerian government has been prepared to tax women who procreate beyond 'the optimal level'; at the same time, it subsidises wealthy transnational oil cartels which pollute arable land.[18] World Bank and IMF structural adjustment policies contributed to the crisis in Rwanda. And despite a UN embargo, a British company, Mil Tec Corp, cashed in on the genocide, supplying East-European-made rifles, grenades and mortar bombs to the Rwanda government secretly via Zaire. The deal brought home a queenly profit of $6 million.[19]

Struggles for 'difference' – cultural autonomy and biodiversity – come together over the matter of Trade Related Intellectual Property Rights (TRIPS) on genetic resources. In Australia, Henrietta Fourmile of Cape York has pointed out that the continent's biodiversity consists of some 475,000 plant and animal species.[20] Further, the system of totem identification within Aboriginal customary law is the oldest surviving system of usage rights. These common law rights are recognised in the Biodiversity Chapter of Agenda 21 and in the Native Title Act, Section 212. But such provisions are little help, given both ongoing bio-piracy by transnational pharmaceutical companies and ongoing nurture of the biotechnology industry by the Australian Department of Foreign Affairs and Trade.

Without due acknowledgement, and no doubt innocent of the laws of capital accumulation, Commonwealth Scientific and Industrial Research Organisation researchers continue to raid the knowledge of biodiversity built up over centuries of Aboriginal groundwork. Hand in hand with entrepreneurial bio-prospectors, scientists rake through this genetic heritage, 'reserving' what they want in seed or gene banks. Fourmile notes that concurvine, a plant with potential to cure AIDS, can draw millions in royalty dollars, but Aboriginal people will see none of that money. Although the Biodiversity Convention allows for 'farmers' rights', so far nothing has been paid out for the use of genetically cultured stock. Part of the reason for this may be infiltration of the administration of the UN's Food and Agriculture Organisation (FAO) by the international business lobby called Consultative Group for International Agricultural Research (CGIAR).

In any event, as people in India struggle to preserve local intellectual property, the USA initiates legal action against them for violating Clause 301 of the US Trade Act (1 May 1996). In another move, led by the Foundation for Economic Trends, the International Federation of Organic Agriculture; the Third World Network and ecofeminists, some two hundred international organisations will challenge the US Patent and Trademark Office for granting W. R. Grace a pesticidal patent derived from the ancient neem tree of the Indian subcontinent. Company lawyers argue that the product is 'a synthetic compound', thus not pirated knowledge. The case should serve to test the new intellectual property rights legislation administered by the WTO.[21]

Arguing from the precautionary principle, activists at the Pacific Concerns Resource Centre in Fiji want nothing less than a moratorium on genetic engineering, to reserve the South Pacific as a 'patent free zone'. However, DNA from the blood, tissue and hair of Aboriginal and Torres Strait Islander communities has already been 'tapped' and 'banked' as part of the Human Genome Research Project. That US research programme is funded by the National Institute for Health and the Defense Department, both having an interest in the topic of biological warfare. In this ugly context, the scientist's use of phrases such as 'the common heritage of Man' reveals profound ignorance. In the face of such powerful international forces, Aboriginal people may look to the UN Convention on Human Rights, the Draft Declaration on Rights of Indigenous People, the ILO Convention, and the International Convention on Civil and Political Rights, Article 29. But

Commissioner Dodson's conclusion is profoundly telling: 'basically the existing legal system cannot embrace what it needs to define'.[22] Nor, it seems, can the M/W=N regime define what it needs to embrace.

The Northern Territory Conservation Commission shares few of these concerns. In the good capitalist patriarchal tradition of instrumental reason, its bureaucrats define biological resources as 'organisms or parts thereof, with actual or potential value for humanity'. And more: they see patenting as 'a way of organising order out of chaos'.[23] To foster research and development, the Northern Territory government has brokered biotechnology deals between the AMRAD pharmaceuticals venture and the Tiwi people; with the Northern Land Council; and with itself for an undisclosed consideration. Meanwhile, expensive international public relations companies retained by the genetic engineering industry sell the whiz-bang benefits of this new 'science' across the media. In fact, what is going on is very half-baked science, with no attention to unanticipated consequences.

MODELS OF SELF-RELIANCE

Any notion of government by the people for the people is plainly an anachronism. The global strategic plan of mining and agro-industry has turned nation-states into handmaidens of private enterprise. The 1995 Jakarta meeting on the Biodiversity Convention set the seal on corporate patenting of live DNA from plants, animals and human beings. A protocol on biosafety had been consistently obstructed by Germany, Japan and Australia on behalf of the USA – since 75 per cent of biotech research takes place there.[24] Like mining giants, biomanufacturers favour 'voluntary regulation'. But unlike mining pollution which remains local, there is no way of determining how genetically engineered organisms will spread; nor what their effects on people and habitat might be.

Langton claims the ecology movement is 'a barometer of colonial anxiety'. And while there is some truth in this, the claim overlooks a world of difference between how the Business Roundtable thinks and how most eco-activists think. There may be some complacently affluent and self-serving environmentalists: in the International Union for the Conservation of Nature (IUCN); the leisure-oriented US Wilderness Movement; the North Queensland minority who dub themselves 'sanctuary' protectors. But there are also healthy and thoughtful green-black efforts. In Australia, the Australian Conservation Foundation (ACF), the Wilderness Society (TWS), Friends of the Earth, Greenpeace, Greening Australia and the World Wildlife Fund (WWF) each work with Aboriginal people to refine land rights policy, Pay the Rent, get better provisions on hunting, fishing and parks.[25]

Seasonally, the 1/0 gaze leaves commerce behind and turns to wilderness as unpolluted, pure and untouched land. Today indigenes are romanticised on colourful tourist posters, but nineteenth-century adulation of the 'noble savage' was equally symptomatic of the spiritual emptiness of industrial civilisation and hideously hypocritical. In Australia, a pastoral idyll of the outback home was sustained only at cost to Aboriginal people held at bay beyond the 'vermin fence'. Modern wilderness 'husbanding' of 'virgin lands' through national parks further extends the conquest, displacing indigenous skills and livelihood. TNCs at the Rio Earth Summit pushed openly for more global 'enclosures' and even privatisation of parks. Yet white men's rhetoric of wilderness 'management' is self-contradictory, and tells the bad faith of liberal rationalist principles designed to gloss over instrumental mastery and ultimate exploitation.

By definition, 'the wild' must be what escapes control. History has put the corrupt ideas of wilderness and *terra nullius* together, but that does not fix the meaning of wilderness for all time. When indigenous activists argue that 'wilderness' is an oppressive term, they essentialise and kill off a highly subversive conceptual tool. To totalise the *terra nullius* connotation of wilderness is to internalise the master's racism. It also plays into the hands of extractive industries such as mining or bio-prospecting, which would love to see wilderness go by the board. For the wild speaks potentials to rediscover in ourselves. Moreover, by the ecocentric ethic, land is never vacant as in *terra nullius*, but an intractable subject in its own right. A similar notion is found in customary law.

Movements beyond virtual politics can make good use of the wilderness idea, by rejecting the 1/0 projection of wilderness as out there and separate from ourselves. Moreover, working out just how to do that is important political work for environmentalists. For unless we develop an analysis that heals the artificial split between Man and Nature, civilised and native – and the self-denial that it thrives on – our efforts will simply be gobbled up by the ideology of growth and control. Consider the as-yet-unspoken costs of using geographical information systems (GIS) to 'preserve' indigenous knowledge. Does not the digital methodology of GIS itself instantly subvert indigenous ways of knowing which are fine-tuned by sensuous interaction with land? When an oral knowledge tradition is extracted from its generational context, what impact will that have on the well-being of a community where elders are pivotal to social integration? Surely the very translation of indigenous knowledges into resource management betrays indigenous cultural meanings?

If GIS data get to be available only to those with computer access, is that democratic? Who will glean profits from the sale of local knowledges copyrighted on CD-ROM, international encyclopaedias, or transferred by media satellite? Will GIS play into the hands of overseas corporate interests, currently attempting to centralise the global food industry, and what hope then for self-sufficiency? Ideally, in a democratic, nonracist, nonspeciesist world, the research process would flow in the opposite direction. People would want to understand how customary classification systems are put together and to acquire – for themselves, not for sale – hands-on skills passed on by generations of elders. The knowledge would be honoured in its entirety, not picked over by outsiders in the race for efficient management and a quick buck.

In the long run, to base 'value' on human labour and markets is to adopt the founding assumptions of capitalist patriarchal economics, where only what is 'improved' by Man – the commodity – has worth. Oxford-based academic Darrell Posey calls the Biodiversity Convention a double-edged sword, because although it 'recognises' indigenous or farmers' innovation of wild species, 'genetic patenting' puts that knowledge under state or commercial control. Posey urges activists to take an ecocentric not human-centred view of animals and plants, one much closer to indigenous ways of thinking where value is relational and intrinsic. He asks, Who owns wildlife anyway? Let's stop talking about property and speak rather of 'traditional resource rights' which are inalienable and cannot be commodified. Communities in India have led the way by making inventories and seed banks using traditional methods.[26] Yet even well-meaning radical groups such as Cultural Survival Enterprises promote indigenous forest products for trade on the international market; this is a secular equivalent to the missionaries' saving of souls which simply validates the 1/0, dissolving indigenous lore in the process.

In practical terms, hunter-gatherers would have to be the affluent societies *par excellence*.[27] They are self-sufficient and thus genuinely autonomous. They have a stable interchange with their habitat; they use low-impact technologies; they work only a few hours a day, and give energies to social bonds, ceremony and art. Ecologists taking a lesson from Aboriginal cultures might discover how to devise low-demand, low-impact economies where sustainability and social equity can go together. Closing the gap between rich and poor nations will depend on the West scaling down its taken-for-granted levels of resource use, but that alternative is yet to take hold. The ghost of corporatespeak is everywhere it seems, in discussions of indigenous self-determination and in feminism too.

9

A BAREFOOT EPISTEMOLOGY

THE NEOFEUDAL ORDER

One major reason why the capitalist patriarchal mode of production is so destructive of life is that its underlying ontology divides History from Nature. Measurement and the commodity fetish continually reinforce this 1/0 split; calibration reduces substance to discrete units and time is reified, even priced.[1] Jet travel, TV, electronic bank transfers – each displace lived materiality and further reconstitute the experience of time. Too many green entrepreneurs, socialists, techno-environmentalists, Third World elites and even feminists buy into this virtuality; their 'solutions' to ecopolitical crisis are linear.[2] But there is a 'global class' that spends its days outside the mega clock and its tele-pharmo-nuclear complex. Better, these people, with hands-on knowledge of sustaining work, are even a statistical majority.

Discovery of the nexus between 'women and development' on the part of international agencies was not exactly an ecofeminist insight, however. Rather, it was a response to the desire of transnational corporations and their instruments – the World Bank and the IMF – to forge a fresh approach to globalisation. These bodies having passed through 'manpower development', 'rural development', and 'basic needs', with more social and ecological degradation following hard on each approach, a fresh colonial strategy was now required. By the 1990s it was women's turn to feature, although this phase was soon overtaken by the 'no sustainability without development' slogan.[3] Capitalist patriarchal elites in the South now caught the corporate North by its own petard and used it in a cynical trade-off: 'You give us more aid and we'll preserve our forests for your carbon sinks.' At the same time, the ecological contradiction between industrialising aid projects and sustainability went unspoken.[4]

A merry-go-round of UN-sponsored summits – Cairo, Geneva, Copenhagen – grinds on, while the 'development' goal now ravages life conditions in the South, just as it already has in the industrialised North. For as Larry Lohmann puts it

> only by atomizing tasks, redefining women as unproductive and separating workers from the moral authority, crafts and natural surroundings created by their communities, has it been possible to transform people into modern universal individuals susceptible to management … [and] to open up local societies to global trade.[5]

The US Chamber of Commerce has successfully vitiated the 1992 Global Warming treaty, using free-market instruments such as the North American Free Trade Agreement (NAFTA) to reverse controls on gas emissions. The Biodiversity Convention faces ongoing species erosion from toxic dumping and corporate pharmaceutical tinkering. With slogans like 'technology transfer' and 'capacity building', the Rio Earth Summit promoted a colonialism of exportable environmental repair and caretaker services, further breaking apart the integrity of rural communities in the Third World.

According to Winston Langley, this technology transfer is immensely costly.

> A study by the OECD (Organisation for Economic Cooperation and Development) concluded that the techniques of certain pharmaceutical products … were overpriced between 1,000 and 5,000 per cent. Technology is frequently transferred via a number of prearranged or combined component units and transactions, including 'tie in' clauses in contracts which oblige licensees to buy unpatented goods from the licensor.[6]

Another feature of such transfer is the 'turnkey operation', whereby suppliers are responsible for design, construction and management, until 'indigenous personnel are judged ready' to take over. By this time, of course, capital infrastructure is run down, even obsolete. Since the collapse of the Berlin Wall, former communist states have become prime sites for 'offshore industry' ventures by transnational firms, replacing cheap labour havens in the Third World. At Rio, NGOs from the South and East were left to slang it out over the privilege of factory employment opportunities under the supracapitalist patriarchal European Union.

The Rio Earth Summit gave birth to new institutions such as the Global Environment Facility (GEF) and the World Trade Organization (WTO) which would enable corporate pillage of local resources right down to human DNA itself. This low-intensity warfare against the 'commons' is as old as the market. Once an English aristocracy alienated peasant landholders by enclosing land for grazing. Now even Third World nation-states alienate farmers and forest dwellers from their livelihood by facilitating enclosures for logging and mines. If the apparent aim of the Rio Conference was ecological protection, its essential purpose was to involve a global middle class in legitimising globalisation. At the same time, US President George Bush announced that future

CIA surveillance would focus on those whose activities undermine corporate enterprise.[7]

The Earth Summit and its economic infrastructure, the General Agreement on Tariffs and Trade (GATT), would soon empty out the meanings of 'sovereignty' and 'citizenhood'. Under the New World Order, governments tacitly redefine their role as mediating advantages for a transnational ruling class. This means that local environment regulations or workplace health standards have to go. Under an Australian Labor government, this was to be achieved with the passage of an Administrative Decisions (Effect of International Instruments) Bill. Introduced to the Canberra parliament by Attorney-General Michael Lavarch in June 1995, the bill would 'release' the federal government from international treaty obligations such as the Ramsar Convention on wetland protection. The futile pursuit of citizen rights following Bhopal had already demonstrated that TNCs could not be held to account. Consider too the biocolonisation to which populations may be subjected by unknowingly drinking milk treated with Monsanto's genetically engineered bovine growth hormone. According to a Vermont-based doctor, it is highly probable that this will stimulate cancer cells.[8]

The Rio meeting provided a template for the neofeudal order and its key stratifications. At the top of the hierarchy were transnational corporations, flagged as the Business Council for Sustainable Development. Their personnel included Carl Hahn, Volkswagen; Kenneth Derr, Chevron; Alex Kauer, Ciba-Geigy; Akira Miki, Nippon Steel; Frank Popoff, Dow Chemicals; Paul O'Neill, ALCOA; Lodewijk van Wachem, Royal Dutch Shell; Ed Woolard, Dupont.[9] Tourism tycoon and conference secretary-general Maurice Strong was a member of this class. They put forward garbled preliminary drafts of Agenda 21, while UN bureaucrats carried out the conference administration at public expense. The next echelon in the emerging political hierarchy were heads of government and their advisers, 'official' participants whose function was to give political legitimation to Earth Summit proceedings by ratifying the Global Warming and Biodiversity conventions.

The other face of nation-state activity was its downward 'dialogue' with civil society made up of representatives from selected NGOs. Through these 'consultations', governments North and South encouraged a divide-and-rule situation among their constituents, splitting the global green movement horizontally between experts speaking the language of technocratic power and a bottom rung of unregistered grassroots activists representing the voices of everyday life. The 'properly political' exchanges were carried out in eurocentric masculinist terms, among participants who were mainly men in suits. Outside the frame of this *Realpolitik*, and standing at the bottom of the newly engineered global hierarchy, 'special interest groups' were permitted to make input to Agenda 21. Each of these groups – women, youth, indigenous peoples – was, and remains, marginal to the dominant commodity society and its productivist economics. However, in good liberal pluralist form, the business class inserted its voice a second time among the 'special interest groups', thereby neutralising the discourse of marginality.

Despite these conservative consolidations, Rio was not futile. In the huge Planeta Femea tent, women across continents, classes, tribes, shared their efforts for and frustrations about life-on-earth. Their global counter alliance, shaped around an emergent ecofeminist politics, is finding ever new ways to disrupt, shame and subvert the master categories. This is not to deny differences – insensitive remarks by metropolitan feminists to indigenous women; unconscious vanguardism by well-heeled liberals; or political clashes between women of North and South over population control. But the lapses occurred inside a framework of re/sisterly collaboration and resulted in strong policy statements.

GROUNDED SOLIDARITY

These positive developments were possible because indigenous and Third World women bring clarity and conviction from the moral authority of their communities, as well as from lived experiences of exploitation and suffering. The moment of Gayatri's Spivak's postmodern pessimism is past.[10] In postcolonial struggles, women are taking leadership positions against comprador elites who have sold out to globalisation in order to keep their imitative consumerism alive. In the North, it is grassroots housewives, as opposed to so-called emancipated feminist women, who are generally the strongest fighters. They are less affected by the masculinist privilege that can so readily compromise professionals.[11]

The women's tent at Rio was a university in the true sense, but the material optimism of ecofeminists is not always shared among advocates of change. Reflecting on the future of political alliances against globalisation, Lohmann writes this:

> People seeking anti-global alliances are likely simply to have to drop the idea that there are going to be any interesting neutral criteria of rationality or democracy embedded in any particular local language or system and instead content themselves with adopting *certain ethnocentric virtues of inquiry: watchfulness, curiosity, tolerance, patience, humour and openmindedness.*[12]

Now, these were precisely the attitudes that reigned in Planeta Femea: a yet invisible but universal public caring. It is curious, though, that Lohmann calls for new alliances based on an 'ungrounded' solidarity. Is this because, under postmodern influence, he assumes that sociability belongs exclusively to the realm of language?

The problem is that arbitrary systems of linguistic representation are often just what keep people in separate enculturated realities. Lohmann is right to say that universals of the Western Enlightenment kind are not always helpful in postcolonial activism, but he is wrong to assume that democratic unity can rest on idealised discursive constructs alone. Solidarity and equity need to be embodied in objective activities. What Lohmann calls 'ungrounded virtues' – watchfulness, patience, humour – are in fact qualities embedded in the material practices of social reproduction. The temporal structuration of common household labours and exchanges with the natural habitat are each, in part, independent of discourse and persist as 'complex orders of causality'.

Postmodern thought reveals a familiar blind spot when it comes to the comprehension of time, though there is no good reason why this should be so. A not especially fashionable mid-twentieth century French thinker, Georges Gurvitch, was captivated by the notion that time/s might be multiple and relative to our senses, shaped by the material work that we do.[13] With this hypothesis, Gurvitch hoped to explain conflicts between and within societies. His taxonomy of time frames listed the deceptive time of agitated cities such as New York; the erratic time of transitional societies; the cyclical time of mystic communities; the retarded time of professional societies; the proletariat's time in advance of itself; alternating time; and explosive time.

But the time frame most relevant to ecopolitics is his category 'enduring time'. Gurvitch characterised family, local and rural groupings as engaged with enduring time, a sense of past projected into the future. For him living things are joined across time as well as space; possessing an indwelling structure invisible to the positivist methods of science, which prioritise the eye over all other senses.

Oblivious to the pulse of life, Western reason and its instruments cut across nature's intricate score. Consider agroforestry, mining, nuclear weapons, road transport, genetic engineering: the plan is mastery, but complex rhythms are disrupted and ecological disintegration results. Some ecofeminists use web imagery for the cycles of wholeness and decay, entropy and growth. I like to imagine these organic, self-feeding, transformations following a Möbius pattern. Barbara Adam speaks of a temporal structure whose

> parts resonate with the whole and vice versa. Rhythmicity, therefore, forms nature's silent pulse. All organisms, from single cells to ecosystems, display interdependent rhythmic behaviour. Some of this rhythmicity constitutes the organism's unique identity, some relates to its life cycle, some binds the organism to the rhythms of the universe, and some functions as a physiological clock by which living beings 'tell' cosmic time.[14]

The sensibility of people who work within the phenomenal frame of enduring time dovetails with these flows. As distinct from specular 'seeing', a kinaesthetic knowing from somewhere in the gut is probably best for understanding temporal movement. Hence, the age-old wisdom of Middle Eastern belly dance as ritual preparation for birthing; the way some African villagers measure their chores in syncopated chanting; or the relentless drone of a Koori didgeridoo breathing into a desert night. Contrast these vital rhythms with the tortured intentionality of European music, reflecting the sad division of head and hand; Jean-Paul Sartre's nausea, and Simone de Beauvoir's too. For she unwittingly demonstrates the disconnected solipsism of the industrial North when she writes:

> Humanity is not an animal species, it is a historical reality. Human society is an antiphysis – in a sense it is against nature; it does not passively submit to the presence of nature, but rather takes over the control of nature … objectively in practical action.[15]

Indigenous feet tread the soft earth in awe and respect. But the coloniser arrives with bald visual metaphors such as 'regard' or 'viewpoint'; technology gives way to microscope and laser; ·and politics becomes spectator sport. Enduring time is the 'negative' of the photographic mind, but it is no shadow. By dividing what is inextricable, dualisms such as space versus time, culture versus nature, set up a profoundly repressive code.[16] The myth that, as against Man's cultural production, things natural are inherently inferior and impoverished has a particular significance for eurocentric civilisation. As Marcuse taught, this myth comes from an ancient splitting of the so-called higher faculties from immediate sensuous experience; a predilection for the static visual and manipulable properties of objects; their formal objectification in specular language and re-presentation through binary analytical logic as against dialectics; the cogito; the ostensible dissociation of pure fact from value in what passes for science.

The outcome of this strange epistemology based on the suffocation of enduring time is that product takes precedence over process. Artefacts of culture

> are created apart, frozen for contemplation, fixed in their uniqueness. They take on a material existence with a difference: externalised, abstracted, bounded and isolated. ... Their existence constitutes a finite time, encased in things and isolated from the processes of life and ecological interconnections. Consequently, their temporality is governed by entropy not development and growth.[17]

This is the real meaning of essentialism. Hence the therapeutic exposure by ecofeminists of artificial linguistic 'identities' and facticities like Man/Woman, light/dark, 1/0. Some feminists, including de Beauvoir's nemesis, difference theorist Luce Irigaray, connect specularity, productivism and its commodity fetish to the masculine libidinal habit of treating women as 'goods'. Further, they surmise that 'Western thought has been dominated by the physics and mechanics of solid matter whereas the feminine refers much more to a mechanics of fluids, which has barely been elaborated'.[18]

So the elimination of time and movement in the primitive self-estranged functional rationality of the eurocentric fathers yields knowledge only of a dead world of matter. For the physicist, matter becomes mathematical and topographical relations; events, projections, possibilities. Sensitivity to the flow of nature is lost as knowledge emphasises the precise operations to be used in nature's transformation. Under the medical paradigm, the human body comes to be apprehended in terms of fungible atomic units, to be reduced and reassembled at will.[19] With

Vandana Shiva, I have observed this same illusory epistemology in the hubris of hydrological engineers who would control water flows by stochastic calculation. 'When ... flood control measures accentuate floods and fertilisers rob soil of its fertility, the problem is not merely between use and misuse of technology. It is rooted in the very process of knowledge-creation.'[20]

PLEASURES OF ENDURING TIME

The time-negating separation of body and mind, earth and water, is an early gesture toward the steadying of women's subaltern wisdoms. But as late as the 1970s, feminist challenges to marxist mentors have helped us understand a great deal about this aspect of the dominant tradition. In marxism, an ostensibly dialectical theory designed to explain change, and acknowledging our human metabolism in nature, moved sustaining reproductive activities off the historical stage. The phallic enthusiasm for *making* and *having* forgot that the reproduction of life itself, not the production of visible goods, is always already the first historical act. The term 'reproduction' means to be engaged in restoring living processes by enhancing our human interchanges with nature. Domestic labour still has this function in as much as women cook and clean, tend young and old bodies. Obviously, women and men caught up in urban consumer societies have less give and take with external nature than cottage-dwelling folk once did. But in the international division of labour, the domestic functions of indigenous and Third World women farmers are still bound up in care for Earthly cycles, albeit increasingly compromised by the spread of maldevelopment.

'Enduring' is a beautiful word. It connotes the enfoldment of time in pleasure and suffering, hardiness and commitment, stability and security. These ways of being are of interest to ecofeminists because they are the qualities of engagement that marginalised workers, women and subsistence dwellers bring to their material conditions. Against the lost 'working class' of Marx's vision, those who hear the throb of enduring time carry an alternative way of knowing and doing and a new bioethic – one that is sorely needed if we are to build an earth democracy. Moving into a new millennium, modernist science and politics will have to respond to the dance and holler of this conceptual challenge.

While not an ecofeminist himself, development critic Wolfgang Sachs paves the way for such a project in his *Global Ecology*:

> the task of global ecology can be understood in two ways: it is either a technocratic effort to keep development afloat against the drift of plunder and pollution; or it is a cultural effort to shake off the hegemony of ageing Western values and gradually retire from the development race.[21]

The ecofeminist revaluation of the mode of reproduction coincides with Sachs's own 'search for societies which live graciously within their means, and for social changes which take their inspiration from indigenous ideas of the good and proper life'.[22] This does not mean going backwards in history, as ethnocentric Western fundamentalists sometimes claim. It means becoming fully conscious of what we are about. Something of this materially embodied ecological being is expressed in how the Tiwi people of Northern Australia celebrate seasonal time: variously as clap sticks, flowers, tall grass, knock-emdowns (winds), fire, cold, fog, dry creek bed, hot feet, thunder, breeding mangrove worm, and muddy possum tracks.

During the 1990s, a sliver of liberal, marxist and poststructuralist feminists have objected to the association of women and nature. Their academic response has been to label any theory that examines this nexus as 'essentialism'. But this routine misses out on some very radical implications – epistemological, political, personal – contained in the ecofeminist strategy. Against the one-dimensional reasoning of a handful of North-identified women, many more re/sisters access another conceptual space, and one that is very apposite to ecological thinking. This takes in its goal by concentric rather than direct scan, the object being experienced from several tangential points, kaleidoscopically. Knowledge rests not on mere appearance, formal visual properties, but is derived from touch, or the even-more-diffuse kinaesthetic modality that responds to pulse.

The effect is an empathic, reflexive logic without incisive categorical boundaries between the knowing subject-in-process, object-in-process, and its poor representation.[23] Hélène Cixous alludes to this embodied materialism, as I like to call it, in her typification of feminine difference.

> Listen to a woman speak ... it's with her body that she vitally supports the 'logic' of her speech ... she *inscribes* what she is saying because she doesn't deny her drives the intractable and impassioned part they have in speaking. Her speech even when 'theoretical' or 'political' is never simple, or linear or 'objectified', generalised. She draws her story into history.[24]

Masculinist dualisms of Man/Woman, History/Nature, signifier/signified, are here replaced by a metabolism of subject-in-field, the very body of the noun being dissolved in the liquid realism of non-identity: a both/and logic rather than an either/or.

Time and contradiction are enjoyed. Nor are there qualms about 'objectivity', for a new definition of it is offered. This is not so much antisystem as a moving comprehension of the whole in all its moments. There is no interest in control, invariant factors, functions and expedient significance levels. Instead a knowledge of the texture and timbre of qualities in their intricate perversity is sought: communion with the object rather than penetration by the divisive agency of technological reason. In parallel vein, Adam points to a flowing world of uncertainty, implication, invisibility, transience, temporal embeddedness and rhythmicity.

The privileging of solid land over liquid water, like the suppression of ecological time by modern science, deletes both feminine difference and nature's diversity. For just as political 'difference' can be defined by the life-affirming practices and labours of enduring time that mostly women do, so 'biodiversity' is integral to the orchestration of life. Again, Shiva reminds us, 'The construction of women as "the second sex" is linked to the same inability to cope with difference as is the development paradigm that leads to the displacement and extinction of diversity in the biological world.'[25] Feminism in the North should watch that it does not become another monoculture by accepting these masculinist tendencies.

Global crisis is the outcome of a capitalist patriarchal system that treats both women and nature as 'resources'. Ecofeminist literature, conversation and correspondence shows that this shared political intuition arises among women from Vietnam to South Africa, regardless of ethnic background, class, age, or education. Their common perception can be attributed to the kinds of *work* they do. For in most cultures, women – a statistical majority – inhabit a 'minority' subcultural niche outside of specific economic class or national identities. But an argument for ecofeminism as womanist politics, and more, as 'an indigenous knowledge' may be unpalatable to upwardly mobile femocrats in the North. Third World elite women who believe themselves to be emancipated by high-tech gadgetry may also object.

INDIGENOUS KNOWLEDGES

Let us take this idea a little further. According to the *Concise Oxford Dictionary*, the word 'indigenous' means: native, belonging naturally, to soil. So women's labours almost universally mediate nature for men. In a sense, 'women within nature' and 'nature within women' have 'co-evolved' reciprocal practices over centuries. This nature–woman–labour nexus certainly supports a proposition that ecofeminist insights constitute an indigenous knowledge informed by hands-on experiences that are marginalised and devalued by productivist economics. Among housewives, the nexus includes the sensuality of birthing and suckling labours; historically assigned household chores; gardening or making goods; creating and implanting meanings in the next generation. Similarly, peasant and indigenous men and women are organically and discursively implicated in the material rhythms of enduring time and, like domestic workers in the North, they develop practical expertise grounded in that materiality.

In a paradigmatic statement of this agency in complexity, Shiva observes:

> It is in managing the integrity of ecological cycles in forestry and agriculture that women's productivity has been most developed and evolved. Women transfer fertility from the forests to the field and to animals. They transfer animal waste as fertilizer for crops and crop by-products to animals as fodder. They work with the forest to bring water to their

> fields and families. This partnership between women's work and nature's work ensures the sustainability of sustenance.[26]

Enduring activities embrace biological generativity, daily sustenance, social and generational cohesion. Cutting across ethnicity and class, these roles are almost invariably the province of women's rights, responsibilities, and skills. Even in so-called developed societies, women spend a large part of their lives outside the dominant industrial time frame. Women's embeddedness in the mode of reproduction is more common than not, despite a guilty claim from some serviced middle-class feminists that ecofeminists have no right to 'speak for' Third World women. The reality is that women from centre or periphery have quite enough overlap of experience to speak together.

It is no surprise that women's energies and time are treated as an economic 'externality'. This silent annexation of true productivity has been intensified historically by industrialisation and consumerism in the North. In the South, technology transfer and the imported hegemonies of science and bureaucratic planning complete nature's and women's enclosure. Under the eurocentric division of labour, women, North or South, become 'dump sites' for men's laundry, sexuality, and emotional crises. Technocratic environmentalists add to women's domestic load in the name of progress by demanding they conserve water or recycle garbage. Yet toxic heavy metal discharges from male-managed industries spill into nature's streams unchecked.

In the positivist unconscious, time flows, femininity and water are wedded at many levels. For Vietnamese writer Trinh Minh-ha

> Woman's writing becomes 'organic writing' … it draws its corporeal fluidity from images of water – a water from the source, a deep subterranean water that trickles in the womb,

> a meandering river, a flow of life, of words running over or slowly dripping down the pages. This keeping-alive and life-giving water exists simultaneously as the writer's ink, the mother's milk, the woman's blood and menstruation.[27]

The 1/0 approach to water is evinced by the Australian Genetic Manipulation Advisory Committee (GMAC) 1995 guidelines on genetically engineered organisms. This committee's Good Industrial Large Scale Practice proposes that factories using engineered micro-organisms to produce drugs, food agents or chemicals may discharge these live organisms into sewers 'at levels agreed' on a case-by-case basis. The GMAC is supposed to assess the risk of artificial micro-organisms colonising waterways or the atmospheric water cycle, but it is simply not possible to test such things by controlled experiment.[28]

The political expression of many women's sense of continuity with the natural world is nudging forward a subaltern paradigm shift with implications for metaphysics, epistemology, logic, ethics, and of course 'science'. The feminist and ecological revolutions converge on the productivist *a priori*, the substitution of natural human needs by manufactured needs destructive of both the human body and its ecosphere. But meantime, societies from which a lesson in living harmoniously, substantively, with nature might be learned are sliding quickly into the pathology of obsessive production. Theorists who overemphasise science as the radicalising force behind new social movements need to take more account of indigenous knowledges.[29] Their lapse tells us more about a gender-blind sociology than it does about environmentalism.

German ecofeminist Ulla Terlinden connects 'feminine' labour skills and ecological reason in this way:

> Housework requires of women [or men] a broad range of knowledge and ability. The nature of the work itself determines its organization. The work at hand must be dealt with *in its entirety*. 'Typically, housework is seen as ideally all-embracing, functionally nonspecific and diffusely organised. The worker must possess a high degree of personal synthesis, initiative, intuition and flexibility.'[30]

Terlinden notes that the structural features of housework shape the way women organise politically too. Her account calls up principles of 'reciprocity', 'holism' and 'contingency', which determine how most women labour in their material environment. The 'controlling', 'analytic' and 'linear' character of the scientific method is inappropriate to maintenance of living things. A parallel analysis applies to subsistence farming or hunter-gathering activities. Good farmers foster the earth to metabolise these connections; women give up their bodies as alchemists to make life. The enduring time horizons of these meta-industrial workers are not compatible with the truncated time sense of a profit-driven market.

In contrast to the self-interested maximisations known as 'best practice', sustaining labours involve following through with long-term goals in complex systems. In contrast to planning with abstract economic indicators, the indigenous labour process knows its material intimately. Delphine Yeyet affirms this, along with its connection to women's political status in Gabon:

> In a subsistence economy, men are obliged to earn their livelihood in cooperation with women without exploiting them. In a monetary economy, however, the thirst for comfort and profit pushes men to exploit women and chase them from the domains of political and social action.[31]

Another account of vernacular labours 'immersed in details of the physical world' occurs in Sara Ruddick's book *Maternal Thinking*.[32] Although far from the timeless essences of the eurocentric performance, this mothering labour does have its rationality. As Ruddick reminds us, maintaining a household requires harmonising a complex of subsystems, as well as considerable decision-making and diplomatic skills. To reappraise the mode of reproduction in this way is therefore not to argue from victimhood – that the oppressed have a monopoly on good behaviour; nor is it to fall back into unreconstructed masculinist readings of some innate essential 'naturalness', or 'pro-family' assertions about the moral superiority of the female sex. Rather, the argument makes a materialist epistemological claim about cognitive capacities derived from certain skills: a unity of body and mind found in those who work with head and hand in a self-directed way – something unusual in a class-divided public sphere.

Christine von Weizsacker uses the term *Eigenarbeit* for this labour.[33] Nevertheless, while biology is not fixed, social expectations are; thus Ruddick observes that even women who are not mothers must uphold the gendered division of labour. However, men can equally take on caring. Political theorists such as Mary Dietz are unfounded in claiming that an ethic of care is undemocratic because it privileges qualities of a particular group.[34] These learned qualities are open to any group that works at the socially constructed margin where culture meets nature. Ecofeminist respect for enduring time is profoundly democratic. It challenges all existing political stratifications, including the speciesist split between Humanity and Other nature.

HOLDING AND SUSTAINABILITY

Through its attention to physical space, fresh air, cleanliness, food, raw material, bodily discharges, ecofeminism brings eurocentric arrogance back to its senses. To quote Ruddick:

> The value of objects and accomplishments turns on their usefulness in satisfying needs and giving pleasures rather than on the money to be made by selling them. ... Hence [women] are continuously involved with connection, separation, development, change, and the limits of control.[35]

Such flexibility is a most precious 'resource'. But it is the antithesis of the current trend to labour specialisation which leads only to alienation and entropy – in physical and philosophic systems. Ruddick's concept of 'holding' is especially relevant to ecopolitics.

> To hold means to minimize risk and to reconcile differences rather than to sharply accentuate them. Holding is a way of seeing with an eye toward maintaining the minimal harmony, material resources, and skills necessary for sustaining a child in safety. It is the attitude elicited by 'world protection, world-preservation, world repair ... the invisible weaving of a frayed and threadbare family life'.[36]

Paradoxically, holding is the ultimate expression of adaptability. As opposed to the physicist's separation of space and time, interconnectedness is commonsense in the mater/reality of those who 'hold things together'. With ecofeminism, this precautionary principle comes to be applied beyond home and neighbourhood to politics at large. Holding practice is the work of resisting entropy.

Australian indigenous workers also practise a kind of holding in their traditional nurture of sustainability:

> The pods containing ripe seeds are collected, and the seeds are separated through threshing and rubbing. The seeds are yandied to separate them from the remaining bits of pod, and then parched in hot sand and ashes. They are winnowed and yandied again, and then moistened with water and ground into an edible paste. In addition, there is a type of insect gall which is found on these trees at certain times which is edible. Mulga is hard wood, and is used to make spear throwers, barbs for spears, and spear heads, as well as spears, boomerangs, and digging-sticks. And, on top of that it makes excellent fire wood. … Some mulgas are the homes of honey ants who dig themselves in under the roots, and some are home for grubs who burrow into the roots. Some mulgas are called honeydew because of the sweet juice which collects on them, and others have a type of sugar leaf – a sweet substance produced by sap sucking insects.[37]

Unlike capitalist patriarchal Man, Aboriginal peoples do not dig in to territory for fear of losing it, so emptying out its life-giving force; rather they move through country in the knowledge that nature will replenish and provide for them again when they return. Self-managed Aboriginal provisioning richly meets many needs at once: subsistence, learning, participation, innovation, ritual, identity and belonging, freedom and partnership with habitat.[38]

On the other hand, the engineered satisfiers of modern industrial societies – bureaucracies or cars – cost great effort and frequently end up sabotaging the very convenience that they were designed for. The Kalahari Bushmen also compare favourably. According to Gerry Mander's analysis, their work averages only three hours a day, so environmental resources are not economically stressed. When food is available directly from nature, storage, ownership, and accumulation, are not necessary. Bushmen eschew possessions beyond the loin strap, skin blanket and leather satchel. By eurocentric calculation of number of hours spent in toil per mouths fed, Bushmen's food collecting is far more efficient than French farming; and the daily food variety and nutritional intake of hunter-gatherers are beyond that of one American in every six.[39] The Lapp village movement and people of Ladakh too are among those groups increasingly acting to preserve their ingenuity and rationality.

Reproductive labours are embedded in a matrix of social relations which in turn are sustained by subsistence activities embedded in cycles of biological time. In the care-giving labour that Ruddick names 'mothering practice', a woman or man has no choice but deal with the material before her or him. Unlike the physicist or social scientist, she cannot invent categories to deny what is natural. What characterises this understanding is reciprocity with what nature provides. Nancy Hartsock has noted how this gentle labour by mediation distinguishes enduring work from slave or proletarian labour, which must break Nature's back at the master's command. Evelyn Fox Keller's notion of a gender-free science repeats the theme of subject-object collaboration. Nature is known as a subject with a heart of its own, and one that pulses through our own body cells.[40]

Recalling Mary O'Brien's account of the alienative consciousness, we may understand why the Western failure to come to terms with creation and flow cannot but express itself in an obsessional drive for artificial principles of continuity. The legal term 'incorporation' resounds its own lack. By contrast, Winona LaDuke, activist with the Indigenous Women's Network, shows how native American societies where manual and mental labour are not separated can boast a cyclic epistemology and ethic of reciprocity:

> all parts of the natural order flow in cycles – whether those cycles belong to the moon, the tides, our bodies, seasons, or life itself. Within this understanding is a clear sense of birth and rebirth and a knowledge that *what one does today will effect one in the future,* on the return. ... A second concept, reciprocal relations, defines the responsibilities and ways of relating between humans and the ecosystem. ... Thus, one could not take life [for food] without a reciprocal offering ... you take only what you need and leave the rest.'[41]

Holding labour is the practice of a 'sense of place', very different from environmental management conceived under the 1/0 sign. Such work is usually designed mechanically in theoretical terms, computer-simulated, then superimposed over the wild. This approach creates an illusion of human control, unanticipated consequences being called 'accidents'. Worster illustrates the trouble with the top-down capitalist patriarchal approach to planning:

> The first and perhaps most difficult problem ... is the time frame that ought to be assumed. Is a sustainable society one that endures for a decade, a human lifetime, or a thousand years? It is not enough merely to say 'sustainable for a long time', or even 'for the next generation', if we want to *set targets for our institutions.*[42]

Worster asks if boom-and-bust cycles of economic growth – ecological depletion followed by innovative response – may not be inevitable for 'human creativity' to be realised. He wonders whether 'taking off', making 'great strides', and 'keeping up', may reflect a pragmatic decision about 'the degree' of sustainability acceptable. But ecofeminists ask, What is the class, race, gender, species of those who make these ostensibly human decisions? And what is the class, race, gender, species of those who must deal with their consequences? In Daniel Botkin's *Discordant Harmonies,* lived time is again abstracted and projected outwards as population and biosphere. The 'great leap forward' of an earlier socialist generation comes to mind. Needless to say, the gulf between this telling of time and Ruddick's 'holding' is the same as exists between agro-industry's Dust Bowl techniques and careful peasant cultivation. Botkin's postmodern 'permissive ecology' simply clears the way for more open slather by the corporate raiders.[43]

Holding opens people to a self-consciousness that is quite at odds with the cogito of the masculine unitary subject. Women, says Carol Gilligan, are inclined to work out their ethical 'responsibilities' integrating thought, feeling, and relational context. Feminist ethics move away from abstracted formulas such as 'rights' into an extrapolation of caring experience.[44] Holding is based neither on separation and control of Others, nor on some ephemeral cosmic fusion, but on practical deferral. It exemplifies a strong, decentred subject. The origins of this non-identity are overdetermined.

Daring to carry her analysis right into the taboo ground of female biology, but without losing sight of the 'always already', if partial, inscription of gendered experience, O'Brien provides this explanation:

> There are a series of what our culture treats as boundary challenges inherent in female physiology [and its labours],

> challenges that make it difficult to maintain rigid separation from the object world. Menstruation, coitus, pregnancy, childbirth, lactation, all represent challenges to bodily boundaries.[45]

Similarly, women's caring for sick infants and ageing parents brings them in touch with permeability and 'contamination'. Bodies on the margin of nature dribble, smell, ooze, flake, even decay before our eyes. Women have the patriarchally accorded privilege of touching and holding together the fragments of human non-identity in this mesh of enduring time. Men bleed, urinate, ejaculate, but the discourse of mastery forces them to be contemptuous of bodily flows. Capitalist patriarchal languages and institutions offer men an armoury of externalising gestures to bolster their separateness from matter. What they get is desensitisation, a false sense of individualism, crippling loneliness, and destructive compensatory drives.

Since women's social positioning in the gendered division of labour means they do not feel fundamentally separate from unruly nature, they tend not to build an oppositional ontology, M/W=N. Aristotle's law, A cannot equal notA, is fairly inadequate in a world where A may well be in the process of transforming into notA. Further, since women do not have much to do with power and control, they do not project causation as a unilinear sequence. Working in complex open-ended systems, women understand that events can have multiple determinations at once. An embodied materialism rests on fusion of consciousness with field, and sensitivity to the impermanence of both, as they shape each other. Maybe the sensual symbiosis of having another human alive right inside one's belly is the quintessence of this unbounded subjectivity?

10

AS ENERGY/LABOUR FLOWS

BOUNDARY CONDITIONS

With the rise of transnational corporate globalisation, strong socialist critique is more urgent than ever before. But at the same time, ecological crisis has reframed History inside of Nature, calling for all politics to become gendered and ecologically literate. This means that a renewed socialism must take up green, feminist, and postcolonial concerns, as much as those of its old constituency in labour. The difficulty here is that in some respects Marx's work was complicit with the Promethean ethos of capitalist patriarchal economics. A committed critic of the entrepreneur, Marx was nevertheless similarly gendered – a man shaped by the M/W=N assumptions of his time.

The exuberance of burgeoning industrial revolution was supported by the scientific preoccupation with manipulating Nature. In seventeenth-century Europe, Newtonian physics had created an illusion of rational control over process by spatialising lived flow on the clock face. In this world of appearances, change was calculated as an extensional relationship between position *x* and position *y*. Absolute time, somewhere in Mother=Nature, was treated as a necessary ground, but remained untheorised. Enlightened man's specular order depended on a clean libidinal break from such boundary conditions, which might create friction, or otherwise threaten the unitary concept on which measurement depends. The narcissistic omnipotence of the 1 is surely reflected in the claim that matter, 0, can neither be created nor destroyed.

Our earlier review of Marx's views on those outside of mechanised production – peasants, women, animals – has shown how this instrumental climate of discourse underpinned much of his argument. The patently ideological features of his text are found in (1) dualisms, (2) leading to speciesism, (3) sexism, and (4) ethnocentrism; (5) a growth-oriented claim that production disconnected from need is properly human; (6) a separation of necessity and freedom, which unhinges sustainable emancipation; (7) too much faith in rational human control, (8) and the linear idea of progress that goes with it; (9) an undialectical treatment of technology; (10) and, finally, a too narrow theory of value as labour objectified.

In sum, Marx's standpoint is what today's nature ethicists call anthropocentric. That same vision continues to inspire much contemporary writing on the left, even work that addresses the environment question. Reiner Grundmann, for example, maintains that

> Anthropocentrism and mastery over nature, far from *causing* ecological problems, are the starting points from which to address them. … Freedom, for Marx, can be gained only in human objectifications, in second nature. The more first nature is transformed into second nature, the more its laws are understood and the more mankind *[sic]* is able to free itself.[1]

Looking for a deeper level of reflexivity than this, ecofeminists ask, free itself from what, exactly?

The physicist's paradigm is still active when marxists such as James Devine introduce the labour theory of value as a tool for explaining the laws of motion of capitalist production.[2] The argument is that value derives from labour time expended, that is, spatialised, in making a commodity. According to Marx's theory of surplus value, the use value of a worker's labour is invested in a product only to be appropriated by his employer for sale. What the worker receives in return as a wage is only his own exchange value or price in the labour market. Because the worker must use earnings for subsistence to maintain his labour power, he is not fully reimbursed for time and energies expended. In this short-changing, the difference remaining in capitalist hands is called surplus value. This is why marxists say that profit contains its opposite in poverty.

Feminists as diverse as Lise Vogel and Luce Irigaray have pointed out that an unspoken economic transaction between a man and wife exists in nested frame to capitalist patriarchal production. Here a parallel extraction of value occurs.[3] This is why capitalism is essentially patriarchal. What is given by the woman in her role as the worker's personal carer is the labour time of restorative mothering. Moreover, she may labour in a multiple sense: first, making domestically useful things with her hands, use value; and, second, making new commodities for sale on the market, exchange value. Third, she will make the next generation of labour power inside her body. The reproductive worker can expect provisions from her employed partner, but neither capitalist nor husband identify with the domestic labourer as a subject with bourgeois right, thereby feeling obliged to offer a formal wage. Similarly, a woman's adult sons, products of her embodied labour, are not sold by her, but go off to seek their own wage. In this economic system, the product of a woman's labouring body has exchange value, where she has none. This is why feminists say that sexual affection contains its opposite in predation.

The appropriation of a gendered surplus remains a boundary condition in both capitalist and marxist economics. Writing in the anthology *Red on Green*, Devine even calls the daily subsistence work that women do 'imported labour', because it is brought in from some Other mode of production. The sexed breach is very apparent in his somewhat apologetic text:

> The exclusion of surplus arising from household production … is a common *simplifying* assumption of many Marxian analyses. … [And in footnote] After all, that labour does produce use-values that are *quite important, indeed totally necessary* to human existence as sane and sentient beings.

A majority of the global workforce is potentially affected by this theoretic 'simplification', but Devine does not undertake to amend it. Instead, he draws another tacit parallel between women and nature as elements external to the productive process. Although their shared status is empirical, it belongs, according to him, to the sphere of ethics and therefore, by definition, is not economic.

> Just because nature, in the Marxian view, produces no surplus value does not imply that nature is (or should be) either ethically or empirically unimportant to socialists or capitalists … all it says, is that the relationship between capitalism and nature is not a relation among people.[4]

As economic man adopted the models of classical physics, field conditions such as Nature, including women, were named externalities: M/W=N. The labour theory of value amplifies that trend, but the so-called organic composition of capital could do with gendered examination.

EXTRACTING THE SURPLUS

Devine's socialism reinforces the orthodox labour theory of value with a dualist hierarchy of economics over ethics, real work over imported labour, Man over Nature. He rejects Nancy Folbre's proposal that socialised costs of production be made explicit by replacing the quantity of priced transactions, GDP, with an index of Net Economic Welfare (NEW).[5] Instead, he protects the powerful space of the 1 by recourse to a further dualism: GDP and NEW should be used in conjunction, representing 'the two sides' of economic life – jobs versus environment.

On closer inspection, this 'jobs versus environment contradiction' appears to be an artefact of unexamined masculinist assumptions. These rest on the socially constructed invisibility of feminine reproductive labours and the uniquely masculine attraction to mechanically mediated production. The tension between jobs and environment that has beset red–green alliances since the 1980s is compounded by the belief that historical agency belongs to working-class men. However, if marxists assimilated the international statistics on who the global proletariat actually is, their conclusions – not to say starting assumptions – might be different. Using UN indicators, Marilyn Waring shows that it is women who carry out two thirds of all work done and these subsistence labours are relatively free of technology and thus have a benign effect on nature.[6]

In terms of modelling reality, the possibility for a major challenge to the closed-system thinking of patriarchal capitalism was introduced in the nineteenth century by Clausius. His second law of thermodynamics postulated nonreversible transformations of matter and energy. Thermodynamics destabilised the 1/0 bar, adopting a time frame closer to daily horizons, where material processes are seen to run down by entropy. The way was now prepared for ecologists to recognise that energetic structure in nature is damaged by certain kinds of social activity. It is quite possible to think nature thermodynamically without accepting the liberal gloss of economic scarcity. That old association tells more about masculine aggrandisement than it does about living internal relations. In fact, entropy is tantamount to pollution.

Reading Marx's theory of value with ecofeminist eyes, it becomes plain that the negative term in the 1/0 regime represents libidinal energy, whose contribution is silenced by the stroke. On the side of 1, the universal standard, qualitative difference is reduced to quantity, pulverisation, dust. Every great metropolis, for instance, speculates in energy leaving disorder at its peripheries. Uncritical greens resort to technocratic policy 'tools' such as market-based 'instruments' which prop up the capitalist system for a further round of exploitation.[7] Corporate directors, tacitly aware of the energetic theft from workers, ensure just enough reciprocation to keep them around. Welfare benefits for youth in the West, or micro-credits to Third World women, are other tokens that keep the economic system in sufficient equilibrium to ward off crisis. Closer to home, capitalist patriarchal ethics permit men to extract energies from mothers, wives, secretaries and whores, freeing up their own subsistence time for self-actualisation. This is why feminists claim the personal is political.

Devine admits that Marx's theory of value needs to be complemented by knowledge from the 'natural sciences', but again he does not begin this revision. When Folbre, using Piero Sraffa on price determination, asserts that the labour theory of value is irrelevant to sustainable production, he protects the status quo with a positivist formula. 'The Sraffian view that nature (or steel or peanuts) produces a surplus is simply a result of unexplained assumptions about coefficients in the technical input-output matrix.' Yet Devine goes on to say that 'The natural fertility of the soil can raise the productivity of labour, allowing an individual to receive land rent. ... Whatever nature's value to capitalism, it definitely has use-value and is used to produce use-values.'[8] By his reckoning, it is also possible for use values such as raw materials, or goods such as air, to have an in-principle market price, but no value.

Devine is mainly interested in Nature through its economic transmutation as rent. This occurs if natural fertility raises the productivity of labour or capitalist technology increases nature's yield. Grundmann and Devine are both aware that so-called side effects of technology, such as the greenhouse effect and global epidemics of auto-immune disease, may well foil industrialised abundance. But the predeliction for keeping GDP and NEW in separate spheres undermines reasoned assessment of these things. Nor is the recent trend to biocolonisation factored into the equation of progress. When transnational pharmaceutical companies extract DNA from human body tissues to make genetically engineered products, mining occurs without on-site infrastructure costs. A geneticist adds labour time to rearrange the highly mobile resource and a lawyer patents it as a commodity. What happens to rent, the labour theory of value, and boundary conditions now? Eco-socialists need to address these things.

Capitalist patriarchal value is dissociated from bioproductive processes, and anthropocentric readings of Marx repeat that defect. The exclusive focus on economic activities prioritises the moment of Man-to-Man exchange, equivalence, 1:1. It overlooks the fact that all structures of production, social and sexual reproduction consist of environmental energies. The price of an object on the market gets to be accepted as its value, and matter stripped of kinetic pulse is laid waste. The material reciprocity embodied in, say, photosynthesis is inconceivable to the masculinist measures of industrial production. In a dialectical economy, which is simultaneously an ecology, value would represent the deep underlying metabolic cost to workers who give their lived time and bodily energies to sustaining the whole.

Equally, it would be acknowledged that nature must have time to replenish itself. An ecological economics would resonate with the flows and ruptures in nature's holograph. But men's games of choice based on commodity circulation delete the many-dimensioned circuitry of nature. This is why green activists say that growth contains its opposite in breakdown. The only way to bring economics to its ecological senses may well be to move past Man/Woman=Nature relations, rounding out Marx's political insight into surplus extraction with a bioenergetic theory of value. By attending to where human=nature energy transformations really occur, we see clearly where productivity comes from and where value should be accorded.

BIOENERGETICS

Certainly, the concept of rent conflates two contradictory processes: natural fertility which is negentropic and technology which is entropic. An undisturbed ecosystem is a continuous metabolism of energetic substances. Humans are an intrinsic part of these elemental exchanges. A mother enjoys fruit from the vine, then gives up her substance to the child inside. A tooth is lost for each endurance. But the honey-smooth child returns its gift to her in the ecstasy of suckling. Later, their bodies in death and decay dissipate those pleasures in the earth – carbon, nitrogen, phosphorus – and the vine grows heavy again. There is no surplus, only an ever-turning enfoldment of internal relations through time. When human senses are severed from nature by mechanical re/production, the counterpoint of giving and taking, extracting and restoring, is broken.

The argument for bioenergetics has surfaced before. Sergei Podolinsky, a Narodnik who corresponded with Marx and Engels, wanted to reformulate the theory of surplus value as appropriation of usable energy in order to account for the exploitation of peasants and their lands. Later, in the Soviet era, Vladimir Stanchinski would research the energy budgets of biotic communities, convinced that 'by studying the energy flows in a whole range of biocenoses, humans would be able to calculate the productive capacities of these natural communities and would be able to structure their own economic activity *in conformity with* them'.[9] Sadly, the opportunity for an ecocentric marxism passed. Energetics was taken over by positivists and systems theorists in the West. At home, Stanchinski's project perished under Stalin's Five Year Plan. In a political context, Reich pursued a bioenergetic psychoanalysis of the repressive 1/0 culture – albeit in an ungendered way. He too was soon marginalised.[10]

What do production, growth and decay consist in but energy transformations? In measuring the calorific value and distribution of each exchange, economists would find energy utilised in a socially upward manner by men drawing on women's labour, or by the North extracting resources from the South. While such calibration smacks of positivism, it may entice one or two accountants to review M/W=N presuppositions, thereby coming to a material understanding of what racism and sexism really mean. Ecofeminism also invites those concerned with governance to think about power not as 'divide and rule', but an energising force shared by the human species with the rest of its ecosystem. A conscious attention to maintaining the ecological rhythms in which we are implicated brings new meaning as well to political notions such as 'internal security'.

In contrast to the Promethean tendency of Grundmann and Devine, marxists such as William Leiss have opted for liberation through a minimalist mastery over nature. Tim Hayward also argues in favour of an emancipatory humanism.[11] The naturalistic aspects of Marx's thought are explored by Ted Benton, who is particularly opposed to the hierarchical placing of humans over other animals. Benton's intricate discussion of humans developing powers that go against their own needs begs gendered scrutiny. For he is among those who have read ecofeminism dualistically as essentialist or biological determinist for its suggestion that women are linked with nature in ways that can be usefully studied.

The irony is that Benton's own approach to socialism actually reinforces an ecofeminist project. In *Natural Relations*, he suggests areas from which a trans-species ethic might draw insight.[12] These are: an organically limited lifespan; birth and death; temporal phasing of organic growth; sexuality; social cooperation in the meeting of organic needs; stability of social order, and the integration of social groups. Benton does not point out that in almost every culture these areas are ascribed to women's holding labour, and hence, that women might have a specific advantage in helping to create an ecocentric ethic. After all, this is a reasonable proposition, given that Marx himself saw each form of thought as a reflection of work relationships.

Hayward is critical of Benton's attempt to reconstruct marxism's naturalistic foundations, preferring Richard Lichtman's approach to humanity/nature relations. This emphasises the acculturation by which natural-born infants become properly human.[13] Yet Lichtman and Hayward again tend to sideline the mediating role of women's labour in the processes that turn children into social beings. It is not 'culture' but the unvalued agency of daily mothering work that enables one individual to talk, think, and empathise with another in a way that feral children cannot. The humanly species powers that women, and the exceptional man, elicit through this energetic outlay are transcultural, if discursively mediated, yet the invisibility of 'feminine' contributions is ubiquitous. Paula Caplan, for example, cites a US Labor Department work skills index on which 'the skill needed to be a home maker, childcare attendant, or nursery school teacher is rated 878 on a scale of 1 to 887, where 1 is the highest skill level ... [and] the rating for a dog trainer is 228'.[14]

In related vein, women's knowledges may for the most part be grounded in meta-industrial skills, yet learning from them does not mean returning to the past. The peripheral world of subsistence is everywhere with us. It is simply a site of human = nature transactions outside the personal horizon of shared masculine significances. Hilkka Pietila's ecofeminist economics shows that women's unpaid activities actually have higher rates of productive turnover than either the state or private sectors.[15] The profound split between masculine and feminine, within our psyches and without, is rarely a political concern beyond the rubric of feminism. Thankfully, gendered identities are never fixed, just as time and space depend on socially created boundaries of relevance.

NATURE'S HOLOGRAPH

Curiously, the symptomatic urge to install boundary conditions does not seem to have cast science in patriarchal China in the same 1/0 mould. According to scholars such as Joseph Needham, the Chinese remained responsive to internal linkages and transformations in nature.[16] But while organismic thought in the West was pushed aside by men's optimistic commercial ideas of progress and fascination with mechanical models, another mind of Europe carried the agonies of industrialism. There were public stirrings of this sensibility in the dialectical writing of Marx, Engels and even Freud, although it was Haeckel who gave formulation to the ecological idea, naming it after *'oikos'*, the household: 'a unified economic system in which each member works in an intimate relationship with everyone else'.[17]

In contrast to the ecologist's concern for holding together internal relations, hegemonic science in the West has persisted in studying the single 'variable' in controlled isolation. Everywhere, application of the one-dimensional calculus cuts across real nutrient flows. And as Vandana Shiva demonstrates, in the name of development engineered plans have degraded the interactive cycles of carbon, water and minerals, killing off the habitat of creatures depending on them.[18] Overgrazing, deforestation and mining continue to express the linear mindset; its instrumental technique is intrinsically tied to the goal-driven mysteries of Western individualism.

If Newtonian physics hypostatised matter as a hierarchy of elements suspended in space, twentieth-century quantum science and the physical chemistry of Prigogene and Stengers allow for internal relations as mutually responsive rhythms coursing through time like an orchestral score.[19] Knowledge derived from the social planner's structural cross-section of lived reality now becomes inadequate, even ideological, for the dualism of structure and function simply reaffirms the primal 1/0 severing. In fact, ecofeminists and process thinkers from Whitehead to Marcuse begin to approach nature as a subject in its own right.[20] Among other challengers of the metaphysical schism between humanity and nature are biologists Richard Lewontin and Richard Levins, with their observation of active historicity in animal life:

> ant 'workers' switch among a variety of tasks over the course of the day in response to changing environmental circumstances. ... There is, moreover, a 'daily round' of slowly changing colony activities from morning to night and a long term change in the activities of a colony as it occupies the same site over years.[21]

Whereas humanly built machines are supposed to be closed, self-referential entities, natural systems are far from equilibrium, and paradoxically their stability increases with openness and relational complexity. Each habitat is said to have a characteristic field of tensions which oscillate within and against others: identity and difference. Whilst thermodynamics destabilised the 1/0 bar providing the bourgeois subject with a mirror of his entropic achievements, complexity theory now delves into the hitherto invisible generative potentials of the chora and its dissipative structures. Can women now turn these narratives of postmodern physics to their own and nature's liberation?

Just as plants and animals have unique time periodicies, so the time frames of humans engaging with them will vary.[22] At its deepest level, sexual communication between individuals is about letting disparate pulses become attuned. With violence and loss, human energies misfire. When dissipative motions go awry, sending ripples of response across the ecosystem, an abrupt shift to a qualitatively different periodicity can result. Musicians describe this as a harmonic shift. Dialectical thought describes it in terms of contradiction, a quantitative change having a qualitative effect.

The zones of contradiction such as discourse, 0, are often sources of contestation and creativity in nature so-called, as much as for human folk. Frank Fisher tells it this way:

> The zones in which ecosystems overlap, such as forest with plain or land with sea, 'generate' a profusion ... there are, for instance, the species of the plain and those of the forest but there are also species unique to the overlap. Such zones also generate ideas. The places that attract children, like the sea shore, are sources of insight and fun; and fun is precisely the making and breaking of tensions. ... Difference, then, is not just where things happen; it is the happening itself ... sites of disjunction, even dislocation; and where they occur, energy is used.[23]

Under capitalist patriarchal colonisation, indigenous peoples, women, children, the disabled, each in their own way inhabit the meta-industrial margins of difference. Each is differently abrased and in-sighted as a result. But common sense is not helpful for thinking about such things; rather its hegemonic motor always simplifies and consolidates the territory of 1. It focuses on objects, and measurement becomes fundamental. In economics, science and political decision making, artificial monocultures displace the grounded sense of place. So I am told that in the death camps of Europe old women wrote down their recipes for dumplings as an act of resistance to the cold brutality of instrumental reason.

Positivising reality is the ultimate act of foundationalism. When people take words and labels as representing fixed identities, essences, they adopt a naive realism whereby mutually transforming processes in nature or society are held artificially still and constant. Positivism and systems theory invariably go hand in hand. But like Reich's bioenergetic armouring, the manipulation of numerical indicators for 'environment', 'population', 'organisation', 'technology' cancels out internal relations and with them contradiction as the possibility of change.[24] Dialectics is by definition counter-essentialist; it undoes positives like the 1 and conventions like Man/Woman=Nature. Growing out of labour with life processes, dialectical thought defies the semantic boundaries that organise our world as given. In Freud's psychoanalysis the language of humanity=nature metamorphoses included libidinal sublimation, condensation, and displacement of energies. Reich spoke of bio-energetic armouring.

In Marx's dialectic, it is the lines between the points or the interactive processes that are more important than the points themselves: 'the particular ways in which things cohere become essential attributes of what they are'.[25] Hence, the crucial notion of non-identity, which expresses the transgressive/transformative moment. By intuiting reality as a holograph of internal relations, self-identity too becomes relational and constantly negotiated. We can act to unfold the potential of these relations or we can choose to deny it. Right now, for example, many feminists are so confused by the ideologically imposed Woman=Nature grid, they try to suppress any analysis of it.

Hope exists in the fact that crisis can come to signify new growth, even political insight. But for most people in the West, it takes an experience of contradiction, loss, despair, to disconnect from the ideological sediment of everyday meanings and look for other ways of making sense. This emancipatory moment is grasped in this wonderful passage written by Susan Griffin:

> Behind naming, beneath words, is something else. An existence named, unnamed and unnameable … we can pull the grass free of the earth and see its separate roots – but when the grass is free, it dies. … Hand and breast know each one to the other. Wood in the table knows clay in the bowl. Air knows grass knows water knows mud knows beetle knows frost knows sunlight knows the shape of the earth knows death knows not dying.[26]

Another ecofeminist, Caresse Cranwell, calls this rediscovering our erotic genealogy with the Earth. Most indigenous men and women already share these links; are they willing to teach us how?

SELF AS ENSEMBLE

Since Newton's optic, the image of the lens has guided men in focusing on discrete objects. The art of aiming the cannon in war, perspectival drawing, and causal argument in philosophy are each guided by this linear mastery. The discipline of philosophy also serves the thought police of modernity by keeping debate locked into the synchronic grid and its either/or, theory/praxis, fact/value. The argument by Reason always proceeds by 'drawing a clear line between'. When it comes to envisaging complex, weblike patterns, where each part resonates information from the whole, nonsequentially, the holograph is a more useful metaphor than the lens. Even so, the way we have come to talk about it still favours the patriarchal organ of sight.[27]

Marx's own dialectic can be characterised as holographic in that it traced mutually referring internal relations back and forth across a multidimensional field. Several of these relations have already been encountered:

- identity and difference (for example, when women and men, or men and animals, both share common features and yet are also unlike);
- interpenetration of opposites (for example, when women's gendered labours are both a source of their oppression and a source of privileged insight);
- quantitative increase to the point of qualitative change (for example, when human waste in soil at the base of a tree stirs growth of new fruit);
- contradiction, the negation of the negation (a spiral, for example, when antagonistic developments inside one relation, M/W, cause a rearrangement of internal relations, W=M=N).

Marx's sinuous analysis of natural and historical linkages held on to subversive transformations. Ecofeminists and Third World marginals also make good use of decentred oscillation, and of the generative resonances of time lived simultaneously inside and out of History and Nature.[28]

Humans create order out of chaos by calling different internal relations into focus. Women do this as they labour to mediate conflicts in family life. Peasants pacify biological systems by catalysing exchanges between hens, cows, and orchard plots. People who are privileged enough to work with all their senses together, come to a kinaesthetic awareness of the multiple timings embedded in what is handled. They learn holding, synchronising their agency with the rhythms of growth. Feminist cyborgs notwithstanding, the time scales of pregnancy, washing small bodies, planting and gathering, and laying out the dead remain largely the province of women. Most of these activities involve intergenerational needs, demanding planful thought, sensitive to consequence.

Given that these invisible pulsations are integrated with

material practices, socially situated humans have typically ethnic, class, or gendered time frames. The phenomenologist Alfred Schutz inadvertently converged with Marx's sociology of knowledge by calling for an understanding of consciousness as crossed by multiple realities.[29] As he saw it, the paramount reality of everyday life would be bracketed out to construct the time horizon of science. Thus, as mechanism became the bearer of white masculine progress, the separation of plan from action and action from consequence became the social norm. This disastrous fragmentation was institutionalised by capitalist patriarchal commonsense as a division of mental versus manual labour. But technocratic efficiency did not 'save time', it simply displaced matter and disturbed the motility of life forms. In short, the abstracted systems of instrumental reason have created ecological 'noise'.

A doing self is decentred, implicated in many layers of experience at once. This is what is meant when feminists describe women as socialised for contingency. Women's traditional chores demand flexibility and attention to the diversity of human and natural rhythms inscribed across the social score. A constant pull between expectation and encounter demands that care givers attune temporal skills; internal body clocks adjust and anticipate what might impinge on daily survival. The point here is not that sensitivity to periodicity in nature is some sex-specific essence, but rather that the enculturation surrounding life maintenance work gets to be refined by hands-on practice.

Ecofeminist thinking moves away from discrete living entities to their characteristic interactions, processes, and time frames. Complexity. It supersedes psychologising accounts of self that leave the political dimension out. Conservative interests deal with men and women as isolated individuals or sets of gendered attributes negotiating interests. This anthropocentrism stresses intention above all else, and commemorates social life as conquest and submission. By contrast, Marx saw self-identity as an outcome of interacting social processes – 'the ensemble of social relations'. This goes very much against the grain in a society based on competition, serial extraction, and accumulation.

Post-Einstein, reality is increasingly spoken of as layered or, more accurately, relative to how it is conceptually framed. For example, using a sociological lens, a woman can be seen as the routine carrier of learned roles in a social system that functions by certain time coordinates; using another lens, she becomes a dissipative flux in an environment whose temporal context is elsewhere. As Julia Kristeva records it, pregnancy is an experience in which a woman comes to know herself in contradictory ways at once.

> Cells fuse, split, and proliferate; volumes grow, tissues stretch, and body fluids change rhythm, speeding up or slowing down. Within the body growing is a graft, indomitable, there is another. And no one is present, within that simultaneously dual and alien space, to signify what is going on. 'It happens, but I'm not there.' 'I cannot realise it, but it goes on.' Motherhood's impossible syllogism.[30]

A process without a subject; identity in non-identity? The body of the mother is light wave and particle, metaphorically speaking. Only the 1/0 logic of eurocentric philosophers rules this relational truth out of court.

Women's relation to nature, and therefore to labour and to capital, is qualitatively different from men's in at least four ways. The first such difference involves experiences mediated by female body organs in the hard but sensuous interplay of birthing and suckling labours. The second set of differences are historically assigned caring and maintenance chores which serve to 'bridge' men and nature. A third involves women's manual work in making goods as farmers, weavers, herbalists, potters. A fourth set of experiences involves creating symbolic representations of 'feminine' relations to 'nature' – in poetry, painting, philosophy and everyday talk. Through this constellation of labours, women are organically and discursively implicated in life-affirming activities, and they develop gender-specific knowledges grounded in that material base. The result is that women across cultures have begun to express insights that are quite removed from most men's approaches to global crisis – whether these be corporate greenwash, ecological ethics or socialism.[31]

A POSTMODERN MARX?

In his book *Dialectical Investigations*, Bertell Ollman's elucidation of Marx's procedure shows a thinker who readily apprehended social life from many vantage points and at different levels of abstraction or generality. Marx moved between these levels in order to focus on one problem or another. In this respect, there is much for ecopolitical activists to learn from his approach to social theory. Differently constructed experiences of natural processes provide different standpoints from which to conceptualise the human condition. Or, putting it another way, Ollman writes:

> Society has many levels of internally related qualities that we get to understand by using different kinds of lenses, some intimate, others more general, *with each lens or vantage point having a time scale of its own.* This means that seemingly contradictory views can often be true.[32]

If the content of Marx's theory is limited by the anthropocentric values of an industrialising era, his method certainly drove hard against prevailing Western thought habits. Marx's opus exemplifies many different discursive lenses in use, just as with complementarity in physics, where the object may be treated as either light wave or particle. In sociology, a worker may be conceptualised as an individual husband, a sample of an economic class, or a member of the human species. Each distinction describes objective activities in the material world, and each has 'a theoretical vantage point' with conceptual tools honed for different purposes.

Ollman points out that the canvas of social analysis can be intimate or distancing in its 'level of generality': wide or narrow, diachronic or synchronic. In scientistic jargon one might say that the discursive scoping that gives boundaries to an investigation is called its 'extension' and this has both spatial and temporal aspects. With a diachronic or temporal extension, Marx might typically

> abstract a particular group to include where they seem to be heading, together with the new set of relations that await them but which they have not yet fully acquired. In the case of peasants who are rapidly losing their land and of small business men who are being driven into bankruptcy, this translates into becoming wage-labourers.[33]

More recently, ecofeminist dialecticians have focused on the global feminisation of poverty under a transnational capitalist patriarchal system and the emergent unity of interests among women North and South.[34] If only 'productive' workers are heard, our understanding of living rhythms will be limited by the horizons of their industrial labour role. If only men speak about power, again we will have a very partial politics. The way to move beyond old-established boundaries and stratifications is to uncover the texture of internal relations in which we are implicated.

Marx's own thought processes constantly moved back and forth between several levels of generality, just as ecofeminism must do in its deconstruction of the M/W=N attitude. Thus, he might paint a compassionate psychological picture of the 'individual person', as in his heart-rending descriptions of a miserable proletarian man or child. Sartre's existential reading of socialism pursued the ramifications of this personalising vantage point. In contemporary movement politics, deep ecologists such as Arne Naess and postmodern liberal feminists such as Donna Haraway focus on self-realisation as political goals in themselves.[35] At other times, Marx would angle his view of the individual through his or her 'sociological role', like mother or worker. This kind of analysis emphasises the functional status of individuals in the system as a whole. Within socialism, Louis Althusser's effort to describe the citizen bearers of ideology fits here. Similarly, radical feminism and its byproduct in gender studies focus on the complementary socialisation patterns that construct masculinity and femininity respectively.[36]

Third, Marx might provide an economic account of the worker as part of the capitalist 'economic system' and its colonising history. This vantage point would focus on questions of exploitation and equity. It became the preferred level of generality for both socialist feminism in the 1970s and the emerging eco-socialism of the 1990s.[37] But Marx could also pitch his text towards a historical view of capitalism compared with other possible 'political traditions'. Frankfurt School critical theory and Bookchin's social ecology of domination seem to work at this level.[38]

Marx's early work is a naturalistic reading of history as 'species development'. But equally, he recognised that ethical naturalisation has been a favourite device of the Church with its Great Chain of Being and of bourgeois liberal ideologists such as Hobbes and Locke. Conservative-leaning deep ecologists such as Warwick Fox perpetuate this uncritical naturalism. Mies's ecofeminist work on patriarchal accumulation and my own epistemology critique offer a deconstructive reading of it.[39] Finally, to the bioenergetic ground of social life. Engels's dialectical materialism argues a 'biological account' of dialectical and social phenomena, suggesting that the same laws of transformation run through all matter. This line of thought has been cultivated by philosophers in the Soviet Union, and reappears in the process arguments of Fritjof Capra and Jeremy Rifkin.[40]

Since each level has its own characteristic vocabulary and style it works as a discourse in its own right. Marx's capacious intellectual reach across these various problematics surely puts him in place among the masters of postmodernity. But twentieth-century practitioners of socialism, mainly men, have become fixated on economistic explications of capital – the third discourse cited above – unable to articulate other levels of focus. Feminists have also tended to reify specific kinds of analysis. Feminism in the North began with a sociological analysis of gender roles – Ollman's discourse two. At the same time, it entirely rejected the stultifying naturalisation of history, the M/W=N formula by which men situated themselves as part of culture while their mothers and wives remained 'natural creatures'. The radical moment in feminism therefore works deconstructively, using sociological critique from the second level, to deconstruct the ideological naturalism of discourse five.

But radical feminism was quickly overtaken by a need for

dialogue with the political mainstream. Hence the bourgeois moment in the ongoing dialectical development of feminism involved a struggle for women's individual subjectivity to be recognised and then accorded equal political entitlement – discursive levels one and four. Other feminists tried to make sense of their experiences through socialist theory, only to find that here, too, gender stereotyping objectified women as role embodiments. Hence the failure of socialists to see domestic work as economic labour under capitalism – level three. Attempts to remedy this lapse constitute the *socialist moment* in feminism's history.

While building on these earlier feminist analyses, an *ecofeminist moment* has come to explore the reciprocal implications of ecological and gender crisis. Seeing feminism as a continuum of discourses, each with a specific site of political intervention, enables women to bring the full strength of their movement into play. This is why ecofeminism is a dialectical politics. Women activists tread a zigzag course between:

- their liberal and socialist feminist task of establishing the right to a political voice;
- their radical and poststructuralist feminist task of undermining the very basis of that same validation; and
- their ecofeminist task of demonstrating how women – and thence men too – can live differently within nature.

THE META-INDUSTRIAL VANTAGE POINT

Ecofeminist and other postmodern critiques of eurocentric disciplines are occasionally allied. So all capitalist patriarchal discourses, from economism to penis envy and on to Gaia, are treated as failures of masculine reflexivity. Indigenous knowledges at the 'periphery' and housekeeping skills at the 'centre' both typify meta-industrial connections between Man and Nature. In speaking about these ways of doing and knowing, ecofeminists honour women's metabolic bridging of ecology and culture. As opposed to mining and smelting or genetic engineering, which leave disorder and waste, women's subaltern labours give life back to the biosphere.

Epistemologically speaking, these labours are discursively mixed transactions, light wave and particle, productive and reproductive. But everyday language fails dialectics, for talk of reciprocity is itself limited by the dualist fracture of material life into separate realms. In an embodied materialism, these catalysing moments are not exactly identical with the role-gendered labour that turns 'first' nature into 'second', nor are they strictly biology. Women's holding work is relatively autonomous.[41]

A new mode of abstraction is called for in the process of reconstructing our historically deleted human identity with/in nature. An ecofeminist analysis suggests that the psychosexual edge where women 'mediate' nature provides the most common and therefore most democratically useful meta-industrial vantage point for an integrated ecopolitical analysis. Attention to that silenced nexus is long overdue. In taking this political initiative, ecofeminists emulate Marx's sociology of knowledge, which grounds the perceptions of each class in its habitual field of praxis.[42]

Against the tendency of dominator thought and the vanities of eurocentric philosophy, which sees 'everything from nowhere', an ecofeminist standpoint is historical. It temporarily prioritises the vantage point of that working majority who live the deepest contradiction on the margin of human metabolic exchange with nature. As a level of generality, this new discourse can be proudly labelled 0. In the marxist schema just outlined, it can be found between individual agency, discursive level one, and biophysical matter, level six. It is attuned to both. Reciprocally, social and ecological conditions both enable and constrain our activities. Ecofeminists argue that the metabolic limits of biology should not be counted as frustrations of human will, but trusted and enjoyed.

Marxists who write that face-to-face interaction takes us backwards in history celebrate the masculine myth of technological production, forgetting that humanity only survives by dint of domestic relations with its environment. David Harvey calls up the Promethean vision when he writes that

> For Marxists there can be no going back, as many ecologists seem to propose, to an unmediated relation to nature (or a world built solely on face to face relations), to a pre-capitalist and communitarian world of non-scientific understandings with limited divisions of labour.[43]

Sensuous practice, 0, Mother=Nature as body, these boundary exclusions remain in the shadow of Enlightenment.

Men and women across most cultures, but especially in developed societies, are required to engage differently with the natural world. This political engendering is disguised again when Rifkin writes that 'humanity [*sic*] has created an artificial time environment punctuated by mechanical contrivances and electronic impulses, a time plane that is quantitative, fast-paced, efficient, and predictable'.[44] It is true that when humans interact with machines their bodies are unconsciously captured by the fantastical but solipsistic laws of motion by which such objects are designed. But there are striking contrasts in class, race, gender and species exposure with respect to the technological environment.

Artefacts do indeed mediate and filter experience, but not for all people to the same extent. When the material substrate of life is reprocessed by manufacture and offered up for a price, what is seen gets to be the stuff that fills extensional space. Energy flows are reified and priced as coal or sugar or a stand of forest. But the socially contrived focus on 'things' misses the myriad of reverberations that hold matter together. Furthermore, because people's sense of time as multiple is denuded by the administered state, its citizen consumers are disempowered by only being able to grasp 'what is' as distinct from 'what can be'.

Humans can never know what nature wants outside their own perceptual limitations. The challenge is to meet nature in hands-on dialogue. A kinaesthetic knowing is wanted in order to mend ruptured M/W=N energies. We cannot defy modernity with rationalism, nor by simply 'loving what is given' as some ecophilosophers suggest. What is given, including eurocentric reason, is complicit in the oppression of far too many earthly beings. Harvey speaks for the left, both marxist and ecofeminist, when he claims that values are 'arrived at through a process of inquiry embedded in forms of praxis'.[45] In careful labour, the enfoldment of internal relations is known. If a concept of intrinsic value and a precautionary ethic is possible, then this is surely it.

It can be argued that the dialectic of internal relations of Marx and Engels is postmodern in a quite exemplary sense. It also converges with an ecofeminist standpoint through (1) its dialectical and transformative epistemology; through (2) an ontology of nature as multidimensional and processual, (3) with human identity embedded in nature and human interaction with nature as self-affirming; through (4) a claim that only sensuous praxis is the basis of valid knowledge; through (5) key notions of labour and appropriation as defining the human interface with nature, (6) as defining the history of class struggle, (7) and, implicitly, defining gendered, species and postcolonial relations as well; through (8) a view of social institutions as first/second nature, interlocking and mutually effective; and through the concepts of (9) alienation, (10) ideology, and the fetishism of commodities.

In the late twentieth century we are becoming aware of how the Great Chain of Being theology has penetrated day-to-day practice; and the discourses of science, economics, politics and marxism too. It is effectively a hierarchy of estrangement and predation of lower orders by those at the top of the line of denial. To his credit, Marx described his ideal of a communist society as 'the consummate oneness in substance of man and nature – the true resurrection of nature – the naturalisation of man and the humanism of nature both brought to fulfilment'.[46] Marx also spoke about economic and spiritual relatedness to nature in the same breath; and this makes sense to many women and environmentalists.

When it comes to the popular dualistic debate over anthropocentric versus ecocentric ethics, it is plain that both are fabrications of the M/W=N ideology. As ecofeminists see it, the main obstacle to a sustainable future is the androcentrism of both political left and right. The labour theory of value especially demands reformulation in a way that takes account of the materially embodied reciprocity of men, women and nature. Men, especially, need to open up and hear what ordinary women have to say. And, more, to share holding labours. In the long run, this direction of structural change will be more emancipatory all round than wholesale entry of the oppressed into public institutions that are both gender-dysfunctional and unsustainable.

11
AGENTS OF COMPLEXITY

ENFOLDMENT AND RESONANCE

As every *campesino* knows, there is fishing time, resting time, ripening time for fruit, baking time, time for elderly walking. But the Man/Woman=Nature ideology detaches the signifier 'time' from enduring material referents. The outcome is a fatal lack of commensurability between Western knowledges and living thermodynamic entities. Martin O'Connor writes that global economics and the 'capitalisation of nature' through science raise up a 'semiurgical' time.

> For the industrial *episteme*, time connotes continuity and predictability, more specifically, an irreversible accumulation: the expanded reproduction of capital. … [But that] Time is in fact the Nemesis of any pretension to have determined the future, and connotes the indeterminacy, ambivalence, and mutability of historical trajectories.[1]

The social constructionist world of signifying chains without referent mirrors commodification just as much as the naive realism of positivist science did two generations ago.[2] The post-modern objection that ecofeminism 'appropriates' indigenous knowledges is a byproduct of this ungrounded solipsism. The common denominator of women's struggles for survival North and South is their holding work and consciousness of enduring time. This creates empowerment and solidarity between people on the wrong side of the 1/0 code.

Catriona Sandilands has expressed concern that there may be a self-contradictory moment in ecofeminism that loses touch with the multiplicity of voices when it universalises itself: 'The moment in which ecofeminism claims to have found the truth of women's *being in nature* is the moment in which it loses its promise.'[3] But again, this perception seems to drag capitalist patriarchal dualisms along with it. On the other hand, when we think about ecofeminism in a multidimensional way, issues like privileging the Woman=Nature link, seeing 'women' as a cross-cultural category, theorising feminine subjectivity as decentred, recede as problems.[4] Sandilands comes close to this view herself, when she talks about focusing on 'a different kind of politics, one that does not spring naturally from "being" or "identity", but that sees itself as a temporary and flexible, politically produced representation of specificity.'[5] Ecofeminism is indeed a transitional intervention by specific subjects at a specific historical point.

Underlining how experiences are shared by women across spatial and discursive boundaries is crucial to ecofeminist mobilisation. Ecofeminists try not to reify attributes such as class, race, or age; rather, they move across these identities in ways that are ideologically transgressive. It is actions that count. Moreover, increasingly women have complex, mixed-race or mixed-class non-identities. However, as noted before, many eurocentric liberal, socialist, and postmodern feminists reject this inductive gathering of commonalities as a politically incorrect 'essentialism'. The old feminist fear is that ecofeminists further women's oppression by relying on traditionally ascribed 'feminine' psychological attributes to build unity among women. The misinterpretation results from reading 'difference' with a naive realist mindset, so losing the radical structuralist meaning of deferral: a creative movement in language, product of internal relations.

Cultural critic Megan Morris lends clarity to the ecofeminist position with her contrast between 'an essentialist cultural politics dependent on inherited traditions of identity and community ... and a "differential" or "diasporic" identity politics understood as an historical, as well as cultural, production carried out in the midst of, precisely, flux and change'.[6] Morris's notion of a diasporic identity is stronger than Gayatri Spivak's proposal for a 'strategic essentialism'.[7] The latter suggests simply a pragmatic, cognitive choice, whereas the 'self making' that occurs in crisis intimates an underlying libidinal struggle. Dialectically speaking, to uncover an essence means to make explicit structural relationships between people in a social totality, not fixed psychological traits. This is what the ecofeminist deconstruction of Man/Woman=Nature assumptions does.

In this political work, women from many class and race backgrounds are well placed and well motivated to unravel the Boromean knot with its historical identification of femininity and social reproduction. At the same time, the majority of women are well situated to create new bonds between Man, Woman, and Nature, so-called. Those who challenge ecofeminism as 'essentialist' theory fail to draw the fundamental sociological distinction between 'first' and 'second' nature. If their thesis is right – that all we can ever know is a constructed 'second nature' from technologies to political institutions – then we can never address a radical vision of what our full potential might be, only a reformist one.

Far from being premised on simple polarities of masculine and feminine, culture and nature – as some critics of ecofeminism have implied – the ecofeminist standpoint rests on a dialectical negation of received dualisms. As an emerging political consensus among women, ecofeminism is overdetermined in the structuralist sense. We have already outlined the ecological holding skills that domestic care givers, Third World farmers and indigenous gatherers share. But in order to understand what energises political agency, a deeper materialist analysis is useful. Ecofeminist theories draw on an embodied materialism which not only overcomes masculinist essences; by affirming labour as sensuous practice, it goes beyond this to an interior dialectic between bodily drives and discourse.

North and South, women under capitalist patriarchal conditions find themselves lodged inside/outside relations of production in a way that is unlivable. Daily they are broken on the contradiction that has them 'closer to nature'. Even after national independence, ni-Vanuatu poet Grace Molisa says, most women are still colonised:

> Six months pregnant
> kicked
> in the abdomen
> punched
> on the head
> perforated eardrum
> scalp lacerations
> require suturing …
> haematoma
> deep penetrating wound
> fingers chopped off
> epistaxis …
> ruptured spleen
> and (R) kidney

> 2 major operations
> pushed to the ground ...[8]

Canadian psychologist Paula Caplan has analysed the phenomenon of 'momism', an hostility just as virulent as racism, ageism, and class snobbery. Thinking men and women who would scrupulously avoid expressing anti-black sentiments still readily mock 'the mothering class'. This prejudice will be the last domino to fall. Irish and Polish jokes are now considered *passé*, but it has remained

> acceptable to say venomous things about Blacks as long as they were Black *mothers* or about Jewish mothers, Italian mothers, Catholic mothers, funny old grannies, or mothers-in-law ... you [the butt] are expected to find them funny ... to be hurt is to be oversensitive – or ridiculous.[9]

Women are human, but still treated socially as simple reproductive sites or commodities, made use of and exchanged like any other natural resource. Being 'not quite labour', they cannot achieve equality – ideological or financial – in the workforce. Having 'no subjectivity to speak of', their voices remain unheard, unless to chorus the 1/0 discourse thereby affirming their own diminutive role.

How does a woman ever find her way out of this double bind, let alone come to act for social change? The secret exists in the fact that somatic states make and unmake subjectivity. After all, what is the subject but a body that carries intention. Abrased by contradictory meanings, she becomes an active field. In her semanalysis, Julia Kristeva talks of a special state of apprehension where, under stress, body drives and their ideations disintegrate and reassemble. This matrix of apprehensions or 'chora' is the very kernel of historical consciousness, and is renewed again and again, through a multiplicity of libidinal cathexes which feed the link between signifier and signified.[10] Unlike most structuralists, Kristeva joins language, politics and psychology with her unique notion of 'signifiance': 'a process in the course of which the "subject" of the text, escaping the logic of the ego-cogito and engaging in other logics (of the signifier, the contradiction), struggles with meaning and is deconstructed ("lost")'.[11] It is through crisis and moments of non-identity that subjects glimpse new meanings, a hidden historical potential behind what is given. This dialectic rests on a distinction between a relational essence and mere appearance, 'facts', the positives of perception.[12]

ERASURE AND NON-IDENTITY

Sexual violence, economic and cultural marginalisation – these things may fracture a woman's identity. Invalidated by contradictory significations, the object/subject decathects somatic energies which tie her to existing social relations. Becoming free from her status as Other, a subject-in-process begins to predicate a new relation to the totality. To paraphrase Kristeva: when the fragile equilibrium of consciousness is destroyed by the violent heterogeneity of contradiction, the body returns to a state of difference, heavy, wandering, dissociated. It is this moment of annihilation and decomposition, a moment of raw anguish and disarray that gives way to a new productive unity, and reaffirms the subject as active signification in process.

In parallel vein, Ashis Nandy describes the dialectic of signifying practice as experienced by the postcolonial subject:

> when psychological and cultural survival is at stake, polarities such as the ones discussed here do break down and become irrelevant, and the directness of the experience of suffering and spontaneous resistance to it *come through at all planes.* When this happens, there emerges in the victim of a system a vague awareness of the larger whole which transcends the system's analytic categories and/or stands them on their head. Thus, the victim may become aware that, under oppression, *the parochial could protect some forms of universalism more successfully.*[13]

Although we speak of signifying moments, such transformative insights can take years to coalesce. Strange as it may seem to emancipated feminists in the North, in settings such as Brazil this transvaluation of feminine identities has even been facilitated by mothers' groups:

> the collective construction of consciousness of gender opens the possibility for women to surpass their fragmented identity ... the constitution of a new political image for women will eventually lead to a fading of the lines of separation between the 'public' and 'private' spheres.[14]

For those in the front line of environmental impacts, eroded as nature is, social dis/location eventually shatters ideological common sense like a phenomenological laser. But the freewheeling chora with its insurgent energies and multiple significations offers new possibilities for dealing with regimes of erasure.

From this place of non-identity, beyond the 1/0, ecofeminists boldly reframe the Woman=Nature nexus, revaluing what has been problematic in a one-dimensional order and confronting its stagnant totalisation. Some liberal feminists and socialists, still speaking from the unreconstructed side of the capitalist patriarchal contradiction, fail to see the dialectical shift here, and hence employ the 'essentialist' label. This is not surprising, since the scientific hegemony of the West cannot handle irony, the moment of tension when a signifier is suspended between two competing senses. A lived intertextuality.

Further, the power of bourgeois realism is such that the very term 'essence' itself is captured by positivism, losing its negative, unmasking function. Concepts can only be understood when we grasp their limits – what they are not. This is why Minnie Bruce Pratt reminds us:

> The 'self' in this narrative is not an essence or truth concealed by layers of patriarchal deceit and lying in wait for discovery. ... 'The system' is revealed to be not one but multiple, overlapping, intersecting systems or relations that are historically constructed and recreated through everyday practices and interactions, and that implicate the individual in contradictory ways.[15]

Far from the complacent certainties of M/W=N lore, the negative dialectic holds to an inverse relation between power and historical consciousness. Thus, it is not the free-floating intellectual who has privileged access to the critical perception; nor is a theory of class-consciousness adequate to understand the eurocentric contradiction that brackets subalterns together against men of capital and labour. Rather, ecofeminist insights are driven by the profound 'lack' imposed on those who are neither 'human' nor of 'nature'. In Theo Adorno's words, the moment of non-identity is 'the somatic unrest that makes knowledge move', the dialectician's duty being to help this 'fool's truth' attain its own reasons.[16]

But this embodied defiance of inscription is merely the deconstructive moment, negation. Alienation may be necessary, but it is not a sufficient condition for political consciousness. In a time of ecological crisis, free-wheeling punk attitudes give us little direction. However the alternative subculture of women is grounded by skills and values that both challenge the system and rationally affirm life. Women's political awareness is not merely reactive, but expresses qualities of personal synthesis, initiative, intuition and flexibility, learned in caring labours.[17] Women may be the displaced persons of most thought traditions arriving at politics like refugees; but their grounded wisdoms are scarcely nomadic in the glamorous postmodern sense. The Other of one-dimensional rationalism has too long been suppressed as a way of knowing and being. Activist men have embarked on this search with Oriental gurus, only to reinforce the pre-Oedipal dynamic that feeds global crisis. Deep ecologists forge their own transcendent schemes, but again it is not clear that they are looking in the right place for their Other nature.

Empirical knowledge conceived in daily labour sustains the ecofeminist voice. Phrases such as 'women transfer fertility' or 'partnership between women's work and nature's work' convey a dialectical epistemology, discrediting the transcendent dualisms of the West. Feminists should not fear the double-edged metaphor of Mother=Nature. This nexus both describes the source of women's power and integrity, and at the same time exposes the complex of pathological practices known as capitalist patriarchy. Feminists can use this metaphor to encourage their brothers to think about the libidinal source of the pitiful drive to dominate and reassemble what is Other – the tele-pharmo-nuclear enterprise its latest symptom.

AN EMBODIED MATERIALISM

The Man/Woman=Nature hegemony constantly catches oppressed social groupings on a two-pronged dilemma. But there is a way out for those prepared to look behind the facade of eurocentric convention. Just as ecofeminist activists try to steer liberal feminism away from conservative political strategies, they need to guard against its ideology posing as theory. Too much bourgeois academic writing protects the masculinist status quo, suppressing conflict and overlooking the in-process character of lived history. The unwitting essentialism of the disciplines has an elective affinity with time-suppressing ways of using language. Both analytical philosophy and poststructuralism are typically synchronic, for example, yet rarely are they examined as tools of privilege and denial.

For sure, postmodern textual analysis has helped protest movements to expose the social agenda of Enlightenment universalism and instrumentalism. However, in voicing the Other of modernity, the deconstructive technique has been adopted by many marginals as if it were a politics. Sections of feminism, the gay movement, postcolonial struggle, and ecology have each embraced it in this way. Ironically, the pluralism that results from these emancipations becomes neoliberalism by default, because once the moment of destabilisation has passed and discourse effects are exposed, the postmodern exercise has little further to add. It cannot help movements to formulate a programme of action without undermining its own epistemological root in Derrida's dissolution of the fixed referent.

Many scholars who rely exclusively on the critique of representation to dismiss oppressive practices fail to distinguish between the naive realism of everyday life and more culturally reflexive forms. They overlook the marxist truism that objectification is not the same as reification. But unselfconscious liberals are not especially tuned in to the study of structural conditioning, being more at home with manipulation of the social in terms of individual categories and psychological norms.[18] This analytical reason, with its egoistic concept of self, agency and moral will, privatises truths and preserves the capitalist patriarchal paradigm expertly.

Identitarian psychology is inept before the interactive reality of material self in habitat. The latter is never a seamless construct, but a throbbing complex of body organs, imageries and social pressures. Static labels like Woman, Man or Nature are social givens which must achieve the impossible by standing for subjects always in process of being made. People move in and out of these positivities with degrees of integration.[19] For example, in the joy of orgasm, men and women feel what deep ecologists have identified as 'indistinguishable self', just as a mother can with a suckling infant. Afterwards they regain degrees of separateness and come to collaborate, or plan and judge for themselves. Deep ecologists also talk about an 'expanded self' which projects the structures of ego outwards. Women often feel expanded self in conscious-raising groups or in community activism undertaken in the interests of the whole. But the consciousness that is of most interest to ecofeminism is the 'colonised self', with its grasp of intricate and contradictory political relations.

Thus Lourdes Torres describes the perspicacity of her Latina re/sisters in reclaiming

> an identity they have been taught to despise. In order to do this, they must work through all the cultural and gender socialization and misinformation which has left them in a

> maze of contradictions. This results in the fragmentation of identity, and the inability to speak from a unified, noncontradictory subject position. No existing discourse is satisfactory because each necessitates repression of different aspects of the self.[20]

North and South, women suffer these binds. As feminists they fail to achieve citizen equality with men by being of Nature and all it entails. Even as ecologists, their perspectives are not taken seriously, even though they *are* supposedly of Nature. An ecofeminist analysis emerges from the resolution of these contradictions.

Ecofeminist and other postcolonial critiques of eurocentrism move beyond positivist ways of knowing.[21] In contrast to the shamed silence of liberal feminists and their urge to assimilate, awareness of self-in-nature means opening up to the double binds of the M/W=N regime. Maxine Hong Kingston has described her coping with contradiction thus: 'I learned to make my mind large, as the universe is large, so that there is room for paradoxes.'[22] And so she discovered dialectical thought as the way in which individuality and social change are joined. Recursive perceptions defy the essentialising categories of normative dualism; in fact, the pain of ambiguity pierces given 'essences' and hones the critical voice like nothing else.[23]

When thought is not wrapped in denial but 'endures', raw consciousness spins through new possibilities. As subjects-in-process let the energy of suffering break through and fracture the surety of everyday life, contradiction is released in a personal and historical sense. Jim Cheney articulates the making of this vernacular politics drawing on feminist standpoint epistemology: 'A voice is privileged to the extent that it is constructed from a position that enables it to spot distortions, mystifications, and colonizing and totalizing tendencies within other discourses.'[24] This voice does not make an abstract claim to universal objectivity; it is relational, telling the world from a particular sense of place at a particular time in history.

Taking the argument further, Gloria Anzaldúa talks of an identity born on the borderlands, sensitive to multiple frames and negotiations:

> The work of the mestiza consciousness is to break down the subject-object duality that keeps her a prisoner and to show … how duality is transcended. The answer to the problem between the white race and the coloured, between males and females, lies in healing the split that originates in the very foundation of our lives, our culture, our languages, our thoughts. A massive uprooting of dualistic thinking in the individual and collective consciousness is the beginning of a long struggle, but one that could, in our best hopes, bring us to the end of rape, of violence, of war.[25]

Dealing with double binds is crucial in the process of unmaking Western dualisms. However, postmodern approaches to heterogeneity hold the political status quo intact by fragmenting subjective identity. A dialectical theory of signifying practice cuts beneath the social statics of discourse analysis to a conception of agency based on the negotiation of lived contradiction.

This method is consistent with our ecofeminist interest in energy and its multiple forms: enjoyed, commodified, trapped, petrified, stolen, enfolded, transformed, shared, sold, free-flowing, dissipated, recycled. Thus, an exploited worker might be empowered to move from subjective anger to 'objective' consciousness of her unity with a class of others. Similarly, if negative connotations attach to, say, black identity under the logic of domination, when blackness is reframed in transcendent discourse as difference, individual actors together can begin to force immanent structures to realign. What counts as emancipatory is that the contradicted subject 'makes herself'. Liberal feminists should take time out to think about this 'real choice', as opposed to the false needs and artificial options of pre-packaged affluence.

But ecofeminism is much more than just a standpoint and 'a view' from below. It is about that critical eye combined with holding skills already practised by a majority of women across the globe. Living in/with Nature means labouring in a way that does not disrupt the time of ecosystemic processes. The labour-in-reciprocity of Vandana Shiva's forest dwellers or Sara Ruddick's mothers unifies space–time in the technical act of holding together complex biological flows and linkages of meaning between loved ones. In this activity, the subjectivity of others, including nature's constant flux, is fostered, just as the caring worker him- or herself develops through such exchanges. Where holding is practised, Petra Kelly's 1/0 insight that 'disarmament' means exposing one's vulnerability becomes a possibility. Labour-in-reciprocity privileges neither worker nor matter, it annuls that sharp distinction. Holding becomes the moment of knowing, in a carnal sense, between self and nature; an identity/non-identity.

THE PRECAUTIONARY ETHIC

If masculine agency produces knowledge by splitting subject and object, then dividing the object into discrete units in order to remake it, what might be called a feminine or communion approach to knowing expresses a sensibility that is not alienated from itself or its environment. Reflecting the fluid, dialectical, self-feeding and polyvalent character of things in the world, this attitude encloses an epistemology that is well matched to the study of ecosystems. So Susan Griffin reminds us:

> We say you cannot divert the river from the riverbed. We say that everything is moving, and we are part of this motion. ... We say every act comes back on itself. There are consequences. You cannot cut the trees from the mountainside without a flood.[26]

Ecofeminist politics is grounded in women's economic marginalisation and skills, and the painfully won awareness of non-identity that their place in the nature–woman–labour nexus gives them.[27] Formulated as an embodied materialism, ecofeminism gets at the lowest common denominator of all oppressions. As such, it opens up new possibilities for dialogue between classes and social movements resistant to capital.

By reasoning dialectically, then, ecofeminists introduce an alternative ontology to political discourse, one that cancels the frightened dualisms of transcendent subjectivity. In defiance of the eurocentric canon, ecofeminists propose that:

- nature and history are a material unity;
- nature, women and men are at once active subjects and passive objects;
- the woman–nature metabolism holds the key to *historical jouissance*;
- reproductive labours model sustainability.

Tying political perception and motivation to suffering, the phenomenology of deconstruction that women experience results in a materially grounded epistemology.

Concerned with equality for all life forms, ecofeminism is a socialism in the very deepest sense of that word. But it may be noted that 'spiritual' ecofeminism reflects the same ontological assumptions. This feminine voice becomes even more apposite to ecology, as men begin to respect nature itself as a subject with its own needs. Both dominated and empowered, women and other colonised subjects are well equipped, at this conjuncture, to take up the case for life. Again, this is not to argue in a simple-minded essentialist way that women or natives are somehow 'closer to nature'. Rather it is to acknowledge a complex socially elaborated difference and its agency.

For the most urgent and fundamental political task is to dismantle ideological attitudes that have severed the human sense of belonging to nature; and this, in turn, can only happen once nature is no longer fixated, commodified as an object, outside of and separate from humans. Reifications of this sort are endemic to capitalist patriarchal discourse, starting with the very subject of bourgeois right who is supposed to participate in the democratic process with a fixed identity and status. Socialism, too, has traditionally attributed a permanent character to the proletariat as historical agent. But universals or essences such as Humanity, Class, Woman, Nature, are abstractions that do violence to those living under the regime of contradiction. The alternative ecofeminist conception of subjectivity as signification in process, permanently forming and reforming itself in collision with the social totality, is based in a materialism that defies the limits of bourgeois epistemology. Against the theoretically abbreviated notions of capitalist patriarchal common sense, the ecofeminist consciousness is reflexively decentred.

Unlike the 1/0 regime which is geared to short-term profits, women's lives straddling the nature–woman–labour nexus are embodied in the context of conservation. Women's labour experiences house both 'grounds' for ecopolitical critique and actual 'models' of sustainable practice. Transcending the limits of both capital and socialist ideologies, 'if women's lived experience were ... given legitimation in our culture, it could provide an immediate "living" social basis for the alternative consciousness which [radical men are] trying to formulate as an abstract ethical construct.'[28] Thanks to capital and its contradictions, ordinary women, a global majority, already cultivate sustainability in their cycle of reproductive labours. The labour of women from Indian farmers to Finnish housewives and Aboriginal gatherers instantiates this consequential ethic.[29] Here, in practice, are ways of meeting community needs with low disruption to environment and minimum reliance on a dehumanising cash economy.

Honouring the 'gift' of nature, these people outside commodity culture labour with an independence, dignity and grace that those of us looking for sustainable models can learn from. For, as Shiva reminds us:

> Culturally perceived poverty need not be real material poverty: subsistence economics which satisfy basic needs through self provisioning are not poor in the sense of being deprived ... millets are nutritionally far superior to processed foods, houses built with local materials are ... better adapted to the local climate.[30]

Unlike women's work, the market economy is disconnected from daily physical realities; its operational imperatives bear no relation to people's needs; its exponential 'growth' trajectory even kills off its own future options. As global capital becomes increasingly centralised by the transnational management of information flows, nation-states are rendered powerless and men are made marginal in a workforce segmented by enterprise bargaining and subcontracting. The situation of housewives in 'advanced' industrialised societies regresses to a point where they no longer control either their means of production or their fertility.

In the North, women's domestic maintenance functions continue to echo the 'mediation of nature' for men, but they have begun to lose skills and autonomy to consumerism. Meanwhile the very manufacture of so-called labour-saving devices destroys the living habitat beyond repair. Ecofeminists reject the industrial notion that 'necessary labour' is a burden to be passed on to nature through technology. Equally they reject a strategy of 'partnership' with the union movement in an unviable economy. Structurally speaking, all women's labours for subsistence are meta-industrial in character, which is appropriate to a Go Back: Wrong Way critique of modernity. Mies calls for a notion of labour as pleasure and challenge.[31] And most ecofeminists look forward to self-sufficient, decentralised relations of production, where men and women work together in reciprocity with external nature, no longer alienated or diminished by a gendered division of labour and international accumulation. Ecofeminism is about a profound transvaluation, because

> the most radical, activist politics develop when one comes to understand the dynamics of how one is oppressed and how one oppresses others. … [W]hen one comes to understand the basis of one's own pain and how it is connected to the pain of others, the possibility of forming coalitions with others emerges.[32]

12

BEYOND VIRTUAL MOVEMENTS

SOCIOLOGY AND BIOPOLITICS

In 1984, an ecofeminist essay noted that the far-reaching influence of C. P. Snow's 'two cultures' theme was a real obstacle to getting linkages with biology looked at by scholars in the humanities.[1] Born under the sign of Enlightenment rationalism, Western sociology has been especially slow to accommodate interconnections between culture and nature, let alone tackle the Man/Woman=Nature ideology. However, a recent anthology *Social Theory and the Global Environment* from Michael Redclift and Ted Benton takes some tentative steps in this direction:

> physical objects and substances, spatial relations, non-human animals and plants may all be theorised as belonging to the social as objects, conditions and media of social activity … [but] they are *never wholly incorporated into society, and persist as complex orders of causality* which both enable and constrain human social activity in ways which are only partially calculable and predictable.[2]

Marx's observation that people make their history but in conditions not of their own choosing resonates here, and plainly an 'environmental sociology' will call for a dialectical method.

Benton's work on 'the biological' brings home the conceptual gulf between sociology and its material substrate. A generation of feminist theorists has been too intimidated by the Woman= Nature image and the threat of being labelled 'essentialist' to explore these questions. But Benton is more free to address the Humanity/Nature opposition and its role in mapping a professional territory for social science. There is no doubt that Durkheim's ambitious imperial vision of 'the social' as reality *sui generis* has been read far too literally by social science. The nature/ culture dualism is so ingrained in eurocentric thought that even for self-styled deconstructionists it may be the last domino to fall. Benton is well aware that what he, and our ecofeminist re/sisters, are taking on is no easy task. He admits that, 'So pervasive are these ways of thinking that the attempt to transcend them is a veritable exercise of pulling oneself up by one's own boot-laces.'[3] Again, the need for a reflexive dialectical reason is clear. For most people who try the bootstrap trick end up falling over, either into a naturalistic reductionism, or into an oversocialised version of reality that deletes objective nature by turning it into a human construct.

In sociology, both an older hermeneutic tradition and contemporary discourse analysis pass over the sustaining ecological world as much as positivism does. This lack may well be inevitable in a society where mind workers and manual labour rarely meet each other. But the social sciences suffer a related dualism between 'individual action' and 'social structure', a separation that has the practical effect of mystifying people about how historical change can ever happen. By default, this methodological polarity preserves the comfortable class enclave of sociologists, dependent as most are, for a crust and a mortgage, on the status quo. Others offer themselves as technocratic policy experts, playing the credit card of corporate greed while life-on-earth is hollowed out.

So, there is an urgent need for 'a politically sensitised academic intelligentsia to facilitate [grassroots] struggles by doing parallel struggles inside the university, teaching and research, in the way knowledge about others is constituted and produced'.[4]

To be effective as a social change movement, a grouping needs to be able to see *why* a problem occurs; know *who* wants to change it; see *what* alternatives there are; and know *how* these can be put in place.[5] In other words, historical agency cannot emerge where people are disoriented and deskilled. A movement also needs critical mass. Perhaps a focused and well-attuned mass already exist among reproductive workers North and South, but political theorists are simply too culturally blinkered to see it? Certainly, ethnic and gendered presuppositions can easily get in the way. For example, standard American sociology has approached movements as a matter of rational self-interest and careful mobilisation of political resources. Using the individual as unit of analysis, opens up the topic to statistical treatment as well.

Hard-nosed liberal capitalist values feature prominently in this perspective. Rational choice is directed at minimising cost and maximising benefit. To privatised consumers, politics becomes a form of risk assessment, a part-time commitment in well-managed voluntary associations. What this so-called social science does not recognise is the exclusionary nature of its ostensibly universal approach.[6] For whilst unions and political parties are in principle open to any democratic subject, the organisational norm of instrumental rationality is culturally alien to most women, youth, subsistence farmers, and indigenous peoples.

Unable to secure a voice in existing pressure groups, these marginals usually lack resources to form counterinstitutions of their own. Mainstream politics largely excludes non-white, non-adult, non-male Others; being reformist, it does not ask why its who is who it is. Its answer to what alternatives there are and how these can be put in place is more of the same: cars-meat-electronics and GNP. At least a marxist sociology does ask why a problem occurs, and it pushes beyond the narrow statistical empiricism of liberal social movement analysis. Change is seen to become possible once workers are conscious of their shared economic class. However, while rightly claiming that social relations must be treated as a totality, socialists have singled out the 'objectivity' of productive positioning above sex or skin colour. And, more, they have omitted to examine how economics itself is a set of gendered eurocentric constructs.

Jurgen Habermas's neo-marxist emphasis on rational communicative consensus within modernity is thus equally problematic. By promoting essentially urban-middle-class standards as universal, his notion of self-realisation turns the clock back on earlier Frankfurt School insights which placed humans in/with nature.[7] While for Habermas anything other than modernity is conservative retreatism, Ferenc Feher and Agnes Heller have adopted a simple classification of old red movements 'for freedom' and new green movements 'for life'.[8] The contrast is between the sixties politics for freedom – women, gays, youth – and eighties movements for life. Yet the Vietnam protests and commune experiments inspired by 'Eros' were as much movements for life as are today's campaigns over genetic engineering, abortion, pornography, and euthanasia.

A postmodern contribution to social movement theory from Ernesto Laclau and Chantal Mouffe has done little to challenge the eurocentric fetish with freedom and self-expression.[9] A domain assumption of their stance is that knowledge is always relative to the social conditions under which it is produced and that all such 'knowledges' are valid. This is a version of ideology as the reflection of special social interests, but it dilutes the critical marxist understanding that the ideas of dominant groups are marred by a defensive false consciousness. In classical socialist reasoning, those who are oppressed will have the clearest vision, which is why the working class was expected to lead the revolution.

THE DEMOCRATIC SUBJECT

The postmodern answer to the question of agency favours a multiplicity of subject positions or nodal points – a relative autonomy of feminist, ethnic or ecological struggles. Laclau and Mouffe replace Marx's historical totalisation with a logic of disarticulation and contingency. Careful not to 'privilege' one social voice over another, they celebrate this pluralism at the cost of political common ground. Although critical of commodity culture, their radical democracy gives in to the prevailing 'option'-oriented mindset. Its discursive relativism speaks the disconnection of mental labour from manual labour and a society whose products, from computers to jet planes, reinforce a disorientation of the senses.[10]

By locating ecology on the same plane as social identity politics, this neoliberalism misses the chance to deconstruct the 1/0 rule and to theorise new ethical parameters appropriate to humans in/with nature. Left-leaning authors on 'identity and difference', such as Anne Phillips and others, also celebrate plurality and point to the bankruptcy of the West.[11] Phillips wonders about the source of a critical democratic politics and its possible external reference point. But surely environmental crisis provides just such a point: and a universal one at that? For the crux of the matter is, what does freedom mean when humanity itself is in the process of being redefined as bioresource? Ecopolitics demands much more than a balance among competing interests. The bodies of all species are under attack from capitalist patriarchal institutions.

This is why new movements for life are so salient. They are usually postmaterialist, aiming to defend civil society against its colonisation by both technocratic state and corporatised trade unions. They eschew political professionalism, organising themselves as anti-party parties. They do not embrace citizenship as individual autonomy but as a relational sensibility, supporting spontaneous collective action. Alain Touraine has called them 'postindustrial'.[12] However, many new movement actors come from a pre- or rather meta-industrial niche. The Bordeaux wine growers or housewives of Wyhl are distinguished examples. Domestic care givers, subsistence farmers, and indigenous peoples are each meta-industrial groupings. The term 'meta' avoids the value judgement embedded in the ubiquitous Western idea of progress.

Most greens reach for sustainability in practices that honour biodiversity, grassroots democracy, and nonviolence. In the green conjuncture, struggles shift from the workplace to the 'reproductive' sphere as marxists call it – housing, health, education, and now habitat. Somewhat contemptuous of libidinal nurture and 'background conditions', socialists have rejected environmental politics as local, small-scale, citizen initiatives.[13] E. P. Thompson was an exception – and most ecofeminists would agree with his prognosis that the future hovers between industrial disarmament or exterminism.[14]

Contemporary political interpretation has been preoccupied with the relationship between modernity and the postmodern, and its parallel expression in the contrast between old versus new social movements. Old movements are said to seek rights and reforms within the political system.[15] Hence, socialists or liberal feminists will 'mobilise resources', integrating their struggle with the existing state apparatus using a hierarchical organisational style. Similarly, green activists who enter alliances with older political movements such as social democrats are compromised by the process; that fault line has led to ongoing conflict between pragmatists or 'realos' versus 'fundis' or fundamentalists.

Prioritising economic activity as they do, socialists characterise new movements – deep ecology, animal liberation, feminism, peace, gay and ethnic rights – as ideas-based and subsidiary to proletarian leadership. They are judged to be superficial, like civil rights campaigns that throw their lot in with middle-class privilege. The trans-species interest of animal liberation, ecofeminism, and deep ecology defies that categorisation however, since it begins to undermine the basic tenets of bourgeois humanism. With the Man/Woman=Nature hegemony in the process of being reframed by ecology, the right/left dualism has also gone awry.

In fact, ecopolitics has many complexions: the push for population control is authoritarian; nature preservation is both conservative and radical; celebration of diversity is liberal; calls for equality are socialist; and the preference for decentralised solutions is anarchist. It might be argued that the difference between old and new movements is not ideological but simply a matter of maturation. If so, repressive tolerance will surely overtake paradigm shift every time. But for ecofeminists the categorical difference between old and new movements is now arguably obsolete; since most such movements succumb to functional liberation on 1/0 terms, they should all be called virtual movements, having the appearance of opposition only.

Ecofeminist politics exemplifies Alberto Melucci's identification of grassroots mobilisation as stemming from a passionate sense of frustration over contradictory social requirements.[16] From the vantage point of an embodied materialism, ecological crisis is a symptom of structural conflicts much deeper than those elucidated by hitherto-existing ideologies. Ecofeminism deepens the movement agenda, arguing that ecological crisis is profoundly implicated with human feeling, psychosexuality, the bioenergetic level. For all political agents are materially born and sustained by caring labours; even rational contestation depends on noncognitive experiences of identity, loyalty, passion, and commitment.

In the alienative consciousness, both nature and those who labour with nature are treated as 'resources' without intrinsic, that is 'human' value or rights. Modes of production from feudalism to late capitalism elaborate this underlying instrumental logic. The resourcing of animals, women, native Others, and their habitats by an appropriative M/W=N culture is a structural fact. North and South, this violence is legitimated by the global brotherhood of church and state, market and trade union, science and technology. The injury caused by this battery of capitalist patriarchal institutions remains comfortably invisible to those who benefit from them. Malini Karkal demonstrates this when she reads the Constitution of India against the facts of women's lives. In a nation where female foeticide and infanticide are common, where girls' births often go unregistered, and where 60 per cent of women are anaemic, India's Constitutional Preamble assures 'Justice – social, economic and political, Liberty of thought, expression, belief, faith and worship, Equality of – status and opportunity, and to promote among all the citizens *Fraternity*.'[17]

Mystified and canonised as law, the *polis* still infatuates the fragile self of young men coming into gamesmanship. There are good biological reasons for the words 'fatherland' and 'patriot'. Nation-states replay the old drama of corporeal prohibitions.

And the boundaries of this shared masculinity are jealously policed. Meaningful political representation for Other groups within such a civil society is a nonsense, hence Tarja Cronberg's pessimistic prognosis on the new European Union: 'Masculine visions of organisations are very hierarchical … centralisation of power from above. The integration of Western Europe … means enormous strengthening of patriarchy all over Europe.'[18] At both centre and periphery, ruling interests cancel erotic links with the body of Mother=Nature. Management may make good environmental decisions from time to time, but at a deep structural level, other drives readily undermine their implementation. The facts of ecosystem breakdown may be well understood by executives and officials, but a vague and very gendered numbness constantly disempowers the will.

STATES OF MIND

Political debate hovers around questions like: How should the nation-state evolve in an era of environmental stress, regional dissent, and transnational corporate expansion? Conservative ecological thinkers such as Ophuls, Hardin, or Heilbronner imagine new international 'machineries' of administration, just as some left peace activists do.[19] But there are already supranational bodies in existence: the UN Security Council and General Assembly, UN conventions, the European Union, the International Court of Justice, the World Bank, OECD and APEC. They remain incoherent as legal instruments, hence well suited to ongoing capital accumulation. Is the solution to systematise these organisations under a federating World Constitution? Transnational corporations are unlikely to want this. For a start, negotiations would make existing class interests far too transparent. Not to speak of gender interests, for these trans-boundary institutions remain exclusively framed by the norms of white middle-class standing.[20]

Arguing by homology, economic transnationals need political nation-states, the way men need wives: to service industry, pacify the underlings, and repair the territorial body. Naturally, as the historical influence of national sovereignty withers away, women are permitted a place on the parliamentary benches. But the main game has shifted elsewhere. Taking a lesson from the era of welfare, business now milks the state to provide free infrastructure and cultural legitimation. Since the 1992 Earth Summit, however, a plethora of corporate-sponsored local government initiatives around Agenda 21 is assisting globalisation by legitimating local council politics. Thus, venal capital keeps the nation-wife in tow by threat of a local mistress.

When an urban proletariat demands a share of the spoils, bourgeois laws of contract and arbitration may accommodate them. But, as Maria Mies writes, the 'truly human' sphere of masculine privilege is widened only at the price of sharpening the ideological 'naturalisation' of Others. If emancipation of working men is achieved, on the one hand, by forcing women deeper into a precarious domesticity, on the other hand, it is achieved at the expense of people of colour, drawn in around the margins of the paid workforce. The cost of economic justice for a masculine proletariat has meant intensified sexual abuse, racism and environmental assault.

Closer to ecofeminist hearts are the decentralists: eco-anarchists like Murray Bookchin, deep ecologists like Bill Devall, and bioregionalists like Peter Berg and Kirk Sale.[21] Applying the logic of 'small is beautiful', they urge that large-scale social structures – industrialised production methods, global markets, bureaucracies, political parties – deform human interaction and are insensitive to particular habitats. For decentralists, it is largely a matter of putting power in its place. Yet, as with voluntary associations, unions and churches, which each tap into the communitarian ethic, a residue of gender hierarchy still contaminates their radicalism.

Helen Forsey's fine essay 'Two Kinds of Power' comes close to recognising a post-gendered ecopolitics. Discussing the blockade for bioregional support of Mohawk people against Canadian authorities at Oka, she writes:

> Vital to our power was our groundedness, our direct connection to the Earth, living there beneath that wooded hill under the September sky. Our daily activities – gathering wood, cooking, caring for the children, building shelters, cleaning up, keeping warm, and sharing everything we needed in order to do so – drew us together as a community and bonded us to that piece of ground. It is no accident that much of the work that forged these bonds was 'women's work'. In cultures the world over, women traditionally are responsible for the tasks most directly concerned with maintaining and nurturing life and people's connectedness with each other and with past and future generations. Such work is concrete and essential … we were discovering the things that really matter.[22]

So, in the end, will the world federalists or decentralists carry the day or is there an Other alternative? North and South, ruling elites consist of big men and their families, including the occasional well-situated feminist. But in the debate over global governance, the masculinist imperative that structures state formations is not questioned. Whether it be proposals for supranational entelechies or levelling committees of correspondence, politics is conceptualised on a one-dimensional specular plane, a matter of size and extension. While sovereignty is the privileged term, along with comforting references to a viable civil society, transnational might is backgrounded. But so are other kinds of governance in social life – like the intrinsic control by integration among subalterns whose citizen self is relationally constituted. One kind of relational politics can be seen at work in the collective conflict resolution practices of indigenous peoples, such as the Jawoyn of Northern Australia.[23] Other skills pertinent to a concept of *relational governance* are found in mothering processes.

Gendered ecological crisis is an opportunity for a radical delinking from the counsels of competitiveness. An ecofeminist analysis suggests that the way to survive is not by constructing ever-further political hierarchies, with more grey-suited mullahs or more electronic decrees enshrining ostensibly universal rights. Rather, by acknowledging our libidinal grounding in the cycles of nature, we begin to talk sense about security and sustainability. Through connectedness, relational selves already exercise communal integration with sensitivity to the needs of future generations and other species.[24] Being responsive to other selves, only relational self has the reflexivity to examine its contingent identities and actions. If ecology is the matter and internal relations its theory, then a relational psychology and politics are the practice.

Mastery is not the only model of agency. An alternative occurs in holding actions such as mothering or organic cultivation. These activities are not 'just running around in circles', as women are taught self-deprecatingly to say about their daily chores. They are exercises in balancing internal relations with decentred foresight. Returning to the dialectic of alienation paradox, it is estrangement of consciousness that provides reflexivity and the possibility of new insights. By capitalist patriarchal logic, women are positioned as heterogeneous subjects – simultaneously absent from public institutions yet positively competenced in dealing with nature and its powers.

Today, the idea of self as heterogeneous and socially enfolded is drowned out by the chorus of possessive individualism. Even harder to think against the drone of the factory floor is a notion of self as ensemble inside a holographic web of ecological relations. Given that human bodies are implicate with nature, they take part in thermodynamic and dissipative exchanges of energy. But the ideologies of physics and economics operate with an imaginary of 1/0 appearances, becoming thermodynamically reductive. Conversely, in the face-to-face reality where subsistence and productive human=nature transformations happen, embodied activities are timeful and dovetail with generative structures. That is why ecofeminists say that unfree subjects in an M/W=N regime occupy a privileged epistemological site.

FOUR REVOLUTIONS IN ONE

Under the eurocentric regime, all discourses become property systems, ways of dividing up matter and suppressing the amniotic flow of lived time. Thus it is futile to take cue from the economists, planners and scientists with their illusory trajectory of managed progress. Men, or women, with little practical experience of the humble world of necessity have inadequate grasp of the limits of Enlightenment reason in the many-sided human interchange with nature. Our first step is to get back in touch with that reality. As a result of this impasse, and other modernist knots, ecofeminists urge recognition of the path-breaking significance of women's reproductive labours.

It is impossible to encompass complexity and simultaneity in discursive rationalism of the Cartesian subject/object kind. The master narratives of philosophy let alone the anorexic methods of postmodernism were devised precisely to exclude corporeality. But given the death-denying excess of eurocentric masculine dreams, it is crucial to nourish Marx's passionate intervention. An ecopolitics that ignores dialectical contradiction will prove insufficiently materialist and politically regressive. Needless to say, warding off a phallic subsumption of ecofeminist critique by the proud socialist tradition may take continual effort.

By approaching discourses as representative of different positions in a many-dimensioned field of internal relations, seemingly irreconcilable differences between say eco-socialism and deep ecology can be resolved epistemologically. They turn out to be a product of the level of generality at which their proponents make sense of their experience. Marxism has exposed the inversion of reason involved in bourgeois liberal accounting practices. But the twists and turns of reason surrounding gendered labours beg explanation too. The deterministic language of causality is inappropriate to workers grappling with lived contingency and simultaneous intergenerational connections.

Some ecologists looking for a way beyond the modern malaise turn to indigenous cultures for holistic social models. And there is much to be learned from peoples untouched by the rigidities of capitalist patriarchal development. As Serge Latouche concludes in his evaluation of the eurocentric development paradigm:

> If we were to pursue a true and genuine internationalism, or universalism, the proper approach would be to invite 'experts'

> from the last remaining 'primitive' regions of the world to draw up a list of the 'lacks' from which we, the people of the developed countries, suffer: loneliness, depression, stress, neuroses, insecurity, violence, crime rates, and so on.[25]

But while movement activists open up dialogue with indigenous Others, they need to avoid reinforcing the domestic exclusion of feminine knowledges. After all, an alternative approach to being in/with nature already exists inside Western culture itself. The unheroic work that mainly women do already shows the precautionary principle in action.[26]

The holding ethic of ecofeminism should not be confused with the no-regrets principle of greenwash and its wealthy promoters. A corporation is a legal entity designed to absolve men from liability for their decisions and it expresses the quintessence of the 1/0 achievement. It is futile to speak of a precautionary principle in an economic system that is dissociated from consequence. Despite the great leap forward to globalised electronic markets, women and natives still enjoy a contradictory status, treated as human subjects and animal-like resources at the same time. But the very discourse that has us 'closer to nature' lends insight to complexity.[27]

Sadly, the partial absorption of Second Wave feminism by capitalist patriarchal objectives has blurred many women's political focus. Yet with the advent of biocolonisation, our bodies are more invasively resourced than ever before. Technologies are reshaping sexual reproduction and dissolving identities – sexed ones, even species ones. Transnational business, environmental degradation, regional conflicts – all intensify the need for a multicultural response. Ecofeminist theory is negotiating these emerging interfaces and, in doing that, revitalises both socialist concerns for equity and the original radical feminist project of changing how men in the West work, think, love and rule. This is where our politics converges with the men's movement wish to free 'masculinity' from deforming social structures.[28]

A favourite move of liberal equality feminists is to present women's oppression as simply 'a model' or 'logic' for understanding the domination of nature, and certainly no more basic than domination by race or class. Such intellectualism simply reflects the capitalist patriarchal tactic of dividing and ruling the assorted Others. The outcome is that making common ground between social change moments becomes a kind of add-on coalition building. Unreconstructed pluralism means functionalist stasis. The ecofeminist way, is to pursue the connection between dominations, while yet developing an integrative subaltern standpoint. After all, in today's world, class, race, gender and habitat are each permutations of 'variable' capital; energies held in reserve, and readily substitutable for each other.

It seems that every emerging radical voice gets trapped by the M/W=N grid, unable to move beyond a virtual politics.[29] Matthias Finger's pessimism is symptomatic of that centripetal process: thus, he writes:

> ecology has created a 'political' vacuum, which waits to be filled by a new form of 'global politics' yet to emerge. … What remains is *a profound absence* of vision and leadership. No project is in sight to get us out of the crisis.[30]

Ecofeminism refutes that claim: as a transitional praxis by historically contingent subjects, it carries forward four revolutions in one. Ecofeminist politics is a feminism in as much as it offers an uncompromising critique of capitalist patriarchal culture from a womanist perspective; it is a socialism because it honours the wretched of the earth; it is an ecology because it reintegrates humanity with nature; it is a postcolonial discourse because it focuses on deconstructing eurocentric domination.

A dialectical ecofeminism asks not What political vision is true for all time? but Which way of knowing is most helpful in a time that cries out for affirmation of life? Our practical strategies for change include Hilkka Pietila's subsistence economics, Carol Adams's vegetarianism, Maria Mies's neighbourhood communities, Janis Birkeland's playgarden designs; Vandana Shiva's vision of indigenous science, Rosemary Ruether's alternative metaphysic, and Charlene Spretnak's spiritual renewal. Caring women and men can get such ideas across through academia and social movements, by global networking and alternative media. Moves to delink from the tele-pharmo-nuclear complex can be made by using boycotts and urban-rural consumer associations and by setting up bioregional institutions to dual power mainstream political bodies. An international ecofeminist 'security council' is long overdue. Many of these ideas are not new, but from now on men and women need to act together using a full and deep structural analysis of power relations.

CODA

In the beginning, the Judaeo-Christian tradition imagined life-on-earth as a Great Chain of Being. This was made up of a hierarchy of dominations from white men – and their God – at the top, running down through white women, black men, black women, children, animal species, plants, air, water, and rocks. Capitalism and the Whig revolution gave middle-class men sovereign rights, but the liberal pluralist tradition got stuck after that. Socialism has so far failed to get working-class men a fair piece of the pie. Feminism, postcolonial struggles, ecology, in turn, each challenge the 'natural hierarchy' of privilege. But in this structure of patronisation, each link in the chain of dispossession squabbles with the others like anxious, unloved siblings. So black and green, or red and violet, sometimes lock in a battle for political recognition, arguing their case in the discourse of sovereignty and rights. The divide-and-rule that follows simply reinforces the master's control.[31]

Now, through bio-prospecting, corporate colonisation literally undercuts the paternal deal and its domestic protections. For indigenous peoples and women, the semantics of self-determination is annulled by the thrust of white men's science beneath their very skins. Equal pay, contract law and land ownership walk a barren field when blood, sweat, and tears are mined and sold. Most greens, ecofeminists, and Australian indigenous people agree that the great culture of Europe is spiritually sick, economically and environmentally unsustainable. Wilderness in measured doses – usually on Sundays – has been a salve to the West's malaise, but like sexuality it must be contained. The flaccid, unfocused faces of the brotherhood in suits tell it all. If the wild does indeed reveal the crisis of a bankrupt civilisation, then let's keep working away at that point of least resistance. Green, black and ecofeminist politics will each benefit by supporting men's own movement struggle to leave behind the ugly capitalist patriarchal default position.

We do not challenge the monoculture of corporate savages by denying 'difference' and the 'wild'. To dub talk of indigenous specificity as 'primitivising' is to take on board the nineteenth-century evolutionist mentality with its ladder of 'progress' rather than to respect the diversity of people's ways. It is to shun 'women's business' in favour of white men's business. Just because an indigenous people has no division between Culture and Nature does not mean they are closer to Nature in the eurocentric sense of 'inferior'. This is also true of women under capitalist patriarchal ideology. Indigenous cultures offer rational models of how that linkage has been realised by peoples in their history. To say this is neither romantic nostalgia nor a perverse claim that indigenous environmental practices are 'better' than 'modern' scientific ones. All cultures make mistakes. Neither is it to suggest that indigenous peoples should necessarily want to live as their ancestors have – though some may, and some whites along with them. All cultures grow and change.

In times such as these, when the lifestyle of a few brings ecological devastation and poverty to many, there is an urgent need to reappraise economic alternatives to industrialisation, to reframe our political tenets, and to start taking small everyday steps away from the folklore of self-loathing and its pitiful gadgetry. Concepts such as 'management' and 'control', paternalistic beliefs that Western technologies are essential to the good life, these are the most insidious form of invasion. After all, what is this modern civilisation but a time- and energy-consuming process of dismantling living things and turning them into dead matter? The only thing that increases with 'economic growth' is waste. And so a holocaust goes on among us: dammed-up rivers run sour and parched soils crack open; continents swarm with environmental refugees; man-made viruses are unleashed; silently an ozone hole and electromagnetic radiation cull new cancer victims; oil spills suffocate sea life, and melting ice plateaux threaten islander peoples. Will you, too, close your eyes to these crimes, the linear model of development exported by an Enlightened West?

INTERVIEW

EMBODIED MATERIALISM IN ACTION

GERRY CANAVAN, LISA KLARR, AND RYAN VU

Ariel Salleh has been working at the intersection of ecology, feminism, and materialism since the early 1980s. Her emphasis on the need for an embodied materialist analysis of global capitalism offers a crucial antidote to the objective idealisms of postmodern and poststructuralist thought. Her seminal work Ecofeminism as Politics: Nature, Marx, and the Postmodern *(1997) seeks to politicise ecofeminism, a branch of ecological thought often imagined to be 'murky' and 'essentialist,' particularly in its 1970s iteration. In* Ecofeminism as Politics, *Salleh introduces the ideological formation Man/Woman=Nature to underscore how the aligning of 'woman' with 'nature' allows for the instrumentalist appropriation of both nature and woman-as-nature. Climate change, overfarming, ocean acidification – all ecological crises stem from this basic ideological structure. In other words, all of these crises are sex-gendered. For Salleh, this is the hidden complication subtending the human/nature split, holding it in place despite the work of otherwise astute critical analysis. Her work is thus a key intervention into the fields of marxism, socialism, and ecology, and it was with the intent of bringing the insights of feminism into conversation with scholars striving after eco-socialist aims that Salleh joined the editorial board of* Capitalism Nature Socialism *in 1988, a position she continues to hold. Salleh's embodied materialist understanding of nature, society, and capitalism has evolved through decades of activist work. She has been a co-convener of the Movement Against Uranium Mining, founding member of the Greens, a participant in local catchment campaigning, the representative ecologist on the Australian government's Gene Technology Ethics Committee, and an original signatory of the 2001 Eco-Socialist Manifesto. Editors of the Duke University journal* Polygraph *spoke with Ariel Salleh over email in Autumn 2009.*

Polygraph. *You've had a lot to say about the conceptual dualism of humanity versus nature over the years, but there are contributors to this issue who would contest any notion of nature – even calling for an 'ecology without nature.'*

Ariel Salleh. Well, I think we are talking about different preoccupations here. Tim Morton's thesis in *Ecology Without Nature* is rather like Judith Butler's ejection of the idea of woman from feminism.[1] Each author sets out to demonstrate how language is never adequate to its object. Yet paradoxically there is a de facto quest for positivist certainty beneath this restless constructionism. And it seems to me that Morton's deferrals actually end up reifying his elusive nature and personifying it as a trickster, a move that echoes Donna Haraway's earlier seduction by the coyote figure.[2] Three decades of poststructuralism, 'the linguistic turn' and its flight from essentialisms, suggests that the voyage to conceptual purity inevitably founders in a semantic swamp. On the other hand, it is possible to acknowledge politically fraught terms like nature or woman and yet still work with them. In fact, if political theory is to be grounded in praxis, it has to bracket out or suspend these epistemological nuances to reach people in everyday in life. To reinforce the ecological resistance of ordinary women or to encourage sex-gender sensitivity in activist men, one must use the words they understand. This means working both in the ideological medium and against it at the same time – with people, so that they can develop reflexivity. Morton himself is vaguely dismissive of ecofeminist politics, though in a rather unscholarly way, without citations to substantiate his view. However, if he engaged with our literature, he would find that it resonates with his desire to push ecocriticism deeper than deep ecology by taking it to the realms of 'dark ecology.' Morton's rejection of deep ecology's naive entrancement with the scientism of systems theory was already part of our thinking 25 years ago.[3] The ecofeminist analysis also predates Morton's use of Adorno's philosophy of non-identity, the chiasmus, and quantum theory, to challenge the nature/humanity dualism in a deconstructive way.[4]

For there is no denying it – humans are nature in embodied form. If people were not earthly flesh, the metabolism which keeps us alive could not happen. This humanity/nature split is thoroughly historical, rooted in depth psychology, a *dispositif* of capitalism, and pre-capitalist patriarchal formations before that. But the static essentialised deformation of nature should not be confused with the material potentiality of nature, just as the deformation known as womanhood should not be confused with the material potentiality of a specific embodiment. Just as humans exist in continuity with nature, so beneath culturally inscribed sex-genders there is no binary opposition either, but a continuum of body types and dispositions.[5]

Human knowledge of the green wild and of embodied nature is corrupted by politically contaminated discourses but this does not mean that such entities have no existence outside of language. That popular, if fading, postmodern assumption simply defies commonsense; so where did it come from? Certainly universities in the global North have had a fair bit to do with propagating it. As materialist ecofeminists observe, capitalist patriarchal economies rest heavily on a profound human alienation from nature, one that is generated in the exploitation of people's labour and resources. The rationalisation of this condition permeates all capitalist practices and structures, including hegemonic institutions like the academy. The radical grassroots feminism emerging in the 1970s was quickly contained and sanitised by a new discipline called gender studies. Soon enough, more critical strains of environmentalism would be de-politicised by cultural studies. If the practitioners of poststructuralism began as methodologists, they soon came to serve as ontologists for capital.

PG. *To further problematise the humanity/nature divide, what are we to make of iterations of the binary that aligns European men with nature against the influence of an overly feminised culture? How do such figurations complicate the nature–culture binary from which ecofeminism draws so much of its interpretative strength?*

AS. I've not come across any research that scrambles the masculine/feminine, history/nature, progress/regress pairs which ecofeminists have used to expose the operations of the globalising mindset. But I can see how somebody in an idiographic field like literature or cultural studies might turn up odd instances that slip through the dualisms. However, the only thoroughly 'feminised cultures' I am aware of are residual matriarchies in South China and Mexico, and these are no threat to the tele-pharmo-nuclear complex. The Biblical creation myth puts Eve in with the serpent, while Adam stands with civilisation and a transcendent father-god. So too, during the European witch burnings, women were accused of bestiality. This said, the traditional concept of woman is hybrid. Sometimes she is constructed as the madonna (tamed by patriarchal mores), and sometimes as whore (filthy nature). But each of these femininities is an object of resourcing by men. In the private sphere, the madonna/mother/housewife 'mediates nature' for the family; but even in public employment, women service workers are implicitly understood as 'closer to nature' and receive significantly lower wages than men do. Of course, living women are neither of these essences – madonna/whore – but a blend of many learnings including so-called masculine attributes. The Muslim argument that women should cover themselves because of men's potent natural drives adopts the madonna route to oppression, but the dualism and othering process is still there. Occasional identifications of men with nature appear in the utterings of down-home right-wingers. But theirs is an image of masculine nature as brute strength and control – which does not upset the familiar categories too much. I think the question to ask is: who is subject and who is object in these formulae? These irrational strictures will get to be assembled in different combinations in order to legitimate the exercise of power.

In the very welcome anthology *Material Feminisms*, brought out by Stacy Alaimo and Susan Hekman in 2008, a number of academics visit the ecofeminist epistemological terrain by addressing the humanity/nature split.[6] As Alaimo observes, for too long nature and the biological 'served as feminism's "abject" – that which, by being expelled from the "I" serves to define the "I".'[7] What is so interesting about this collection of essays is that women who were previously taken with the linguistic turn – Elizabeth Grosz, Donna Haraway, Vicki Kirby – are now taking seriously 'the very stuff' of bodies and natures. Theirs is not always a full emancipation from the body as inscribed text, but a new appreciation of material agency is emerging. Alaimo herself uses the term 'trans-corporeal' to describe the space between humanity and nature as a site for new theoretical work. For indeed the body comes to know itself, through its environmental interactions.

Discursive allusions and permutations can carry on to infinity, but political action calls thinking people to test their analysis in material doing. Here, the woman=nature metaphor draws attention to the massive theft of women's reproductive labours, a theft that is the very foundation of capitalism. This woman=nature metaphor speaks of resourcing; an appropriation of time and energy that might be quantified as 'embodied debt.' The paradigm shift is not complete though. The move from an elusive post-modern 'materiality' of the corporeal body is just a beginning.

The next step is to spell out women's unique implication in the humanity-nature metabolism. Then, this must be articulated with the materialism of economic domination. For this, the linguistic turn will be complemented by multiple lenses and transdisciplinary thinking. In addition, it is impossible to write sense-fully about politics without practical experience at the grassroots. My own activism has criss-crossed the movements from social justice to ecology and back, and I have found that analysis of the humanity/nature binary helps interconnect the diverse political strands. The positioning of humanity (read man) over nature marks eurocentric knowledge-making from religion to philosophy to science, and the same convention is complicit in the breakdown of Earth life-support systems. Yes, I am saying, for example, that climate change is sex-gendered. The domination of nature is intrinsic to masculinity as we know it – a preconscious but social identity for whom the mother (and women, as bodies in general) exists as primal ground.[8] The sublimation of this attitude is amplified in geopolitics when the Intergovernmental Panel on Climate Change reduces the regenerative powers of nature (and women) to 'source and sink.' The sociological effects of this sex-gender dissociation play out in violence on women, economic dispossession, and political silencing. But the humanity/nature binary can undermine the efforts of radical movements too – from deep ecology on the right to eco-socialism on the left. There will be no lasting change until this libidinally charged sex-gender rift is recognised as a political phenomenon. No easy matter. The call for historical reflexivity threatens to open up an abyss of doubt; masculinist disorientation. It is far easier to fantasise a higher-order control over the meat of nature through technological transcendence of its/her powers. By my ecofeminist interpretation of Michael Hardt and Antonio Negri, this 'affective' management is the real agenda of the cognitariat.[9] Meanwhile, you can be sure that 'Mother Earth' will continue to carry the scientific risks and mop up the industrial spills ...

There is a fair way to go in actualising this layered political understanding. Postings by North American knowledge workers on the ENVIROSOC Listserv offer another glimpse of the humanity/nature disjunction – and indeed the limitations of 'immaterial labour.' Climate change is typically objectified here and treated at one remove, as a matter of policy manipulation or technics. And no surprise that a recent sex-gender challenge to List readers from one Clay Grantham at the University of Oregon, fell into an electronic vacuum. The posting read:

> An 'elegant' collapse seems very needed at this time in history. Of course, having an elegant collapse, rather than an ugly collapse, would have to go hand in hand with freeing ourselves from the patriarchal cultures/structures that have subjugated and destroyed all non-patriarchal culture over the past few thousand years ... I increasingly see patriarchy as the root of authoritarianism, imperialism, global capitalism, racism, and ecological degradation (all of which closely overlap). Nothing inherently wrong with men. Just a culture that privileges

> aggression, emotionally stunts everyone, subjugates women as objects, etc. We are so immersed in it that it's like the water a fish swims in. Most men, and even women, just take it for granted. Otherwise 'enlightened' people end up reinforcing it at every turn. Time to turn it around.[10]

The ENVIROSOC List goes quiet when sex-gender difference is raised in the context of ecological questions, but you'd expect better of sociologists. After all, it's simply a matter of applying one aspect of the discipline (gender analysis) to another (environmental behaviour), and bringing these together, hopefully in tandem with a critical marxist perspective. Last month, the Listserv had American Sociological Association members congratulating themselves on the high visibility of their professional contribution to the climate change debate.[11] But not a single woman sociologist writing about climate was named. As noted already, a significant body of research is uncovering the fact that global warming – causes, effects, solutions, and policies – are sex-gendered and it is plain that the lifestyle choices of affluent white men are primary drivers of the crisis.[12]

PG. *Were you going after this sort of one-dimensional thinking in the exchange with John Bellamy Foster and Paul Burkett published by* Organization and Environment *(2001)?*[13] *As we recall, this took the form of a conversation over how to schematise methodological articulations of the nature of reality, or the reality of nature. Can we revisit this debate?*

AS. Yes, the essay 'Sustaining Nature or Sustaining Marx?' was about hidden sex-gendered tensions in ecopolitical thought – among other things. Don't get me wrong, Foster and Burkett, separately and together, are major theorists of eco-marxism. And they are absolutely right that the environmental crisis will not be resolved until capitalism is dismantled. However, if the end of capital is a necessary condition for sustainability, it is not a sufficient one. For capitalism itself is a modern version of patriarchal social relations, and so a parallel political devolution is called for. In other words, the ties between hegemonic masculinity and the diminishment of nature and of women still have to be unravelled. So far, neither Foster nor Burkett carry their work to this level, which means that their political remedy for the emancipation of nature may be self-defeating in the end. Sex-gender silence is prevalent across the social sciences, among political economists, environmental ethicists, and so on – and as I say, the bias is not just intellectual but fuelled by embodied libidinal energies. Perhaps some kind of Reichian practice will be found to release these deeply enculturated attitudes?

PG. *So you differ with Foster and Burkett over the causal relevance of gender, but you share with them a determination to avoid positivist scientism, on the one hand, and culturalist, postmodern scepticisms such as deconstruction, on the other.*

AS. Not exactly this. I mean ecofeminist politics is itself deconstructive in its exposure of the triangular ideological dynamic between iconic 'men,' 'women,' and 'nature.' To reiterate: you can't address the oppression of nature by men without simultaneously addressing the oppression of women by men. This deconstructive moment has been a domain assumption of our politics from its beginnings – well before postmodernism came to academic ascendency. But to say this, is not to say that we focus on the discursive. Environmental struggles cannot be resolved simply by some corrective intervention or symbolic displacement from nature to trickster. The man-woman-nature triangle is thoroughly material, solidly embedded in biological, social, and economic structures. A purely cultural or philosophical analysis has no purchase when it comes to engaging in political action over embodied processes – like rape or domestic labour. Postmodern feminist articulations that are limited to discursive politics risk idealism, becoming complicit with the invisible hand of mastery – the logic of the market, in other words.

I thoroughly agree with Foster and Burkett on the need for a materialist analysis vis-à-vis such idealism. But then again, they tend to apply the idealism label across a too broad spectrum of folk – basically to whoever interrogates some aspect of Marx.[14] Curiously, I believe they do this, precisely because their own materialist stance is itself somewhat idealised and reified! What I mean by this is that Foster and Burkett bypass the concrete particularities of sex-gendering in everyday life; the embodied materialist character of social and natural relations – and even of theory making itself. The nineteenth century master text is thin in this area – which fact explains why classical socialist theory fails women, peasants, and indigenes – labour outside of the factory. So while I stand with Foster and Burkett in their opposition to capitalism and with their case for a materialist analysis, I try to draw them towards an embodied materialism.

PG. *But how is it possible to maintain a materialism, and a broadly realist ontology, without succumbing to positivism?*

AS. Foster and Burkett themselves aspire to a 'non-determinist materialism' or 'ecological humanism,' but this call has a certain rhetorical feel to it. As you point out they are at heart ontological realists – strong on economic structures, thermodynamics, evolutionary processes, and they convey a rather positivist reading of Marx. This is why my *O&E* reply to them sketched out a more critical dialectical approach, materialist, realist, yet reflexively aware of its own social construction and permanent re-visioning as a knowledge. But both of our realisms contrast with the postmodern idealism that has nature and society exclusively constituted by discursive practices. Take for instance, the 'production of nature' theme popularised by Neil Smith and others in the 1990s. Nor is it any coincidence that Smith's commodification-speak appeared in the heyday of neoliberalism.[15] This tension between realism and constructionism seems to have been greater in a right-leaning US than it was elsewhere. In the UK, sociologist Peter Dickens' critical realism offered a way to mediate the two epistemological extremes. In Germany, Jurgen Habermas's blend of phenomenology with Freudo-Marxism gave permission for the subjective dimension.[16] In any event, my agenda in conversation with Foster and Burkett was to bridge ecofeminism and eco-marxism, to help build left resistance as a more inclusive social force. As long as marxists have no sex-gendered sociology of their own theoretical knowledge, this movement alliancing will remain very difficult. There is a certain irony here, because Bertell Ollman demonstrates that Marx himself was exemplary in his capacity to shift between lenses and levels of abstraction in order to unpack different facets of the political object.[17] This dialectical method is about as far from positivism or naive realism as you can get.

PG. *How would you characterise the major fault line within ecopolitical thought, and how does the 'embodied materialism' you have been proposing negotiate this conceptual difficulty?*

AS. The globally dominant culture is crossed by many political fault lines – class, ethnicity, and so on – but in my view, the sex-gender fracture cuts beneath the others because it is not only sociological but heavily somatic, material, infused with psychological energies. To say this might be to risk the accusation of essentialism, but only if one assumes that nature and/or the body, is somehow separate from historical influence. Whatever its originary force field, the capitalist system diminishes the maternal body and sets up a predisposition for othering. The value of 'reproduction' gives way to value in 'production' and man-to-man exchange. Today, G20 politicians ramp up the machine – mining, banking, electronics – but the harnessing of natural resources and human labour for capitalist aggrandisement was always a substitute, an elaborate compensation for the denied abject body. What is needed right now is a movement coalition mature enough to acknowledge this; one ready to organise social life around the logic of regeneration.[18] This would put human well-being before egoistic competition, industry, and war; put ecosystem integrity before accumulation.

An embodied materialism reaches out to re-ground left thought and action by remembering our human origin as nature.[19]

- Embodiment joins the human condition to its natural condition, making politics deeply and consistently material. This is a message for idealists and postmoderns.
- Embodiment joins theory to praxis, making politics historically sensitive and accountable. This is a message for realists and positivists.
- Embodiment joins the experience and knowledge of workers, mothers, peasants, gatherers, making left politics whole. This is a message for all movement activists.

Too many political programs rest in ossified and disembodied belief systems, whereas an embodied materialism is a transitional idea, a tool for making change at this moment now. Once attitudes and structures shift, the ecofeminist critique can be discarded. Ecopolitical thought from eco-socialism to social ecology to deep ecology, stares into the humanity/nature divide but does not neutralise it. A tacit sex-gender investment, an embodied fault line, holds the regressive aspects of this opposition in place. Our analysis offers to cut the knot, but achieving this means personal reflexivity among activists. An energy shift.

PG. *Among the obstacles, theoretical and practical, that deter steps toward political unity, how has the charge of gender 'essentialism' hindered the collaboration you are seeking between the various green and socialist formulations?*

AS. Morton writes that essentialisms are everywhere – and thus nowhere. Whole civilisations are built on them, so there's nothing especially essentialist about ecofeminism. That charge has often been tossed off before any effort is made to understand what our epistemological claims actually are. And sometimes, the prosecutor has only a very hazy idea of what essentialism itself actually means. I've written about this in all sorts of places, but nothing beats Diana Fuss's classic treatment of the problem in *Essentially Speaking*.[20] In our anthology *Eco-Sufficiency and Global Justice*, I explain how everyday life and political thought is rife with taken for granted essentialisms – bureaucratic, economic, humanist, liberal feminist, marxist, and patriarchal ones. For example, a common essentialism in ecopolitics is the humanist assumption that men and women are implicated in environmental degradation in the same way, or that men and women are able to practice citizenship responsibilities in the same way. Our analysis has always been about deconstructing essentialising concepts and practices. Despite this, my writing has been subjected to this theoretic charge on several occasions. When the old chestnut turns up in eco-socialist or deep ecological writing, I interpret it as a resistance on the writer's part to the embodied rethinking that our politics calls for.[21] But when the charge is laid down by one's ecofeminist sisters, then it's a worry! One case concerned the rhetorical essay 'Deeper than Deep Ecology' where I used the phrase 'closer to nature' and all hell broke loose from literal minded readers who missed the teasing tone of the text.[22] In another case, my discussion of the Man/Woman=Nature formula was stripped of critical context and turned into a case of hetero-sexist imperialism and homophobia. The author was apparently unaware that I've always considered sexualities to be a continuum (not binary) and was writing about the liberation of transgenders as early as 1981.[23]

The attribution of essentialism is often a category mistake made by synchronic thinkers like analytical philosophers or people untrained in recognising a text designed as provocative intervention. The charge illustrates what critical marxists call one-dimensional reasoning and as such, it plays into establishment hands. Unfortunately, the contemporary hegemony of measurement-based science favours fixed terms (parameters, variables) and identitarian logic, so there is an increasing tendency for scholars and publics alike to use or read words in a concrete essentialising way. I've noticed as well, that in US writing, the noun (solid commodity) will be preferred to a verb (action, change). The phrase 'the American People' is one such objectification, whereas the open adjectival form 'American people' allows for difference and agency. As Herbert Marcuse pointed out some decades ago, capitalist culture is prone to one-dimensionality, where movement, complexity, and paradox in language is suppressed.[24] A dialectical methodology offers an antidote to this by focusing on meaning in transformation. Thus, woman is not an essence fixed for all time, but a being with multiple political potentials. So too, an embodied materialist perspective which has people's consciousness formed in the labour that they do, sees identities like transgenders, indigenes, men, etc. continually being re-made through their practical action in/on the world. We are all works-in-progress.

PG. *You have been using the journal* Capitalism Nature Socialism *as a platform for dialogue between eco-socialist and ecofeminist factions within the left in the hope of initiating a kind of integrative stage of discovery. What is the current status of this hoped for fusion?*
AS. I joined the editorial of *Capitalism Nature Socialism* at its inception in 1988 and had a little round of the tables with eco-socialists Jim O'Connor and Dan Faber in 1991. Needless to say, I was often frustrated by marxist misconstruals of our politics, that is, until Joel Kovel took over as chief editor in 2003.[25] At that point, I came forward with a plan for at least one ecofeminist article per issue to get eco-socialist readers engaging with women's writing. Then, in 2006, we brought out a 12 piece special issue entitled 'Ecosocialist-Ecofeminist Dialogues,' which symposium ran conversations between a variety of women thinkers and respondents.[26] I can't do justice to the richness of these texts here, but themes included the complicity of working class men and capital in the economic subsumption of women, the betrayal of women by international development agencies and Third World elites, the displacement of women from livelihood resources by designated national park enclosures, and the ecological impact of unnecessary technologies.

If my vocabulary appears more explicitly marxist these days, it simply reflects my more proactive movement alliancing; but my domain assumptions have not changed much since I first started writing about ecofeminism. My hope is that eco-socialism will eventually join women's, peasant, indigenous' and ecological struggles in a single force for sustainability and global justice. But integrating these groups in political action means dealing with questions like:

- How are productive and reproductive labour interrelated?
- What is the political economic function of woman=nature or native=nature ideologies?
- How is gender constitutive of class and how is materialism embodied?
- Can eco-socialism coexist with cultural diversity and with ecocentric values?
- What technologies are compatible with democracy and sustainability?
- Who are the key agents of alternative globalisation and struggles for the commons and resource sovereignty?
- Is a new theory of value called for to build an ecologically sustainable society?

Questions like these might be discussed on the Listserv of the Eco-Socialist International Network (EIN), but they are not. In fact, in the first two years of this List, 99 per cent of contributors have been men, and I cannot think of any contribution by a woman that got a reply.[27] For sure, the *CNS* journal project brings ecofeminism into the peripheral vision of marxists, but I have to say that the intellectual apartheid by which feminist writing is passed over as 'women's stuff' is not giving way yet. The odd citation of our work is not enough. Ideally, the comrades will engage with our ideas and apply them in their own theory and praxis.

PG. *In* Eco-Sufficiency and Global Justice, *you argue for a reflexive ecological economics, a hybrid discipline capable of investigating 'all forms of debt': economic, ecological, and embodied, as are incurred in the global production of goods. But how do we call these debts to account without at the same time falling back into the instrumental logic of the market?*

AS. Yes, written with a team of scholar-activists, *Eco-Sufficiency and Global Justice* does call for a critical examination of the objects and methods of ecological economics.[28] It highlights everyday problems like the systemic devaluation of women's labour, the violence of development, the futility of neoliberal mainstreaming, sex-gender blindness in economic indicators, women for nature swaps, and the precarity of capitalist accumulation. The studies reinforce the ecofeminist focus on subsistence and reproductive labour, global struggles for the commons, solidarity economies and ecologically sound indigenous provisioning. Thus, the essays contest the ad-hoc separation of political economy (man), feminism (woman), and ecology (nature), and suggest their triangulation as a single discourse dealing with meta-industrial labour, embodied debt, and metabolic value. These rhetorical challenges are directed at liberal professionals, but my forays into deep ecology and eco-socialism were part of the same agenda. Of course, I am not literally committed to the idea of building a new ecological economics, a remedial study that will remain necessary only as long as capitalism stands. Rather the book is about consciousness raising in ecological economics, to begin the process of structural change. By my reckoning, practitioners in this field are less bound by an overarching theory than say marxists are, which fact could make the interrogation of sex-gender easier.

PG. *So is this why you write that yours is not 'an argument for reproductive labours to be waged, just as the case for ecological debt is not literally about monetising nature's "services" across the globe'? Do you reject the notion of postcolonial reparations then? How do you see your ecological and embodied debt being politically activated?*

AS. This activation was already underway at the climate conversations of COP15 in Denmark, December 2009 – even while nation-states were unable to agree on how to stabilise nature. The idea of reparations has had currency since Jubilee 2000 prompted the global South to ignore World Bank loan repayments. The group Acción Ecológia based in Ecuador and Belgium extended this to include a claim for the environmental damages of colonial plunder by Europe and the US. The movement of movements known as Climate Justice Action has ecological debt high on its list – no surprise that Tadzio Muller and other leaders wound up in jail at Copenhagen. The debt concept forces free riders of the global North to think twice about how international market economies really work, and I would be very happy if the UN or World Bank reversed South to North monetary flows. However, it's not so simple. The methodological problem of commensurability – i.e. dollars for what exactly – might be met by lateral thinking combined with good will. But the political reality is more challenging. The recipients of reparation would most likely be the ruling class clones of the North who manage nation-states in the global South, so it is doubtful that impoverished communities would benefit from the payments. This is already written in the failed history of overseas AID projects and more recently, the faltering administration of REDD schemes in Africa or Southeast Asia.[29] There is no guarantee that money will reach the grassroots. Even more apposite is the material fact that financing the adaptation or mitigation of a damaged environmental metabolism does not itself restore nature. Reproduction of humanity-nature flows involves hands-on work by people who understand the history of their habitat in its complexity. This is the class of meta-industrial labour.

And so we move to embodied debt – an ambit claim, riding pillion to its political brother ecological debt. Environmental protection programs already acknowledge the need to honour indigenous expertise. In Northern Australia, rangers skilled in Aboriginal fire techniques are being employed pre-emptively for climate mitigation, and they receive a salary for their work. On the other hand, the depth psychology of sex-gender leaves mothering work in the trans-corporeal sphere unspoken and unwaged. While a country like Sweden has generous maternity leave provisions, nowhere is the embodied debt accrued to women for the reproduction of society itself acknowledged in its multiple dimensions – biological, social, and economic. I support postcolonial reparations, albeit as a temporary corrective, and recommend sex-gender reparations as well. Even then, this symbolic gesture would be a solitary milestone along the road to global transformation.

PG. *We are very interested in your figuration of this 'meta-industrial' sphere, inhabited by an apparently new class of labour whom you identify paradoxically as both outside of capitalism and completely integral to it.*

AS. The notion of 'meta-industrial labour' is another strategic tool, to help open up hitherto closed notions of class. People who maintain the humanity-nature metabolism are certainly not a new class, but they have not been dignified by sociologists as a social class before this. For sure, there are cultural differences among meta-industrial workers, but materially speaking, these differences are less formative than the phenomenology of the embodied labour that they each do. The non-monetised work of meta-industrials like mothers or peasants not only sustains everyday life; in many 'developing' regions, it backs up the infrastructure of global markets as well. I am thinking here of peasant contributions to the protection of biodiversity and soil quality and the indigenous management of water catchments.

Meta-industrial work, whether domestic care or organic farming, involves principles learned hands-on in the material world. It generates a vernacular epistemology replicating and reciprocating the thermodynamic circuits of nature. This labour is flow oriented avoiding entropy, it is intergenerational and precautionary; its unique rationality is a capacity for economic provisioning in a way that keeps 'metabolic value' or ecological integrity intact. Unlike the extractive capitalist mode of production which sacrifices metabolic value to the manufacture of profitable commodities, locally eco-sufficient economies meet human needs without externalising costs as ecological debt or embodied debt.[30] The seeming contradiction that you pick up on, with meta-industrials both inside and outside of capitalism at the same time, simply speaks the humanity/nature ideology. That is to say, these workers are inside of capitalism as labour resources and natural energy, but outside of capitalism when it comes to recognition of their humanity with a wage or citizenship rights. The most urgent project of twenty-first-century politics is to draw together the social movements in a sustainable alternative to globalisation, and here, it is critical that the voices of this invisible class be heard.

PG. *How would you compare your choice of this group as a kind of epistemically privileged loci to Marx's choice of the proletariat as* *revolutionary class? Or for that matter, Slavoj Žižek's 'de-structured masses' of the urban slums, identified by him as the locus of twenty-first century struggle.*

AS. Marx, writing at the inception of the industrial revolution, was a relentless critic of capitalist depravity and of the metabolic rift it sets up between parasitic towns and ravaged countryside. Even so, Marx was hopeful that well-managed industry would deliver material progress to humanity, universally. History would soon enough prove that technological progress for the few means 'regress' for the many. Then, the proletariat, entranced by the cargo cult of consumerism failed to step up to its anticipated role of overturning their exploiters. Today, global capital replaces viable land based subsistence communities with mining and agro-industry; it throws factory workers into poverty; it captures governments to the service of a death wish. Enter Žižek. And here I have to confess to not reading his work, which strikes me as written for intellectual masochists! So I ask you – am I right to assume that his 'de-structured mass' is similar to Andre Gorz's disaffected 'post-industrial neo-proletarians'?[31] If so, my response is that while alienation and resentment may be good for fuelling political agitation, what is needed is people with aptitudes and skills for creating the alternative to industrial decay – a green, autonomous, just, and eco-sufficient commons. Neither Marx's, nor Žižek's, putative revolutionaries have this capacity – victims of industrial mal-development that they are.

Similarly, I would disagree with the thesis of Hardt and Negri that affective labour is the new hegemon and agent of qualitative change. The thesis panders a little too much to the urban cognitariat, a relatively small and atypical section of humanity.[32] For sure, affective workers prioritise reproductive over productive relations, but that's about as far as the convergence of autonomous marxism and ecofeminism goes. As Hardt and Negri describe the constitution of subjectivity in contemporary societies, their vision of reproduction is fully embedded in the high tech infrastructure of capitalism. The ecological debt that keeps this lifestyle afloat goes unexamined; yet its material base is a vast thermodynamic cost against environmental sustainability. The embodied debt accrued by the cognitariat in its dependency on migrant cleaners or silicon slaves might also be problematised. Immaterial labour speaks the domination of the middle class economic North, but the majority of workers in the world exist outside of that electronic buzz. The meta-industrial class labours at the human interface with nature, and as such is very broad, transhistorical even, beyond cultural differences. One might argue that these caregivers and gatherers are actually autonomous labour in the true sense of the word, since their materially embodied work is not reliant on ecologically destructive technologies. As I contemplate the 2010 Peoples' World Conference on Climate Change and Mother Earth Rights in Cochabamba, the claim of Hardt and Negri that the peasant class is a residue of history seems quite askew to me.[33]

PG. *In your schematisation, the meta-industrial worker operates in the global system where humans directly metabolise nature, where farmers, peasants, mothers, 'oversee biological flows.' But agribusiness now affects the very possibility of such metabolic spaces, introducing hyper-industrialised modes of farming that bypass or speed up metabolic processes.*

AS. True, capitalism expands its global reach and must do, according to Rosa Luxemburg, to find new markets. But the Earth is not yet fully paved in concrete… In this respect the financial crisis may be a boon. You are right that self-sufficient agricultural communities are facing the onslaught of 'green revolution' from the World Bank, UNDP, CGIAR, transnationals, and corporate funded university research centres.[34] On the other hand, since 40 per cent of the world's workers are farmers, there is still a great body of land out there, where eco-sufficient provisioning happens. In the global North permaculture and community gardens are becoming popular too. So do I sense a touch of the hyper-industrial fantasy in your devil's advocate question? Do you tease me with the capitalist soft sell? A deep metabolic rift exists between that abstract spatial imagination and kinaesthetically tended biological transformations. The rift is confirmed in that GM technology has not demonstrated its efficiency as a production method. Ecological feminists have been very focused on genetic engineering, most likely because it concerns reproductive labour.[35] But the argument for recognition of meta-industrial labour belongs to the alternative globalisation movement at large, with its struggles for land and water sovereignty. These political actors gather at the World Social Forum in Porto Alegre; they sit in on Davos and meetings of the G8.

PG. *What do you see when you turn your ecopolitical lens on the new US administration? Nominally it has a green economic agenda and wants global mandates like carbon caps in the UN Framework, but the liquidity crisis and economic collapse threaten to push the environment to the back burner.*

AS. I am horrified that every government response to the financial meltdown has been linear, more of the same: print more money, lend and spend, till the economy grows back again. Global elite decision makers don't recognise that liquidity and solvency are not the same thing. Disconnected, immaterial thinking is the order of the day. Looking at climate change, I'm not sure what the latest political moves in the US are, but I know that they will have been made in dismal ignorance of how the humanity-nature metabolism functions. Besides the absurd cap and trade idea, I understand Al Gore has been talking up solar, wind, and geothermal spots in the deserts of the Southwest; a national low-loss underground grid; hybrid cars and retrofitted buildings.[36] A high-tech wish list like this deflects attention from lived social and indeed, natural thermodynamic realities. And the capitalist economy dependent on permanent consumption remains intact with 'the conversion to green product.' This is because the construction of new solar cities will consume vast amounts of front-end fuels – in welding turbines and grids, road making, water supply, component manufacture for housing; air conditioning for shopping malls. What is offered is yet another mortgage – but this time an ecological one. Moreover, the new urbanisation will mean a loss of farmland, possibly to be replaced by agricultural leases in the Third World. How then will the displaced peasants of Central America feed themselves? And what global warming pollution will be generated by the long haul of food back to the US?

The Green New Deal plans that I have looked at also prime a faltering economic system, postponing consciousness-raising and fundamental structural change.[37] Many middle class critics of capitalism are suspended in ambivalence, because they cannot imagine any other way of life for themselves. Then it's business as usual in the meta-industrial peripheries – where peasant farmers are corralled by the promise of green revolution, indigenous peoples seduced by mining royalties, and housewives by luxury goods. International activists who recognise the moral force of ecological debt demand monetary reparations for peoples in the global South. However, the expectation that technologies can mitigate global warming is very naive. The material bottom line of an economy is a healthy integrated ecosystem represented by metabolic value. That cannot be bought, or restored by mechanical means. A sounder way to avoid human exploitation and natural entropy is to de-link from the global North and its hyper-industrial programs. Ecological debt is best resolved by people holding land for eco-sufficient provisioning. As for embodied debt, the thermodynamic draw down from the bodies of reproductive workers is still to be taken up by scholars and by the alternative globalisation movement.

For me, hope resides in the fact that meta-industrial labour comprises the largest bloc of workers worldwide. The capacities of this class – peasants, mothers, gatherers – have never been fully colonised by eurocentric modernity or post-Fordist immateriality. The contradictory inside/outside sociology of this class gives it a special leverage over capitalism, because it is in principle autonomous, and while capital leans on the free services of meta-industrial workers, their gifts may be withdrawn at any time. This majority is central to transforming the present conjuncture – and that is not mere coalition pragmatism. It does justice to instate hitherto silenced political voices alongside those of urban workers and ecological activists. Now the question for intellectuals and activists in the global North becomes how to create the psychological space to listen and learn from meta-industrial skills and values. The World Social Forum has yet to enact its historical mission. What other options do we have?

NOTES

INTRODUCTION

1 Gerry Canavan, Lisa Klarr, and Ryan Vu, 'Embodied Materialism in Action: An Interview with Ariel Salleh', *Polygraph*, 2010, No. 22, pp. 183–99.
2 Will Steffen, Jacques Grinevald, Paul Crutzen, and John McNeill. 'The Anthropocene: Historical and Conceptual Perspectives', *Philosophical Transactions of the Royal Society*, 2011, No. 369, pp. 842–67.
3 Vandana Shiva, *Earth Democracy: Justice, Sustainability, and Peace* (London: Zed Books, 2005).
4 Patrick Curry, *Ecological Ethics* (London: Polity, 2011); Giacomo D'Alisa, Federico Demaria, and Giorgos Kallis (eds.), *DeGrowth: A Vocabulary for a New Era* (London: Routledge, 2015).
5 Tom Mertes (ed.), *A Movement of Movements* (London: Verso, 2004); Boaventura De Sousa Santos, *The Rise of the Global Left* (London: Zed Books, 2006); Jackie Smith, Scott Byrd, Ellen Reese, and Elizabeth Smythe (eds.), *Handbook on World Social Forum Activism* (Boulder: Paradigm, 2012).
6 James O'Connor, *Natural Causes* (New York: Guilford, 1998); John Bellamy Foster, *Marx's Ecology* (New York: Monthly Review, 2000); Joel Kovel, *The Enemy of Nature* (London: Zed Books, 2002); Ariel Salleh, 'Editorial: "Towards an Inclusive Solidarity on the Left", Symposium on Eco-Socialist–Ecofeminist Dialogues', *Capitalism Nature Socialism*, 2006, Vol. 17, No. 4, pp. 33–38; Eco-socialist International Network: EI-Network-subscribe@yahoogroups.com.
7 Landless People's Movement: www.mst.org.br.
8 Damien Cahill, Lindy Edwards, and Frank Stillwell (eds.), *Neoliberalism: Beyond the Free Market* (Cheltenham: Elgar, 2012); Harris Gleckman, 'WEF Proposes a Public–Private United "Nations"', 23 June 2013: www.environmentalgovernance.org.
9 Tim Jackson, *Prosperity Without Growth* (London: New Economics Foundation, 2009); Qingzhi Huan (ed.), *Contemporary Western Green-Left Political Theories* (Peking: Peking University Press, 2009).
10 Systemic Alternatives: www.systemicalternatives.org; Cormac Cullinan, *Wild Law: A Manifesto for Earth Justice* (Cape Town: Siber Ink, 2002).
11 Hugo Blanco (ed.), 'Mandato I Cumbre Continental de Mujeres Indigenas' [First Continental Summit of Indigenous Women], *Lucha*

Indigena, 2009, No. 34, p. 5: www.luchaindigena.com/wpcontent/uploads/2009/06/lucha-indigena-34.pdf; Ariel Salleh, 'Climate Strategy: Making the Choice between Ecological Modernisation or "Living Well"', *Journal of Australian Political Economy*, 2011, No. 66, pp. 124–49.

12 Gerd Johnsson-Latham, *Initial Study of Lifestyles, Consumption Patterns, Sustainable Development and Gender* (Stockholm: Ministry of Sustainable Development, 2006); GenderCC: www.gendercc.net; World Rainforest Movement: www.wrm.org.uy; Indigenous Environmental Network: www.ienearth.org; John Foran, 'Finding Our Frontlines in Indigenous North Dakota', Resilience.org, 10 October 2016; Via Campesina, *Small Scale Farmers are Cooling Down the Earth* (Jakarta: VC, 2009); Evo Morales, 'People's World Conference on Climate Change and the Rights of Mother Earth', Cochabamba, 19 April 2010: www.bolivia.un.org/cms.

13 Marina Sitrin (ed.), *Horizontalism* (Oakland: AK Press, 2006).

14 Ariel Salleh, 'Fukushima: A Call for Women's Leadership', *Japan Fissures*, 21 April 2012: www.jfissures.org/author/ariel-salleh/; *Chain Reaction Magazine*: www.chainreaction.org.

15 World Watch Institute, *Toward a Transatlantic Green New Deal: Tackling the Climate and Economic Crises* (Brussels: Heinrich-Boell Stiftung, 2009); Australian Conservation Foundation, *Towards a Green New Deal*: www.acf.org.au; UNEP, *The Future We Want: Draft Zero Document* (New York: United Nations, 2012); World Social Forum Dialogue Platform of the Thematic Social Forum, *Another Future is Possible!*, 24 January 2012: www.rio20.net; ETC, 'Who will control the Green Economy? Building the People's Summit Rio+20', Rio+20 Portal, 17 December 2011.

16 World March of Women: www.marchemondiale.org/; Wo-Min: African Women Unite Against Destructive Resource Extraction: www.womin.org.za; Shannon Bell, *Our Roots Run Deep as Iron Weed* (Chicago: University of Illinois Press, 2013); Code Pink Women for Peace: www.codepink.org/; Navdanya: www.navdanya.org/; MADGE: www.madge.org.au/; Chan Shun Hing: http://our-global-u.org; Pamela Odih, *Watersheds in Marxist Ecofeminism* (Newcastle upon Tyne: Cambridge Scholars, 2014).

17 Encyclical Letter, *Laudato Si', of the Holy Father Francis, On Care for Our Common Home* (Rome: Vatican Press, 2015).

18 John Clark, *The Tragedy of Common Sense* (Regina: Changing Suns Press, 2016).

19 Nuit Debout: https://nuitdebout.fr/.

20 Arthur Mol and David Sonnenfeld (eds.), *Ecological Modernization Around the World* (London: Frank Cass, 2000); Ewa Charkiewicz, 'Who is the He, of He Who Decides in Economic Discourse?' in Ariel Salleh (ed.), *Eco-Sufficiency and Global Justice: Women Write Political Ecology* (London: Pluto Press, 2009); Ariel Salleh, 'Ecofeminism' in Clive Spash (ed.), *Ecological Economics: Nature and Society* (London: Routledge, 2017).

21 Timothy Morton, *Ecology Without Nature: Rethinking Environmental Aesthetics* (Cambridge, MA: Harvard University Press, 2007); Diana Coole and Samantha Frost (eds.), *New Materialisms: Ontology, Agency, and Politics* (Durham, NC: Duke University Press, 2010).
22 Manfred Steger, James Goodman, and Erin Wilson, *Justice Globalism: Ideology, Crises, Policy* (London: Sage, 2013); William Carroll, *Expose, Oppose, Propose: Alternative Policy Groups and the Struggle for Global Justice* (London: Zed Books, 2016); Global University for Sustainability: http://our-global-u.org.
23 Marti Kheel, *Nature Ethics: An Ecofeminist Perspective* (Lanham, MD: Rowman and Littlefield, 2008); Pattrice Jones, 'Afterword: Liberation as Connection and the Decolonization of Desire' in Breeze Harper (ed.), *Sistah Vegan: Black Female Vegans Speak on Food, Identity, Health, and Society* (Brooklyn: Lantern Books, 2010).
24 Susan Buckingham (ed.), *Gender and Environment* (London: Routledge, 2015); Mary Phillips and Nick Rumens (eds.), *Contemporary Perspectives on Ecofeminism* (London: Routledge, 2016).
25 Silvia Federici, *Caliban and the Witch: Women, the Body, and Primitive Accumulation* (Brooklyn: Autonomedia, 2004); Mary Mellor, 'Ecofeminist Political Economy and the Politics of Money' in Ariel Salleh (ed.), *Eco-Sufficiency and Global Justice: Women Write Political Ecology* (London: Pluto Press, 2009); Heather Brown, *Marx on Gender and the Family: A Critical Study* (Chicago: Haymarket, 2013); Frigga Haug, 'Marx Within Feminism' in Shahrzad Mojab (ed.), *Marxism and Feminism* (London: Zed Books, 2015).
26 Miriam Wyman (ed.), *Sweeping the Earth: Women Taking Action for a Healthy Planet*, (Charlottetown: Gynergy Books, 1999); Wilma Dunaway, 'Women's Labor and Nature: The 21st Century World-System from a Radical Ecofeminist Perspective', in *New Theoretical Directions for the 21st Century World-System* (New York: Praeger, 2003).
27 Ana Isla, *The Greening of Costa Rica: Women, Peasants, Indigenous Peoples, and the Remaking of Nature* (Toronto: University of Toronto Press, 2015).
28 Rosemary Ruether, *New Woman, New Earth* (New York: Seabury Press, 1975); Carolyn Merchant, *The Death of Nature: Women and the Scientific Revolution* (New York: Harper 1980); Maria Mies, *Patriarchy and Accumulation on a World Scale* (London: Zed Books, 1986); Vandana Shiva, *Staying Alive: Women Ecology, and Development* (London: Zed Books, 1989).
29 George Herbert Mead, *Mind, Self, and Society* (Chicago: University of Chicago Press, 1934).
30 Veronika Bennholdt-Thomsen and Maria Mies, *The Subsistence Perspective* (London: Zed Books, 1999); Ivonne Gebara, *Longing for Running Water: Ecofeminism and Liberation* (Minneapolis, MN: Fortress Press, 1999).

31 Bertell Ollman, *Dialectical Investigations* (New York: Routledge, 1992).
32 Greta Gaard, 'Ecofeminism Revisited: Rejecting Essentialism and Re-Placing Species in a Material Feminist Environmentalism', *Feminist Formations*, 2011, Vol. 23, No. 2, pp. 26–53; Emilie Hache (ed.), *Reclaim: Recueil de textes ecofeministes* (Paris: Editions Cambourkakis Sorcieres, 2016).

1. ECOLOGY REFRAMES HISTORY

1 The word 'nature' is a mystifying construction in capitalist patriarchal discourse, just as 'man' and 'woman' are. In this book, static ideological terms like 'Woman', 'Humanity', 'the State', 'Nature' are occasionally capitalised to convey the false concreteness that must be resisted in making change.
2 Jacques Derrida, *Specters of Marx*, trans. P. Kamuf (New York: Routledge, 1994), p. 59. While not much interested in feminism or ecology, Derrida does note in passing (p. 86) that *Liberté, Egalité, Fraternité* has become a problematic slogan.
3 Karl Marx and Frederick Engels, *Manifesto of the Communist Party* (Moscow: Foreign Languages Press, 1959), p. 86. The present usage of the term 'class' is neo-marxist, referring to economic position but qualified by gender and ethnicity.
4 Andrew Dobson, *Green Political Thought* (London: Unwin Hyman, 1990).
5 Jonathon Porritt, *Seeing Green: The Politics of Ecology Explained* (London: Blackwell, 1984), p. 116.
6 Charles Birch, *Regaining Compassion for Humanity and Nature* (Sydney: University of New South Wales Press, 1993); Warwick Fox, *Toward a Transpersonal Ecology* (Boston: Shambala, 1990).
7 Hans Magnus Enzensberger, 'A Critique of Political Ecology', *New Left Review*, 1974, No. 84, pp. 3–32.
8 'Ableness' is used in preference to 'disability', to emphasise the value of bodily difference.
9 See Stephan Schmidheiny (ed.), *Changing Course: a Global Business Perspective on Development and the Environment* (Cambridge: MIT Press, 1992).
10 Rudolf Bahro, *Socialism and Survival* (London: Heretic Books, 1982), p.65. The words in quotation marks are Bahro's own.
11 David Pepper, *eco-socialism: from deep ecology to social justice* (London: Routledge, 1993).
12 Doniella Meadows et al., *The Limits to Growth* (London: Pan, 1983), p. 19.
13 James O'Connor develops this position in the journal *Capitalism Nature Socialism* from 1988. Joe Weston (ed.), *Red and Green: the New Politics of the Environment* (London: Pluto Press, 1986), p. 154.

14 Robert Bullard, *Dumping in Dixie: Race, Class, and Environmental Quality* (Boulder, CO: Westview, 1990).
15 Dobson, p. 162.
16 André Gorz, *Paths to Paradise* (London: Pluto Press, 1985), p. 36.
17 Ibid., p. 35.
18 Boris Frankel, *The Post-industrial Utopians* (London: Polity Press, 1987).
19 Herman Daly (ed.), *Toward a Steady State Economy* (San Francisco: Freeman, 1973).
20 Michel Foucault, *Language, Counter Memory, Practice*, ed. and trans. D. Bouchard (Ithaca: Cornell University Press, 1977); Jacques Derrida, *Writing and Difference*, trans. A. Bass (Chicago University Press, 1978).
21 Andrew Ross, *Strange Weather* (New Haven: Yale University Press, 1992).
22 Ernesto Laclau and Chantal Mouffe, *Hegemony and Socialist Strategy* (London: Verso, 1985); Fritjof Capra, *The Elmwood Newsletter*, Berkeley, CA; Carl Boggs, *Social Movements and Political Power* (Philadelphia: Temple University Press, 1986); Stanley Aronowicz, *The Politics of Identity* (New York: Routledge, 1992); Dennis Altman, *Rehearsals for Change* (Sydney: Pluto, 1980); Herbert Marcuse, *One Dimensional Man* (London: Abacus, 1964).
23 Murray Bookchin, *The Modern Crisis* (Philadelphia: New Society Publishers, 1986), p. 152. More recently, Bookchin has rejected 'lifestyle anarchism' for syndicalism.
24 Jurgen Habermas, 'New Social Movements', *Telos*, 1981, No. 49, pp. 33–7; Frankel, pp. 234–42.
25 Alain Lipietz, *Green Hopes* (Cambridge: Polity Press, 1995).
26 Werner Hülsberg, *The German Greens* (London: Verso, 1988), p. 77. See also the essay by Tasmanian Greens leader Christine Milne in C. Pybus and R. Flanagan (eds.), *The Rest of the World Is Watching* (Sydney: Pan, 1990); Ariel Salleh, 'A Green Party: Can the Boys Do without One?' in D. Hutton (ed.), *Green Politics in Australia* (Sydney: Angus and Robertson, 1987); Ariel Salleh, 'Shades of Green in Australian Politics', *Economic and Political Weekly*, 28 April 1990.
27 P. Lowe and W. Rudig, 'Review Article: Political Ecology and the Social Sciences – the State of the Art', *British Journal of Political Science*, 1986, Vol. 16, pp. 513–50.
28 Leslie Sklair, 'Global Sociology and Global Environmental Change', in M. Redclift and T. Benton (eds.), *Social Theory and the Global Environment* (London: Routledge, 1994), p. 207.
29 Redclift and Benton, 'Introduction', p. 21.
30 Dobson, p. 203.
31 Petra Kelly, *Fighting for Hope* (London: Chatto and Windus, 1984), p. 32.
32 Steven Yearley, 'Social Movements and Environmental Change', in Redclift and Benton; Swasti Mitter, *Common Fate, Common Bond* (London: Pluto, 1986); Cynthia Enloe, *Bananas, Bases and Beaches* (London: Pandora, 1989).

33 Luke Martell, *Ecology and Society* (Cambridge: Polity Press, 1994), p. 155.
34 Alberto Melucci, *Nomads of the Present* (London: Radius, 1989).
35 Ibid., p. 194. Also Robert Goodin, *Green Political Theory* (Cambridge: Polity Press, 1992).
36 Francis Fukuyama, *The End of History and the Last Man?* (New York: Free Press, 1992).
37 Dobson, p. 203.
38 Hazel Henderson, 'The Warp and the Weft: the Coming Synthesis of Eco-philosophy and Eco-feminism', in L. Caldecott and S. Leland (eds.), *Reclaim the Earth* (London: Women's Press, 1983), p. 207.
39 Karl Marx, *Critique of Hegel's Philosophy of Right*, in T. Bottomore and M. Rubel (eds.), *Karl Marx: Selected Writings in Sociology and Social Philosophy* (Harmondsworth: Penguin, 1984), p. 190: cited in Dobson, p. 156.

2. ECOFEMINIST ACTIONS

1 What follows is a global perspective on the first two decades of ecofeminism; a thorough history of the movement demands a book of its own.
2 Dorothy Nelkin, 'Nuclear Power as a Feminist Issue', *Environment*, 1981, Vol. 23.
3 Françoise d'Eaubonne, *Le féminisme ou la mort* (Paris: Horay, 1974); Rosemary Ruether, *New Woman, New Earth* (New York: Dove, 1975); Anne-Marie de Vilaine, 'La femme et/est l'écologie', *Le sauvage*, 1977, July.
4 Carolyn Merchant, 'Earthcare', *Environment*, 1981, Vol. 23. For more on the Oz history, see Ariel Salleh, 'A Green Party: Can the Boys Do without One?' in D. Hutton (ed.), *Green Politics in Australia* (Sydney: Angus and Robertson, 1987).
5 Friends of the Earth (Australia), *Chain Reaction*, 1978, Vol. 3, No. 4.
6 Susan Griffin, *Woman and Nature: the Roaring Inside Her* (New York: Harper, 1978); Mary Daly, *Gyn/ecology* (London, Women's Press, 1979); Elizabeth Dodson Gray, *Green Paradise Lost* (Wellesley, MA.: Roundtable Press, 1979).
7 Merchant; and Nelkin.
8 Delphine Brox-Brochot, 'Manifesto of the Green Women', in E. Hoshino Altbach et al. (eds.), *German Feminism* (Albany: SUNY Press, 1984), p. 315; Monica Sjoo, *Women Are the Real Left* (Manchester: Matriarchy Publications, 1979).
9 Joyce Cheney, 'The Boys Got Us into This Mess', *Commonwoman*, 1979, quoted by Nelkin, p. 38.
10 Ariel K. Salleh, 'The Big One in Britain', *Chain Reaction*, 1981, No. 26; Jane Jaquette, *The Women's Movement in Latin America* (London: Unwin, 1989).

11 Helen Caldicott, correspondence with the author, 1982. Manushi Collective, 'Drought: God Sent or Man Made Disaster?', *Manushi*, 1980, No.6.

12 Carolyn Merchant, *The Death of Nature: Women, Ecology and the Scientific Revolution* (San Francisco: Harper, 1980).

13 Nelkin.

14 L. Jones (ed.), *Keeping the Peace* (London, Women's Press, 1983).

15 Ibid.; also Alice Cook and Gwyn Kirk, *Greenham Women Everywhere* (London: Pluto, 1983).

16 Dora Russell, *Religion of the Machine Age* (London: Routledge, 1983); Leonie Caldecott and Stephanie Leland (eds.), *Reclaim the Earth* (London: Women's Press, 1983); Wilmette Brown, *Black Women and the Peace Movement* (London: Falling Wall Press, 1983), p. 36.

17 On the deep ecology debate see the US journal *Environmental Ethics*, 1984–94.

18 Petra Kelly, *Fighting for Hope* (London: Chatto and Windus, 1984); Fritjof Capra and Charlene Spretnak, *Green Politics* (New York: Dutton, 1984); Helen Caldicott, *Missile Envy* (New York: Morrow, 1984).

19 Hilkka Pietila, *Tomorrow Begins Today* (Nairobi: ICDA/ISIS Workshop Forum 85, 1986); Troth Wells and Foo Gaik Sim, *Till They Have Faces: Women as Consumers* (Rome: ISIS International, 1987); Mary Pardo, 'Mexican American Women Grassroots Community Activists: Mothers of East Los Angeles', *Frontiers: A Journal of Women's Studies*, 1990, Vol. 11.

20 Women Working for a Nuclear Free and Independent Pacific (eds.), *Pacific Women Speak* (Oxford: Greenline, 1987); Pat Costner et al., *We All Live Downstream* (Eureka Springs, AR: Waterworks Publishing, 1986); Maria Mies, *Patriarchy and Accumulation on a World Scale* (London: Zed Books, 1986).

21 Chellis Glendinning, *Waking Up in the Nuclear Age* (New York: Morrow, 1987); Emily Hiestand, 'An Old Idea', from *Green the Witch-Hazel Wood* (St Paul: Graywolf Press, 1989), p. 102; thanks to Kirk Sale for the gift of this book.

22 Andrée Collard and Joyce Contrucci, *Rape of the Wild* (London: Women's Press, 1988). There are accounts of the attack on Bari in 1990 issues of *Earth First!* and *Fifth Estate*. Subsequently published was: Judi Bari, *Timber Wars* (Monroe, ME: Common Courage Press, 1994). Also Dai Qing, personal communication, Balmain Markets, 1994.

23 Marilyn Waring, *Counting for Nothing* (Sydney: Allen and Unwin, 1988); Irene Dankelman and Joan Davidson (eds.), *Women and Environment in the Third World* (London: Earthscan, 1988); Anne Garland, *Women Activists: Challenging the Abuse of Power* (New York: CUNY Press, 1988); Patricia Hynes, *The Recurring Silent Spring* (New York: Pergamon, 1989). Besides Rachel Carson, acknowledgement should be given to Mira Behn (Madeleine Slade), who throughout the 1940s

agitated the Indian government over flood and erosion from tree felling in the Himalayas.

24 Gail Omvedt et al., *Women and Struggle* (New Delhi: Kali for Women, 1988); Vandana Shiva, *Staying Alive: Women, Ecology and Development* (London: Zed Books, 1989).

25 Mita Castle-Kanerova, 'Czech and Slovak Federative Republic: The Culture of Strong Women in the Making' in C. Corrin (ed.), *Superwomen and the Double Burden* (London: Scarlet Press, 1992); Cynthia Cockburn, 'A Women's Political Party for Yugoslavia', *Feminist Review*, 1991, No. 39; Hilkka Pietila and Jeanne Vickers, *Making Women Matter: The Role of the United Nations* (London: Zed Books, 1990).

26 Carol Adams, *The Sexual Politics of Meat* (New York: Continuum, 1990); Judith Plant (ed.), *Healing the Wounds* (Philadelphia: New Society Publishers, 1989); Irene Diamond and Gloria Orenstein (eds.), *Reweaving the World: The Emergence of Ecofeminism* (San Francisco: Sierra Club, 1990); Lin Nelson et al. *Turning Things Around: A Women's Occupational and Environmental Health Guide* (Washington: National Women's Health Network, 1990).

27 Catherine Boyle, 'Touching the Air', in S. Radcliffe and S. Westwood (eds.), *Viva: Women and Popular Protest in Latin America* (London: Routledge, 1993), p. 171.

28 Karen Warren (ed.), *Hypatia: A Journal of Feminist Philosophy*, 1991, Vol. 6; Janet Biehl, *Rethinking Ecofeminist Politics* (Boston: South End Press, 1991); Ariel Salleh, 'Ecosocialism/Ecofeminism', *Capitalism Nature Socialism*, 1991, Vol. 2; Valerie Kuletz, 'Ecofeminist Philosophy: Interview with Barbara Holland-Cunz', *Capitalism Nature Socialism*, 1992, Vol. 3, No. 2.

29 Personal communication, Erica Kniep, Cafe Otto, Glebe, 1993.

30 Rosina Wiltshire, *Environment and Development: Grass Roots Women's Perspectives* (St Michael, Barbados: University of the West Indies, 1992); *Ecologist*, 1992, Vol. 2, January/February; *Earth Summit Times*, New York: Prepcom IV, 1992, March; Gwendolyn Mikel, 'African Feminism: Towards a New Politics of Representation', *Feminist Studies*, 1995, Vol. 21, pp. 405–24, 419.

31 Anon., 'Women and Nationalism in Yugoslavia', unpublished manuscript, 1992.

32 Michael Hammond, editorial, *Environmental Values*, 1993, Vol. 2; Rosemary Ruether, *Gaia and God· An Ecofeminist Theology of Earth Healing* (San Francisco: Harper, 1992).

33 Mary Mellor, *Breaking the Boundaries: Towards a Feminist Green Socialism* (London: Virago, 1992); Joni Seager, *Earth Follies: Coming to Feminist Terms with the Global Environmental Crisis* (New York: Routledge, 1993).

34 Val Plumwood, *Feminism and the Mastery of Nature* (London: Routledge, 1993); Corin Bass and Janet Kenny, *Beyond Chernobyl: Women*

Respond (Sydney: Envirobook, 1993); Greta Gaard (ed.), *Ecofeminism: Women, Animals, Nature* (Philadelphia: Temple University Press, 1993, p. 1).

35 Maria Inacia d'Avila and Naumi de Vasconcelos (eds.), *Ecologia, Feminismo, Desenvolvimento* (Universidade Federal do Rio de Janeiro, 1993); Maria Mies and Vandana Shiva, *Ecofeminism* (London: Zed Books, 1993).

36 WEDO, *News and Views*, 1993, April; Patsy Hallen, 'Ecofeminism: Reawakening the Erotic', *Habitat*, 1994, February.

37 On El-Khader, *The Other Israel*, 1995, February/March.

38 Lynette Dumble, 'Population Control, Legacy of Shame', *The Age*, 22 September 1994; *Nursing the Environment Newsletter*, 1995, November/December. Regarding MOP, personal communication, Peter Hopper, NSW Nature Conservation Council, 1995.

39 Kerstin Zillman, 'Gender Sensitive Sustainable Urban Development', *Capitalism Nature Socialism*, 1996, Vol. 7, No. 2, pp. 147–54.

40 Annette Greenall-Gough, 'Listening to the Marginalised', *ecofeminist actions*, 1995, No. 16; *Pacific New Bulletin*, 1995, May and September issues; *Cultural Survival Quarterly*, 1995, Fall, p. 5.

3. BODY LOGIC: 1/0 CULTURE

1 Alain Touraine, 'An Introduction to the Study of Social Movements', *Social Research*, 1985, No. 52, pp. 745–55.

2 Sherry Ortner, 'Is Female to Male as Nature Is to Culture?', in M. Rosaldo and L. Lamphere (eds.), *Woman, Culture and Society* (Stanford: Stanford University Press, 1974). While this essay was a textual catalyst for ecofeminist writing, Ortner herself was a Second Wave equality feminist.

3 Elizabeth Dodson Gray, *Green Paradise Lost* (Wellesley, MA: Roundtable Press, 1979) has a wonderful discussion of this theological construct.

4 Adrienne Rich, *Of Woman Born* (New York: Bantam, 1976). The formula Man/Woman=Nature and its abbreviation M/W=N are used in the present text as ironic shorthand for the unreflective positioning of Man as non-identical to Woman, she being identical to Nature.

5 Fatna Sabbah, *Women in the Muslim Unconscious* (New York: Pergamon, 1984), pp. 104, 114.

6 Amanda Davies (ed.), *Third World: Second Sex* (London: Zed, 1983), p. 110.

7 Mary Daly, *Gyn/ecology* (London: Women's Press, 1978).

8 Silvia Federici, 'The Great Witch-hunt', *Maine Scholar*, 1989, Vol. 1, pp. 31–52.

9 Save the Children, *Children: The Invisible Soldiers* (Stockholm: Save the Children, 1996), cited in Agence France-Presse, 'Over 250,000 Youngsters Forced to Fight', *Sydney Morning Herald*, 2 November 1996.
10 Ariel Salleh, 'Contribution to the Critique of Political Epistemology', *Thesis Eleven*, No. 8, p. 33. Compare the misreading of my position in Karen Warren (ed.), *Ecological Feminism* (New York: Routledge, 1994).
11 Julia Kristeva, 'Oscillation between Power and Denial' in E. Marks and I. Courtivron (eds.), *New French Feminisms* (Brighton: Harvester Press, 1985), p. 165.
12 Dodson Gray, p. 112. Barbara Ehrenreich, in *The Hearts of Men* (New York: Doubleday, 1983), explains the feminisation of poverty that follows from this sexed difference.
13 Mary O'Brien, *The Politics of Reproduction* (Boston: Routledge, 1981), pp. 27, 54.
14 Simone de Beauvoir, *The Second Sex*, trans. H. Parshley (New York: Bantam, 1961).
15 O'Brien, p. 35. The reference is to *Capital*, Vol. 1.
16 Georg Simmel, The Relative and the Absolute in the Problem of the Sexes', in *Georg Simmel: On Women, Sexuality, and Love*, ed. and trans. by G. Oakes (New Haven: Yale University Press, 1984).
17 William Wordsworth, 'Ode on Intimations of Immortality' in F. Palgrave (ed.), *The Golden Treasury* (London: Collins, c1937), pp. 289–90.
18 O'Brien, pp. 54–5. Italics added.
19 Frederick Engels, *The Origin of the Family, Private Property and the State* (New York: Pathfinder, 1972).
20 Compare Jean Baudrillard in *The Mirror of Production* (St Louis: Telos, 1975) who like O'Brien claims that Marx was too much taken with the idea of 'production'. Baudrillard also condemns poststructuralists for carrying on this obsession, when, for example, they speak of 'textual production' or of the body as a 'producer of desire'.
21 It is understood that the Rural Advancement Foundation International may pursue a World Court challenge against the Hagahai patent at The Hague. 'Biopiracy Update', *Pacific News Bulletin*, January 1996.
22 Alison Abbott, 'Greens Attack Transgenic Plant Trials', *Nature*, 29 August 1996.
23 Richard Nathan, 'Ebola Bar Creates Monkey Shortage', *Nature*, 29 August 1996.
24 O'Brien, pp. 54–5.
25 Julia Kristeva, 'A New Type of Intellectual Dissident', in *The Kristeva Reader*, ed. T. Moi (London: Blackwell, 1986), p. 296. The reference is to Woolf's *Three Guineas*. See also Jacques Lacan, *Écrits*, trans. A. Sheridan (London: Tavistock, 1977).
26 Julia Kristeva, *Powers of Horror*, trans. L. Roudiez (New York: Columbia University Press, 1982), p. 109. Daly (p. 59) contends that Christianity

is necrophilic, defined as 'love of those victimised into a state of living death'.

27 Rosemary Ruether, *Gaia and God· An Ecofeminist Theology of Earth and Healing* (London: SCM Press, 1993), p. 53.

28 Jacques Derrida, *Specters of Marx*, trans. P. Kamuf (New York: Routledge, 1994), p. 18.

29 Isaac Balbus, in *Marxism and Domination* (Princeton: Princeton University Press, 1982), also recommended that, as a political act, fathers should take over infant care. He in turn was influenced by Dorothy Dinnerstein's path-breaking analysis in *The Mermaid and the Minotaur* (New York: Harper, 1976).

30 Nancy Chodorow, *The Reproduction of Mothering* (Berkeley: University of California Press, 1978).

31 For the mirror's own point of view see Sally Cline and Dale Spender, *Reflecting Men at Twice Their Natural Size* (London: Fontana, 1987).

32 Cornelius Castoriadis, 'Institution of Society and Religion', *Thesis Eleven*, 1993, No. 35, pp. 1, 16.

33 Phyllis Chesler, *About Men* (London: Women's Press, 1978), p. 71.

34 Daly, p. 63.

35 Sigmund Freud, *Moses and Monotheism*, ed. J. Strachey (London: Hogarth, 1974). Freud was fascinated with the question of our human place in nature. He told how his mother once rubbed the palm of her hand to make dirt, teaching him the ground of his ultimate origin and end. He was also convinced that all knowledge would ultimately be reducible to physicochemical components.

36 John Stoltenberg, *Refusing to Be a Man* (New York: Meridian, 1990), p. 72.

37 Significantly, it was the issues of paedophilia and animal experiments that brought the *Grünen* undone in the 1980s: see Rudolf Bahro, *Building the Green Movement*, trans. M. Tyler (London: Heretic, 1986).

38 Carol Adams, *The Sexual Politics of Meat* (New York: Continuum, 1990).

39 Greta Gaard (ed.), *Ecofeminism: Women, Animals, Nature* (Philadelphia: Temple University Press, 1993), p. 297.

40 Elspeth Lambert, 'The Milking of Cows', *The Animals Agenda*, 1986, April, pp. 2–3.

41 Luce Irigaray, *Speculum of the Other Woman*, trans. G. Gill (Ithaca: Cornell University Press, 1985).

42 Ibid., p. 204. Italics added.

43 Claude Levi-Strauss, *The Elementary Structures of Kinship*, trans. J. Bell et al. (Boston: Beacon, 1969). Luce Irigaray, *This Sex Which Is Not One*, trans. C. Porter (Ithaca: Cornell University Press, 1985); see especially Chapter 8, 'Women on the Market'.

44 Irigaray, *Speculum*, p. 140.

45 See K. (Ariel) Salleh, 'Of Portnoy's Complaint and Feminist Problematics', *Australian and New Zealand Journal of Sociology*, 1981,

Vol. 17. This article also argues that the early critical marxism of the Frankfurt School rejected both sex role stereotypes and the nature/culture dichotomy.

46 Ibid., pp. 9–10.

47 Maria Mies and Vandana Shiva, *Ecofeminism* (London: Zed Books, 1994), p. 186; Rita Arditti et al. (eds.), *Test Tube Women* (London: Pandora, 1984).

48 Regarding overdetermination see Sigmund Freud, *The Interpretation of Dreams* (Harmondsworth: Penguin, 1976), pp. 416–18. The concept was applied to political systems by Louis Althusser in *For Marx*, trans. B. Brewster (London: New Left Books, 1969). For use of the concept to account for ecofeminism: Ariel Salleh, 'From Feminism to Ecology', *Social Alternatives*, 1984, Vol. 4.

49 Talcott Parsons and Robert Bales, *Family, Socialisation and Interaction Process* (London: Routledge, 1956); Margaret Mead, *Male and Female* (Middlesex: Penguin, 1962).

50 Robert Greenway, 'The Wilderness Effect and Ecopsychology', in T. Roszak (ed.), *Ecopsychology* (San Francisco: Sierra Club, 1995), p. 129.

51 Lilian Stehelin, 'Sciences, Women and Ideology', in H. and S. Rose (eds.), *The Radicalisation of Science* (London: Macmillan, 1976).

52 Lorraine Mortimer, 'Feminism and Motherhood', *Arena*, 1985, No. 73, pp. 58–77, p. 62; Diane Ehrensaft, 'Feminists Fight (for) Fathers', *Socialist Review*, 1990, No. 4, pp. 57–80.

53 Patricia Hill Collins, *Black Feminist Thought* (Boston: Unwin, 1990), p. 94.

54 Carol Gilligan, *In a Different Voice* (Cambridge: Harvard University Press, 1982), pp. 173–4. Along similar lines are the following: Sara Ruddick, *Maternal Thinking: Toward a New Politics of Peace* (Boston: Beacon Press, 1989); Jean Baker Miller, *Towards a New Psychology of Women* (London: Allen and Unwin, 1978); Jessica Benjamin, 'The Bonds of Love', in H. Eisenstein and A. Jardine (eds.), *The Future of Difference* (New Brunswick, NJ: Rutgers University Press, 1985); Seyla Benhabib, 'The Generalised and the Concrete Other', in S. Benhabib and D. Cornell (eds.), *Feminism as Critique* (Cambridge: Polity Press, 1987).

55 Irigaray, *Speculum*, p. 142.

4. MAN/WOMAN=NATURE

1 Maria Mies and Vandana Shiva, *Ecofeminism* (London: Zed Books, 1994); Rita Arditti et al. (eds.), *Test Tube Women* (London: Pandora, 1984); Wadjularbinna, with Cam Walker, 'The Gungalidda and CRA – Another Form of Genocide', *Chain Reaction*, 1994, No. 71, pp. 25–6.

2 Marilyn Strathern, 'Between a Melanesianist and a Deconstructive Feminist', *Australian Feminist Studies*, 1989, No.10, p. 58. Strathern's

text draws heavily on the anthropological work of Mark Mosko, 'Conception, De-Conception and Social Structure in Bush [North] Mekeo Culture', in D. Jorgensen (ed.), *Concepts of Conception: Procreation Ideologies in Papua New Guinea*, special issue of *Mankind*, 1983.

3 Strathern, p. 61.

4 Asesela Ravuvu, *The Fijian Ethos* (Suwa: University of the South Pacific, 1983) cited in John Young, *Sustaining the Earth* (University of NSW Press, 1991), p. 46.

5 For example, Susan Griffin, *Woman and Nature: The Roaring Inside Her* (New York: Harper, 1976); Mary Daly, *Gyn/ecology* (London: Women's Press, 1978); Dora Russell, *The Religion of the Machine Age* (London: Routledge, 1983).

6 Maria Mies, *Patriarchy and Accumulation on a World Scale* (London: Zed Books, 1986), pp. 45–6.

7 Ibid., p. 56.

8 Rosemary Ruether, *New Woman, New Earth* (New York: Seabury Press, 1975), p. 195.

9 Ibid.

10 Carolyn Merchant, *The Death of Nature: Women, Ecology and the Scientific Revolution* (San Francisco: Harper, 1980).

11 Peter Singer, *Animal Liberation* (London: Cape, 1975), p. 32.

12 Merchant, p. 168.

13 Ibid., p. 209 n. 38.

14 See K. (Ariel) Salleh, 'Of Portnoy's Complaint and Feminist Problematics', *Australian and New Zealand Journal of Sociology*, 1981, Vol. 17, pp. 4–13 for an ecofeminist reading of Max Horkheimer and Theo Adorno, *Dialectic of Enlightenment* (London: Penguin, 1973).

15 Tariq Banuri, 'Modernisation and Its Discontents', in F. Apffel-Marglin and S. Marglin (eds.), *Dominating Knowledge* (Oxford: Clarendon, 1990).

16 Herbert Marcuse, *One Dimensional Man* (London: Abacus, 1972), p. 123. This aspect of masculine culture relates to what difference theorist Luce Irigaray calls 'specularity': Luce Irigaray, in *Speculum of the Other Woman*, trans. G. Gill (Ithaca: Cornell University Press, 1985).

17 Marcuse, p. 5.

18 E. A. J. Johnson, *Predecessors of Adam Smith: The Growth of British Economic Thought* (New York: Prentice-Hall, 1937), pp. 139–40.

19 John Locke, 'An Essay Concerning the True Original, Extent and End of Civil Government', in Sir Ernest Barker (ed.), *The Social Contract: Essays by Locke, Hume, Rousseau* (Oxford University Press, 1971). See notably Part V, paragraphs 25–51, pp. 16–30. The citations are from pp. 17 and 18 respectively; emphasis in original. Thanks to Martin O'Connor for drawing my attention to these texts.

20 Ruether, p. 194.
21 Rosa Luxemburg, *The Accumulation of Capital* (London: Routledge, 1963).
22 Mies, p. 98.
23 Peter Breggen, *Toxic Psychiatry and the War Against Children* (San Francisco: Harper Collins, 1993).
24 Vandana Shiva, *Staying Alive: Women, Ecology and Development* (London: Zed Books, 1989), p. 45.
25 See Betsy Hartmann, *Reproductive Rights and Wrongs* (New York: Harper, 1987).
26 'How Food Production is Hit by Population', *Standard*, 2 October 1987, p. 14.
27 Debbie Taylor (ed.), 'Myth Conceptions', *New Internationalist*, 1987, October, pp. 8–9.
28 Otula Owuor, 'Sound Science Policies Called For', *Sunday Nation*, 4 October 1987, p. 17. Italics added.
29 Shiva, p. 129.
30 AIDWATCH information sheet, Sydney, 1996.
31 Rosalie Bertell, 'The Re-greening of the Planet', in V. Shiva (ed.), *Close to Home* (Philadelphia: New Society Publishers, 1994), pp. 146–7.
32 Amanda Meade and Stephen Lunn, 'Scientists, Greens at Odds on 87 Year Cancer Danger', *Australian*, 19 November 1996; see also US National Research Council, *Orbital Debris – a Technical Assessment* (Washington: US National Research Council, 1996).
33 Gyorgy Scrinis, *Colonising the Seed* (Melbourne: Friends of the Earth, 1995); editorial, *New Scientist*, 12 August 1995; Richard Hindmarsh, 'BioBiz', *Arena Magazine*, 1995, June/July.
34 Adapted from Ariel Salleh, 'Living with Nature: Reciprocity or Control', in R. and J. Engel (eds.), *Ethics of Environment and Development* (London: Pinter, 1990).
35 Shiva, pp. 152–3.
36 Ivan Illich, 'Vernacular Gender', *Co-Evolution Quarterly*, 1982, Spring, p. 7; Louis Arnoux, *Energy Within, Without* (Auckland: NZ Energy Research and Development Committee, 1982), p. 346.
37 Brian Swimme, comments to the First International Ecofeminist Conference, University of Southern California, Los Angeles, April 1987.
38 Griffin, reprinted in *Made From This Earth* (London: Women's Press, 1982), pp. 95–7.
39 Anon., personal communication, Sydney, December 1996, shortly after the Australian government opened the way for the import of the Monsanto pharmaceutical corporation's pesticide-tolerant genetically engineered soya bean product. Monsanto was the manufacturer of Agent Orange spray used in Vietnam.

5. FOR AND AGAINST MARX

1 Jean-Guy Vaillancourt, 'Marxism and Ecology: More Benedictine than Franciscan', *Capitalism Nature Socialism*, 1992, No. 9; Frederick Engels, *Anti-Dühring* (New York: International Publishers, 1936).
2 Alfred Schmidt, *The Concept of Nature in Marx*, trans. B. Fowkes (London: New Left Books, 1971), p. 17. The present exposition retains the linguistic convention 'Man' out of faithfulness to the master text and its preferred level of generality which downplays the 'difference' between men's and women's experience.
3 Frederick Engels, *The Origin of the Family, Private Property and the State* (New York: International Publishers, 1972).
4 Lise Vogel, 'Marxism and Feminism: Unhappy Marriage, Trial Separation, or Something Else?' in L. Sargent (ed.), *Women and Revolution* (Boston: South End Press, 1981), summarises these developments including the 'domestic labour debate'.
5 See Martin Ryle, *Ecology and Socialism* (London: Hutchinson, 1988); David Pepper, *eco-socialism* (London: Routledge, 1993) and the journal *Capitalism Nature Socialism.*
6 Bertell Ollman, *Dialectical Investigations* (New York: Routledge, 1993).
7 Karl Marx, *Grundrisse*, trans. M. Nicholaus (Harmondsworth: Penguin, 1973), p. 542.
8 Karl Marx, *The Economic and Philosophic Manuscripts of 1844*, trans. M. Milligan and ed. D. Struik (New York: International Publishers, 1964), p. 158.
9 Karl Marx, *Capital*, Vol. I, ed. F. Engels (New York: International Publishers, 1967), p. 177.
10 Elizabeth Dodson Gray, *Green Paradise Lost* (Wellesley: Roundtable, 1979).
11 Val Routley, 'On Karl Marx as an Environmental Hero', *Environmental Ethics*, 1981, Vol. 3.
12 In environmental ethics, deep ecology has shown concern about anthropocentrism. For an ecofeminist critique of deep ecology's own 'androcentrism', see Ariel Salleh, 'Deeper than Deep Ecology: The Ecofeminist Connection', *Environmental Ethics*, 1984, Vol. 6.
13 Charles Birch, *Feelings* (Sydney: UNSW Press, 1995).
14 Mary O'Brien, *The Politics of Reproduction* (Boston: Routledge, 1983); Luce Irigaray, *This Sex Which Is Not One*, trans. C. Porter (Ithaca: Cornell University Press, 1985).
15 Howard Parsons, *Marx and Engels on Ecology* (London: Greenwood, 1977).
16 Cited in Schmidt, pp. 41–3. On the Frankfurt School, see Martin Jay, *The Dialectical Imagination* (London: Heinemann, 1973).
17 Marx, *Economic and Philosophic Manuscripts*, p. 112.

18 Ibid., p. 101.
19 Karl Marx, *The Eighteenth Brumaire of Louis Bonaparte*, in *Collected Works*, Vol. 11 (New York: International Publishers, 1979), p. 103.
20 Marx, *Grundrisse*, p. 366.
21 The concept of the emblematic phallus is developed in Jacques Lacan, *Écrits* (Paris: Editions du Seuil, 1986). This ecofeminist argument relies not on Lacan, but on the French feminist reading of phallic logic developed by Luce Irigaray.
22 See Dorothy Dinnerstein, *The Mermaid and the Minotaur* (New York: Harper, 1976) and Nancy Chodorow, *The Reproduction of Mothering* (Berkeley, University of California Press, 1978).
23 Sherry Ortner introduced the important notion of women's labour as 'mediating nature': see 'Is Female to Male, as Nature Is to Culture?' in M. Rosaldo and L. Lamphere (eds.), *Women, Culture and Society* (Stanford: Stanford University Press, 1974).
24 Karl Marx, Appendix to *Capital*, Vol. 1 (New York: Vintage, 1977), p. 1042. Cited in Alison Jaggar, *Feminist Politics and Human Nature* (Brighton: Harvester, 1983).
25 On 'wages for housework', see writings by Mariarosa Dalla Costa and Selma James, especially *The Power of Women and the Subversion of the Community* (Bristol: Falling Wall Press, 1972).
26 Karl Marx, *Capital*, Vol. III, ed. F. Engels (New York: International Publishers, 1970), p. 820.
27 Berit As, 'A Five Dimensional Model for Social Change', *Women's Studies International Quarterly*, 1981, Vol. 4, and Ruth Schwartz Cowan, *More Work for Mother* (New York: Basic Books, 1983).
28 ILO, *Report far the Copenhagen Mid-Decade Conference on Women* (Geneva: International Labour Organisation) 1980.
29 Marx, *Economic and Philosophic Manuscripts*, p. 149.
30 Marx, *Grundrisse*, p. 706. On men's peculiar fascination with technology, see the following: Ruth Wallsgrove, 'The Masculine Face of Science', in Brighton Women and Science Group (ed.), *Alice Through the Looking Glass* (London: Virago, 1980); Liliane Stehelin, 'Sciences, Women and Ideology', in H. Rose and S. Rose (eds.), *The Radicalisation of Science* (London: Macmillan, 1976); Brian Easlea, *Fathering the Unthinkable* (London: Pluto, 1983).
31 Marx, *Capital*, Vol. I, p. 388.
32 Marx, *Capital*, Vol. III, p. 820.
33 Friedrich Engels, *Herr Eugen Dühring's Revolution in Science*, pp. 26–9. Cited in Parsons.
34 See Rachel Carson, *Silent Spring* (Greenwich, CT: Fawcett, 1962) and Evelyn Fox Keller, *A Feeling for the Organism* (San Francisco: Freeman, 1983), a biography of McClintock; Rosalie Bertell, 'Unholy Secrets: The Impact of the Nuclear Age on Public Health', in L. Caldecott and S. Leland (eds.), *Reclaim the Earth* (London: Women's Press, 1983).

35 Cited in Parsons, p. 178.
36 Marx, *Economic and Philosophic Manuscripts*, pp. 70–1.
37 Karl Marx and Friedrich Engels, *The German Ideology*, ed. R. Pascal (New York: International Publishers, 1947), p. 20.
38 Marx, *Capital*, Vol. I, p. 372, n3.
39 Rosemary Ruether, *New Woman, New Earth* (New York: Dove, 1975); K. (Ariel) Salleh, 'Of Portnoy's Complaint and Feminist Problematics', *Australian and New Zealand Journal of Sociology*, 1981, Vol. 17; Carolyn Merchant, *The Death of Nature* (San Francisco: Harper, 1980); Max Horkheimer and Theo Adorno, *Dialectic of Enlightenment* (New York: Herder, 1972).
40 Engels, *Origin of the Family*, pp. 71–2.
41 This is not just a problem for marxist theory: compare Marilyn Waring, *Counting for Nothing* (Sydney: Allen and Unwin, 1989) on bourgeois economics.
42 Ashis Nandy, *The Intimate Enemy* (Delhi: Oxford University Press, 1983), p. x. Colonised men, in turn, are identified by the coloniser as 'feminine'.
43 See O'Brien; Maria Mies, *Patriarchy and Accumulation on a World Scale* (London: Zed Books, 1987).
44 Marx, *Economic and Philosophic Manuscripts*, p. 30. Cited in Bertell Ollman, *Alienation: Marx's Conception of Man in Capitalist Society* (New York: Cambridge University Press, 1971), p. 298.
45 Marx, *Capital*, Vol. I, pp. 571–3.

6. THE DEEPEST CONTRADICTION

1 David Korten, *When Corporations Rule the World* (London: Earthscan, 1995), p.185. See also Joel Kurtzman, *The Death of Money* (Boston: Little Brown, 1993).
2 Kurtzman, p. 231.
3 Kurtzman, pp. 205–6 and Susan Griffin, Plenary Address, First International Ecofeminist Conference, University of Southern California, Los Angeles, April 1987.
4 Scott McNealy, Chief-Executive Officer, Sun Microsystems Inc., quoted by Sandy Plunkett, 'Battle to Rule the Internet', *Business Review Weekly*, 12 December 1996, p. 41.
5 UNCTAD, *World Investment Report* (New York: UN, 1995).
6 Phil Knight, interviewed on *Four Corners*, Australian Broadcasting Corporation TV, 27 January 1997.
7 Tim Doyle, 'Corporations, Power and the Environment', *Chain Reaction*, 1995, No. 73/74; Chee Yoke Ling, 'Earth Summit: Unequal Negotiations in an Unequal World', *Third World Resurgence*, 1992, No. 24/25; James Goldsmith, 'The Case Against GATT', *Multi-National Monitor*, 1994, No. 10.

8 Courtesy Danny Kennedy, Action for Solidarity, Equality, Environment and Development (ASEED), Sydney, 1995.
9 International Appeal to APEC Energy Ministers, Climate Action Network Australia, c/o Nature Conservation Council of NSW, August 1996.
10 Carolyn Deere, 'NAFTA Casualty Update', *Arena*, 1996, No. 24, pp. 6–8.
11 ILO, *Report for the Copenhagen Mid-Decade Conference on Women* (Geneva: ILO, 1980); UNDP, *Human Development Report* (New York: UN, 1995).
12 The notion of 'conditions of production' as used by James O'Connor in 'Capitalism, Nature, Socialism: A Theoretical Introduction', *Capitalism Nature Socialism*, 1988, Vol. 1, crudely brackets together physical resources, human labour and local infrastructure as a single variable.
13 See Carole Pateman, *The Sexual Contract* (Cambridge: Polity Press, 1988).
14 Professor Jane Mangina, Address to the Fifth International Women's Congress, University of Adelaide, March 1996.
15 Selma James, *The Global Kitchen* (London: Housewives in Dialogue Archive, 1985), p. 1.
16 Marilyn Waring, *Counting for Nothing* (Sydney: Allen and Unwin, 1988); *Three Masquerades* (Auckland: Auckland University Press, 1996).
17 National Mutual advertisement: 'If Your Husband Lost you, Could He Afford to Keep the Children?', *Australian Women's Weekly*, 1994, July.
18 Luce Irigaray, 'Women's Exile', *Ideology and Consciousness*, 1977, Vol. 1.
19 Mary Mellor, *Breaking the Boundaries* (London: Virago, 1992).
20 Hilkka Pietila, 'The Triangle of the Human Economy: Household, Cultivation, Industrial Production', paper delivered at the International Association for Feminist Economics Summer Conference, American University, Washington, 1996, p. 11; see also Anne Chadeau, 'What is Household's Non-market Production Worth?' *OECD Economic Studies*, 1992, No. 18, Spring.
21 James, pp. 10–11.
22 Ibid.; Waring; Hilkka Pietila, 'Women as an Alternative Culture Here and Now', *Development*, 1994, Vol. 4.
23 ILO, *Mujeres en sus casas* (Lima: Regional Office for Latin America and the Caribbean, 1984), p. 17; cited by Giovanna Dalla Costa, 'Development and Economic Crisis: Women's Labour and Social Policies in Venezuela in the Context of Social Indebtedness', in M. and G. Dalla Costa (eds.), *Paying the Price* (London: Zed Books, 1995), pp. 114–15.
24 See Lydia Sargent (ed.), *Women and Revolution* (Boston: South End Press, 1981); Hannelore Mabry, 'The Feminist Theory of Surplus Value', in E. Hoshino Altbach et al. (eds.), *German Feminism* (Albany: SUNY Press, 1984) Unlike ecofeminist critiques, these feminists do not make the link to nature.
25 Berit As, 'A Five Dimensional Model for Social Change', *Women's Studies International Quarterly*, 1981, Vol. 4.

26 See also Seymour Melman, *The Permanent War Economy: American Capitalism in Decline* (New York: Simon and Schuster, 1974).
27 Korten, pp. 188–9; p. 192.
28 Silvia Federici, 'The Debt Crisis, Africa and the New Enclosures', *Midnight Oil: Work, Energy, War* (New York: Midnight Notes Collective, 1992).
29 Ibid., p. 313.
30 Irene Dankelman and Joan Davidson (eds.), *Women and Environment in the Third World* (London: Earthscan, 1988); Lin Nelson, 'Feminists Turn to Workplace, Environmental Health', *Women and Global Corporations*, 1986, No. 7; Cynthia Enloe, *Bananas, Beaches and Bases* (London: Pandora, 1989).
31 Vandana Shiva, *Staying Alive: Women, Development and Ecology* (London: Zed Books, 1989).
32 Ibid., p. 45.
33 Naomi Scheman, 'Individualism and the Objects of Psychology', in S. Harding and M. Hintikka (eds.), *Discovering Reality* (Boston: Reidel, 1983), p. 234.
34 Maria Mies, *Patriarchy and Accumulation on a World Scale* (London: Zed Books, 1986).
35 The need for 'self-criticism' in this regard is put forward by Italian socialists Valentino Parlato and Giovanna Ricoveri: see 'The Second Contradiction in the Italian Experience' (Rome: unpublished manuscript, 1993).
36 Adapted from Ariel Salleh, 'Contribution to the Critique of Political Epistemology', *Thesis Eleven*, 1984, No. 8, p. 25.
37 Some postmodern writers object to the empirical category 'women' as well, in an attempt to avoid 'essentialism'. Marxists – with a universalising concept of 'class' – and people who write about 'race' risk the same charge. However, a structural analysis of domination(s) cannot be made without recourse to general categories.
38 For example, young women who apply for cadetships in Indonesian police and military academies are subjected to medical verification of their virginity.
39 Giovanna Ricoveri, 'Culture of the Left and Green Culture: The Challenge of the Environmental Revolution in Italy', *Capitalism Nature Socialism*, 1993, Vol. 4, p. 119.

7. WHEN FEMINISM FAILS

1 NativeWeb-Glen Welker: gwclker@mail.limi.org, 30 May 1995.
2 Alice Walker, *In Search of Our Mother's Gardens: Womanist Prose* (New York: Harcourt, 1983), p. xi; see also the discussion in bell hooks,

Feminist Theory: From Center to Margin (Boston: South End Press, 1984), pp. 134–5.

3 Paul and Anne Ehrlich, *The Population Explosion* (New York: Simon and Schuster, 1990); Charles Birch, *Regaining Compassion* (University of NSW Press, 1993); Robert Birrell et al. (eds.), *Populate and Perish?* (Melbourne: Australian Conservation Foundation, 1994). The alternative view, espoused by ecofeminists, has been pioneered by Malini Karkal, *Can Family Planning Solve the Population Problem?* (Bombay: Stree Uvach, 1989).

4 hooks, p. 75.

5 Julia Panourgia Clones, 'European Women Identify Gender Differences in Emergency Catastrophic Situations', *WorldWIDE News*, 1995, No. 1.

6 Giovanna Dalla Costa, 'Development and Economic Crisis: Women's Labour and Social Policies in Venezuela in the Context of International Indebtedness', in M. and G. Dalla Costa (eds.), *Paying the Price* (London: Zed Books, 1995), p. 96.

7 Lorraine Mortimer, 'Feminism and Motherhood', *Arena*, 1985, No. 73 is one fine example.

8 For samples of disembodied theory see Parveen Adams and Beverly Brown, 'The Feminine Body and Feminist Politics', *m/f*, 1979, No. 3; Toril Moi, *Sexual/Textual Politics* (New York, Methuen, 1985); Alison Jaggar and Susan Bordo (eds.), *Gender/Body/Knowledge* (New Brunswick: Routledge, 1989); Elizabeth Grosz, *Space, Time and Perversion* (Sydney: Unwin, 1995).

9 On ecofeminism and pornography, see: Susan Griffin, *Pornography and Silence* (London: Women's Press, 1981); Ariel Salleh, 'Black Shades and Ideological Blinders', *Fifth Estate*, 1993, Spring; also Maria Mies and Vandana Shiva, *Ecofeminism* (London: Zed Books, 1994). And for an Enlightened masculine perspective see: John Stoltenberg, *Refusing to be a Man: Essays on Sex and Justice* (Harmondsworth: Meridian, 1990).

10 Ashis Nandy, *The Intimate Enemy* (Delhi: Oxford University Press, 1983), p. xiv.

11 Barbara Epstein, 'Ecofeminism and Grassroots Environmentalism in the US', in R. Hofrichter (ed.), *Toxic Struggles* (Philadelphia: New Society Publishers, 1993), p. 151.

12 Lois Gibbs, 'Foreword', in Hofrichter, p. ix. See also Dorothy Smith, *The Everyday World as Problematic: A Feminist Sociology* (Boston: Northeastern University Press, 1987); Harriet Rosenberg, 'The Home is the Workplace: Hazards, Stress and Pollutants in the Household', in S. Arat-Koc et al. (eds.), *Through the Kitchen Window* (Toronto: Garamond, 1990); Anne Bookman and Sandra Morgan (eds.), *Women and the Politics of Empowerment* (Philadelphia: Temple University Press, 1988).

13 CEAS, 'Mulheres da periferia com a palavra', *Cadernos dos CEAS*, 1981, No. 74, July/Aug quoted in Alda Britto da Motta and Inaia Maria

Moreira de Carvalho, 'Pauperisation and Women's Participation in Social Movements in Brazil', in Dalla Costa and Dalla Costa, pp. 84–5.

14 For critical deconstructions of this writing in social ecology, eco-socialism and deep ecology, see www.arielsalleh.info. There are also ecofeminist allies like David Ehrenfeld, *Beginning Again* (New York: Oxford University Press, 1993).

15 Report on the Seventh Nuclear Free and Independent Pacific Conference in Suva, *Pacific News Bulletin*, 1996, December, p. 3.

16 Audre Lorde, 'The Master's Tools Will Never Dismantle the Master's House', in C. Moraga and G. Anzaldúa (eds.), *The Bridge Called My Back: Writings of Radical Women of Color* (New York: Kitchen Table, 1983), p. 100.

17 Kate Soper, *What is Nature?* (Cambridge: Polity Press, 1995), p. 263.

18 Ibid, p. 271.

19 Silvia Federici, personal correspondence, March 1996. Federici is also concerned at the World Bank tendency to offer village women 'micro credits' for small commercial ventures, so tying them to global capital for meeting even the most basic of life needs.

20 Anon., 'CAPOW Forum 21/8/93', *ecofeminist actions*, 1993, No. 12, p. 4.

21 Office of the Status of Women, 'Fourth UN World Conference on Women', *Infosheet*, November 1995.

22 Anon., 'Global Civil Governance', *Ecoforum*, October 1995, pp. 21–3.

23 Bina Agarwal, 'The Gender and Environment Debate: Lessons from India', *Feminist Studies*, 1992, Vol. 19; Cecile Jackson, 'Environmentalisms and Gender Interests in the Third World', *Development and Change*, 1993, pp. 649–77. For mainstream criticisms of growth see: Donella Meadows et al., *Beyond the Limits: Global Collapse or a Sustainable Society* (London, Earthscan, 1992); Ted Trainer, *Abandon Affluence!* (London: Zed Books, 1987); Fritz Schumacher, *Small is Beautiful: Economics as if People Mattered* (London: Sphere, 1973); Edward Mishan, *The Costs of Economic Growth* (Harmondsworth: Penguin, 1969).

24 Anon., 'Scientists Sound Alarm on Quarantine', *Sydney Morning Herald*, 2 April 1996, p. 1, the accidentally released man-made rabbit *calici* virus was not listed.

25 Wolfgang Sachs (ed.), *Global Ecology* (London: Zed Books, 1993).

26 Compare Bob Scholte, 'Toward a Reflexive and Critical Anthropology', in D. Hymes (ed.), *Reinventing Anthropology* (New York: Random House, 1969); Victoria Davion, 'Is Ecofeminism Feminist?' in K. Warren (ed.), *Ecological Feminism* (New York: Routledge, 1994), p. 20.

27 Megan Jones, 'Women Told to Forget the Boys' Rules', *Sydney Morning Herald*, 14 February 1996, p. 29.

28 The phrase 'Two Thirds World' alludes to the number of people in the world living under Third World conditions. As far as I am aware, the

neologism originated with Jan Strout of the Women's Studies Center at Princeton University. Personal communication with Jan, Baltimore, 1989.

29 hooks, p. 19. DAWN is discussed in Hilkka Pietila and Jeanne Vickers, *Making Women Matter: The Role of the United Nations* (London: Zed Books, 1990), p. 36.

30 Joni Seager, *Earth Follies* (New York: Routledge, 1993), p. 7.

8. TERRA NULLIUS

1 Louis Arnoux, *Energy Within Without* (Auckland: New Zealand Energy Research and Development Committee, 1982) seems to reinforce the mater/matter cut by prioritising symbolic exchange; thus Illich and Georgescu-Roegen are said to 'anachronistically' link back into a 'supposedly natural' order, p. 312.

2 Frances Milne, Economic Reform Australia, Green Party Workshop, University of New South Wales, Sydney, November 1996.

3 On the failure of community, see also Kevin McDonald, 'Morals Is All You've Got', *Arena Magazine*, 1995, No. 20, pp. 18–23.

4 On the official doctrine of *terra nullius*, which assumed that Australia was uninhabited land at the time of the white invasion, see Henry Reynolds, *Aboriginal Sovereignty* (Sydney: Allen and Unwin, 1996), p. xi: 'It is possible therefore to draw a direct line from observations made from the quarter-deck of the Endeavour in 1770, through the Privy Council decision in *Cooper v. Stuart* in 1889, and on to Blackburn's judgement in the Northern Territory Supreme Court in 1971.'

5 Marcia Langton, 'Art, Wilderness and Terra Nullius', in *Ecopolitics IX Conference Papers and Resolutions* (Darwin: Northern Territory University, 1995).

6 Adapted from Ariel Salleh, 'TWS: At the Interface', *Australian Society*, 1984, No. 7.

7 Business Council for Sustainable Development, *Changing Course* (Cambridge: MIT Press, 1992); Bob Burton 'Right Wing Think Tanks Go Environmental', *Chain Reaction*, 1995, No. 73/74, pp. 26–9; Kenny Bruno et al. *The Greenpeace Book of Greenwash* (HEIP Campaign, Washington, 1992); Ariel Salleh, 'Earth Summit: Some Reflections on Our Political Times', *Ecofeminist Newsletter*, 1993, Vol. 4.

8 What follows is adapted from Ariel Salleh, 'Politics in/of the Wilderness', *Arena Magazine*, 1996, No. 23. See also Christine Christopherson, with Marcia Langton, 'Allarda! (No to the Ranger uranium mine)', *Arena Magazine*, 1995, June/July; Richard Ledgar, 'Links between Ranger Uranium and France's Nuclear Programme', *Newsletter of the Environment Centre of the Northern Territory*, August 1995, PO Box 2120 Darwin, NT 08013, Australia; and most issues of *Pacific News Bulletin*, PO Box 803, Glebe, NSW 2037, Australia.

9 Martin Lewis, *Green Delusions* (Durham: Duke University Press, 1992), p. 187.
10 In the celebrated 1992 case of *Mabo v. Queensland*, no. 2, the state argued for *terra nullius*, claiming ownership of the Murray Islands. However, a majority judgement in the High Court of Australia determined that Eddie Mabo and his community were not dispossessed of their land by white colonisation, but retained 'native title' by virtue of continuous cultural association with the land.
11 Helen Rosenbaum (ed.), *Principles for the Environmental Management of Australian Mining Companies Operating in Papua New Guinea* (Melbourne: ACF, 1995) and WEEP, PO Box 4830, Boroko, NCD, Papua New Guinea.
12 Workshop on Regional Agreements, Ecopolitics IX, Northern Territory University, Darwin, September 1995.
13 Pat Hynes, *Taking Population Out of the Equation* (Amherst: Institute on Women and Technology, 1993); Betsy Hartmann, *Reproductive Rights and Wrongs: The Global Politics of Population Control and Reproductive Choice* (New York: Harper, 1987); Malini Karkal, *Can Family Planning Solve the Population Problem?* (Bombay: Stree Uvach, 1989).
14 Lynette Dumble, 'Women and the UN: Another Forged Consensus?', *Green Left*, 20 September 1995, p. 3; 'Population Control's Medical Paradigm: Regulation of Fertility or Disruption of Lives', *Newsletter: Women's Global Network for Reproductive Rights*, 1995, No. 50, pp. ii–iv.
15 Lynette Dumble, 'Population Control or Empowerment of Women?', *Green Left*, 2 November, 1994, p. 15.
16 George Caffentzis, 'The Fundamental Implications of the Debt Crisis for Social Reproduction in Africa', in M. and G. Dalla Costa (eds.), *Paying the Price* (London: Zed Books, 1995), p. 19. Italics added.
17 Ibid., p. 31.
18 Silvia Federici, 'The Debt Crisis, Africa and the New Enclosures', in Midnight Notes Collective (ed.), *Midnight Oil: Work, Energy, War* (New York: Autonomedia, 1992).
19 Michael Chossudovsky, 'IMF World Bank Policies and the Rwandan Holocaust', *Third World Resurgence*, 1994, December; Sam Kiley, 'UK Firm in Rwanda Arms Trade', *Australian*, 11 November 1996.
20 Henrietta Fourmile, 'Protecting Indigenous Intellectual Property Rights in Biodiversity', in *Ecopolitics IX Conference Papers and Resolutions*.
21 'Biopiracy Update', *Pacific News Bulletin*, January 1996.
22 Michael Dodson, 'Indigenous Peoples and Intellectual Property Rights', in *Ecopolitics IX Conference Papers and Resolutions*.
23 Bill Freeland, Workshop on Intellectual Property Rights, Ecopolitics IX, Northern Territory University, Darwin, September 1998.
24 Second Conference of the Parties to the Convention on Biological Diversity, 6–17 November 1995, Jakarta: Bob Phelps (ed.), *Newsletter*

of the Australian GenEthics Network, c/o ACF, 430 Gore Street, Fitzroy, Victoria 3065.

25 The Australian Friends of the Earth Pay the Rent scheme involves a commitment on the part of neighbourhood activists to bank a small weekly sum which can be drawn on by local Aboriginal families as needed. The 'rent' is an acknowledgement of white appropriation of indigenous land.

26 Darrell Posey, 'Indigenous Peoples and Traditional Resource Rights: A Basis for Equitable Relationships?', in *Ecopolitics IX Conference Papers and Resolutions.*

27 This argument is not new: see Marshall Sahlins, *Stone Age Economics* (New York: Aldine, 1972).

9. A BAREFOOT EPISTEMOLOGY

1 For more on the commodity form and mathematisation of reality, see Alfred Sohn-Rethel, *Intellectual and Manual Labour* (London: Macmillan, 1978); there is no awareness of gender effects on labour, however.

2 Cecile Jackson, 'Gender Analysis and Environmentalisms', in M. Redclift and T. Benton (eds.), *Social Theory and the Global Environment* (London: Routledge, 1994), exhibits the pro-development eurocentric bias of such groups. As Janis Birkeland so succinctly puts it: 'we in the North have simply lost the plot'.

3 Wolfgang Sachs (ed.), *Global Ecology* (London: Zed Books, 1994), p. 9. Les Levidow has an excellent report on World Bank hegemony in 'The 11th Annual Meeting of the International Association for Impact Assessment', *Capitalism Nature Socialism*, 1992, No. 9, pp. 117–24.

4 A 'reverse technology transfer' in terms of the brain drain from South to North is yet another loss. Susan George, *The Debt Boomerang: How Third World Debt Harms Us* (London: Pluto, 1992), attempts to persuade the North to quit. See also, NGO and Citizens Organisations, *An Appeal to the People of the World Bank and the International Monetary Fund*, World Bank/IMF Annual Meeting, September 1989.

5 Larry Lohmann, 'Resisting Green Globalism', in Sachs, p. 158.

6 Winston Langley, 'What Happened to the New International Economic Order?', *Socialist Review*, 1990, Vol. 20, p. 56.

7 Compare Brian Glick, *War at Home: Covert Action Against US Activists and What We Can Do About It* (Boston: South End Press, 1989).

8 Craig Forcese, 'Tainted Milk', *Multinational Monitor*, September 1995, p. 4.

9 Stephan Schmidheiny (ed.), *Changing Course: A Global Business Perspective on Development and the Environment* (Cambridge, MA: MIT Press, 1992).

10 Gayatri Spivak, 'Can the Subaltern Speak?', in C. Nelson and L. Grossberg (eds.), *Marxism and the Interpretation of Culture* (Urbana: University of Illinois Press, 1988), pp. 271–313.
11 Compare also Gail Omvedt, 'Ecofeminism in Action: Healing India with Women's Power', *Guardian* (USA), March 1992, pp. 10–11.
12 Lohmann, p. 167. Italics added.
13 Georges Gurvitch, *The Social Spectrum of Time* (Dordrecht: Reidel, 1964).
14 Barbara Adam, 'Running out of Time', in Redclift and Benton, p. 95.
15 Simone de Beauvoir, *The Second Sex* (New York: Bantam, 1953), p. 47, quoted in Mary O'Brien, *The Politics of Reproduction* (London: Routledge, 1981), p. 183.
16 Adapted from Ariel Salleh, 'Contribution to the Critique of Political Epistemology', *Thesis Eleven*, 1984, No. 8.
17 Adam, p. 95.
18 Luce Irigaray, 'Woman's Exile', *Ideology and Consciousness*, 1977, No. 1, pp. 64–5.
19 Adapted from K. (Ariel) Salleh, 'Of Portnoy's Complaint and Feminist Problematics', *Australian and New Zealand Journal of Sociology*, 1981, Vol. 17.
20 Vandana Shiva, *Staying Alive: Women, Ecology and Development* (London: Zed Books, 1989), p. 34. See also Farkhonda Hassan (ed.), *Protection of the Environment of the River Nile Basin: Role of Women* (Cairo: Proceedings of the Scientific Association of Arab Women, 1989) and CSE, *Floods, Flood Plains and Environmental Myths: The State of India's Environment A Citizens' Report 3* (New Delhi: Centre for Science and Environment, 1991).
21 Sachs, p. 11.
22 Ibid. p. 4.
23 Salleh, 'Contribution' p. 33.
24 Hélène Cixous, 'The Laugh of the Medusa' in E. Marks and I. de Courtivron (eds.), *New French Feminisms* (Amherst: University of Massachusetts Press, 1980), p. 251.
25 Maria Mies and Vandana Shiva, *Ecofeminism* (London: Zed Books, 1993), p. 164. See also Jyotsna Gupta, 'Women's Bodies as the Site of Ongoing Conquest by Reproductive Technologies', *Issues in Reproductive and Genetic Engineering*, Vol. 4 (1991) pp. 92–107; Liz Armstrong and Adrienne Scott, *Whitewash* (Toronto: Harper Collins/Weed Foundation, 1992).
26 Shiva, p. 45.
27 Trinh Minh-ha, *Woman, Native, Other* (Bloomington: Indiana University Press, 1989), p. 38.
28 Anon., *Genetic Engineering Infosheet*, Melbourne: Australian Conservation Foundation, 1992.
29 A case in point is the chapter by Frederick Buttel and Peter Taylor, 'Environmental Sociology and Global Environmental Change' in

Redclift and Benton, written with a grant from the US Environmental Protection Agency. The tendency to favour the 'intellectually trained' as agents of history occurs in some neo-marxist analyses as well.

30 Ulla Terlinden, 'Women in the Ecology Movement, Ecology in the Women's Movement', in E. Altbach et al. (eds.), *German Feminism* (Albany: SUNY, 1984), p. 320. Italics added.

31 Delphine Yeyet, quoted in Trinh Minh-ha, p. 108.

32 Sara Ruddick, *Maternal Thinking: Toward a Politics of Peace* (Boston: Beacon, 1989). Compare also Gregory Bateson, *Steps Toward an Ecology of Mind* (Frogmore: Paladin, 1973), p. 437.

33 Christine von Weizsackcr, 'Competing Notions of Biodiversity', in Sachs.

34 Mary Dietz, 'Citizenship with a Feminist Face: The Problem with Maternal Thinking', *Political Theory*, 1985, Vol. 13, p. 87.

35 Ruddick, p. 131.

36 Ibid., p. 79; Ruddick's reference here is to Adrienne Rich, *Lies, Secrets, and Silence* (New York: Norton, 1979), p. 205.

37 Deborah Rose Bird, *Nourishing Terrains: Australian Aboriginal Views of Landscape and Wilderness* (Canberra: Australian Heritage Commission, 1996), p. 68.

38 Manfred Max-Neef et al., *Human Scale Development* (New York: Apex, 1991).

39 Gerry Mander, In *the Absence of the Sacred* (San Francisco: Sierra Club, 1991).

40 Nancy Hartsock, *Money, Sex and Power* (Boston: Northeastern University Press, 1985); Evelyn Fox Keller, *A Feeling for the Organism* (San Francisco: Freeman, 1983).

41 Winona LaDuke, 'A Society Based on Conquest Cannot be Sustained', in R. Hofrichter (ed.), *Toxic Struggles* (Philadelphia: New Society, 1993), pp. 99–100. Italics added.

42 Donald Worster, 'The Shaky Ground of Sustainability', in Sachs, p. 134. Italics added.

43 Daniel Botkin, *Discordant Harmonies: A New Ecology for the Twenty-first Century* (New York: Oxford University Press, 1990). Compare the following: 'Continental Shifts', *Socialist Review*, 1990, Vol. 20; Gayatri Spivak, *In Other Worlds* (New York: Routledge, 1988); and Ranajit Guha and Gayatri Spivak (eds.), *Selected Subaltern Studies* (New York: Oxford University Press, 1988).

44 See Carol Gilligan, *In a Different Voice* (Cambridge, MA: Harvard University Press, 1984); Nel Noddings, *Caring* (Berkelev, CA: University of California Press, 1984). Compare also G. H. Mead, *Mind, Self, and Society* (University of Chicago, 1934) who saw the moral sense as a dialogue between the personal 'I' and relational 'me' aspects of self.

45 O'Brien, p. 237.

10. AS ENERGY/LABOUR FLOWS

1 Reiner Grundmann, *Marxism and Ecology* (Oxford: Clarendon Press, 1991), pp. 2–11. On p. 59 he writes, 'In *Capital*, Marx states more explicitly that man can produce nothing without technology'.
2 James Devine, 'The Law of Value and Marxian Political Ecology', in J. Vorst et al. (eds.), *Green on Red: Evolving Ecological Socialism* (Halifax: Fernwood, 1993).
3 Lise Vogel, 'Marxism and Feminism: Unhappy Marriage, Trial Separation or Something Else', in L. Sargent (ed.), *Women and Revolution* (Boston: South End Press, 1981); Luce Irigaray, in *This Sex Which Is Not One*, trans. C. Porter (Ithaca: Cornell University Press, 1985), goes further, arguing that commodity production is predicated on the symbolic exchange of women as commodities between men.
4 Devine, pp. 138 and 152. Italics added.
5 Nancy Folbre, 'Political Economy and Ecology – Comments on Commoner', paper presented at the Allied Social Sciences Association convention, 29 November 1989.
6 Marilyn Waring, *Counting for Nothing* (Sydney: Allen and Unwin, 1988).
7 Robyn Eckersley (ed.), *Markets, the State, and the Environment: Towards Integration* (Melbourne: Macmillan, 1995); Martin Lewis, *Green Delusions* (Durham: Duke University Press, 1992).
8 Devine, pp. 138–9.
9 Arran Gare, 'Soviet Environmentalism: The Path Not Taken', *Capitalism Nature Socialism*, 1993, No. 16, p. 87. Italics added. See also Nicholas Georgescu-Roegen, *Analytical Economics* (Cambridge: Harvard University Press, 1966); Ivan Illich, *Energy and Equity* (London: Boyars, 1976); Juan Martinez-Alier, *Ecological Economics* (Oxford: Blackwell, 1987).
10 Wilhelm Reich, *The Function of the Orgasm*, trans. V. Carfagno (New York: Pocket, 1975).
11 William Leiss, *The Domination of Nature* (New York: Brazillier, 1972); Tim Hayward, 'Ecology and Human Emancipation', *Radical Philosophy*, 1992, No. 62, pp. 3–13.
12 Ted Benton, *Natural Relations* (London: Verso, 1993), pp. 53–4.
13 Richard Lichtman, 'The Production of Human Nature by Means of Human Nature', *Capitalism, Socialism, Nature*, 1990, No. 4, pp. 13–51.
14 Paula Caplan, *Don't Blame Mother* (New York: Harper, 1989), p. 40.
15 Hilkka Pietila, *Tomorrow Begins Today* (Nairobi: ICDA:ISIS Workshop Forum 85, 1986).
16 Joseph Needham, *Science and Civilisation in China* (Cambridge University Press, 1954); on the West, compare Carolyn Merchant, *The Death of Nature* (San Francisco: Harper, 1980).

17 Jeremy Rifkin, *Algeny* (New York: Viking, 1983), p. 180. The reference is to Ernst Haeckel, *The History of Creation*, trans. R. Lankester (London: King and Co., 1876). Even so, Frederick Engels criticised Haeckel for being dualistic and mechanical; see Engels, *Dialectics of Nature*, trans. C. Dutt (New York: International Publishers, 1940), pp. 225–69.

18 Vandana Shiva, *Staying Alive: Women, Ecology and Development* (London: Zed Books, 1989).

19 Ilya Prigogene and Isabelle Stengers, *Order Out of Chaos* (London: Heinemann, 1984). This is consistent with the ideology of permaculture.

20 Alfred North Whitehead, *Process and Reality* (New York: Macmillan, 1929); Herbert Marcuse, *Counter Revolution and Revolt* (London: Allen Lane, 1972).

21 Richard Lewontin and Richard Levins, 'Animals Have a Complex Nature', *Capitalism Nature Socialism*, 1990, No. 4, p. 64.

22 Barbara Adam, *Time and Social Theory* (Cambridge: Polity Press, 1990).

23 Frank Fisher, *Sustaining Gaia* (Melbourne: Monash University, 1987), pp. 78–9.

24 See for example, Riley Dunlap and William Catton, 'Environmental Sociology', in T. O'Riordan and R. d'Arge (eds.), *Progress in Resource Management and Environmental Planning* (Chichester: Wiley, 1978).

25 Bertell Ollman, *Dialectical Investigations* (New York: Routledge, 1992), p. 37.

26 Susan Griffin, *Made from This Earth* (London: Women's Press, 1982), pp. 340–4, extract from the closing pages of *Woman and Nature.*

27 For more on the holograph see: David Bohm, *Wholeness and the Implicate Order* (London: ARK, 1983); Ken Wilbur, *The Holographic Paradigm* (Boulder: Shambhala, 1982).

28 Patricia Hill Collins, *Black Feminist Thought* (Boston: Unwin, 1990), and bell hooks, *Feminist Theory: from Margin to Center* (Boston: South End Press, 1984).

29 Alfred Schutz, 'On Multiple Realities', *Collected Papers*, Vol. 1 (The Hague: Martinus Nijhoff, 1962); George Herbert Mead, *The Philosophy of the Present*, ed. A. Murphy (La Salle: Open Court, 1959).

30 Julia Kristeva, *Desire in Language*, trans. L. Roudiez (Oxford, Blackwell, 1980), p. 237.

31 My argument does not differentiate women by stratifications of class, race, age, abledness, since the nature–woman–labour nexus crosses these conceptual boundaries. This is one reason for arguing that it constitutes a primary contradiction of capital.

32 Ollman, p. 93. Italics added. The value of Ollman's articulation of dialectics in reconciling seemingly contradictory socialist paradigms should not be underestimated. See Ariel Salleh, 'Social Ecology and The Man Question', *Environmental Politics*, 1996, Vol. 5 for an ecofeminist response to Murray Bookchin's dialectical naturalism.

33 Ollman, p. 47.
34 Maria Mies and Vandana Shiva, *Ecofeminism* (London: Zed Books, 1993). Mies adapts Rosa Luxemburg's analysis of the role of the periphery in capital accumulation.
35 Jean-Paul Sartre, *Reason and Violence*, trans. R. D. Laing and D. Cooper (New York: Random House, 1971); Arne Naess, *Ecology, Community and Lifestyle*, trans. D. Rothenberg (Cambridge University Press, 1989); Donna Haraway, *Simians, Cyborgs and Women* (New York: Routledge, 1991).
36 Louis Althusser, *For Marx*, trans. B. Brewster (London: New Left Books, 1972); Robin Morgan (ed.), *Sisterhood is Global* (New York: Anchor, 1984).
37 See, for example, Sargent; David Pepper, *eco-socialism* (London: Routledge, 1993).
38 Herbert Marcuse, *One Dimensional Man* (London: Abacus, 1972); Murray Bookchin, *Remaking Society* (Boston: South End Press, 1990).
39 Warwick Fox, *Toward a Transpersonal Ecology* (Boston: Shambala, 1990); Maria Mies, *Patriarchy and Accumulation on a World Scale* (London: Zed Books, 1987). Ollman suggests that the preferred voice of capitalist ideology prioritises individual experience in a naturalising way. Hence the mainstream interpretation of ecofeminism as 'just blaming men'.
40 Fritjof Capra, *The Tao of Physics* (New York: Bantam, 1984); Jeremy Rifkin, *Time Wars* (New York: Holt, 1987).
41 The term is freely adapted from Althusser.
42 Ollman, p. 69.
43 David Harvey, 'The Nature of the Environment': The Dialectics of Social and Environmental Change', *Socialist Register*, 1993, Part III, p. 42.
44 Rifkin, p. 12.
45 Harvey, p. 37.
46 Karl Marx, *The Economic and Philosophic Manuscripts of 1844*, ed. D. Struik (New York: International Publishers, 1964), p. 104.

11. AGENTS OF COMPLEXITY

1 Martin O'Connor, 'Codependency and Indeterminacy: A Critique of the Theory of Production', in *Is Capitalism Sustainable?* (New York: Guilford, 1994), p. 66. See also the chapter 'On the Misadventures of Capitalist Nature', especially p. 137.
2 An exception in postmodernism would be Gayatri Spivak's plea for the subaltern to be heard, inspired by a blend of socialist concern and deconstructionist technique.
3 Catriona Sandilands, 'Not the Same Difference? Ecofeminism, Universality, and Particularity', in J. Vorst et al. (eds.), *Green on Red: Evolving Ecological Socialism* (Halifax: Fernwood, 1993), p. 62.

4 Sarah Hutcheson, 'Walking the Line: Facing the Complexities of the Woman–Nature Link', *Alternatives*, 1995, Vol. 21, pp. 16–20.
5 Sandilands, p. 63.
6 Megan Morris, 'The Man in the Mirror: David Harvey's "Condition" of Postmodernity', *Theory, Culture and Society*, 1992, Vol. 9, p. 267.
7 Lynne Segal, *Is the Future Female?* (London, Virago, 1987) was an early rejection of ecofeminism on these grounds. Compare Gayatri Spivak, *In Other Worlds: Essays in Cultural Politics* (London: Methuen, 1987). See also the exchange between Cecile Jackson, 'Radical Environmental Myths', *New Left Review*, 1995, No. 210, and Ariel Salleh, 'An Ecofeminist Bioethic and What Post-Humanism Really Means', *New Left Review*, 1996, No. 217. And for more on essentialism, see Ariel Salleh, 'The Politics of Representation', *Arena*, 1990, No. 91 and 'Essentialism and Ecofeminism', *Arena*, 1991, No. 94.
8 Grace Mera Molisa, *Colonised People* (Port Vila: Black Stone, 1987), pp. 10–11. See also Cherrie Moraga and Gloria Anzaldua (eds.), *This Bridge Called My Back: Writings by Radical Women of Color* (New York: Kitchen Table Press, 1981).
9 Paula Caplan, *Don't Blame Mother* (New York: Harper, 1989), p. 43.
10 Julia Kristeva, *Polylogue* (Paris: Editions du Scuil, 1978). Cathexis is a psychoanalytic term implying an investment of bodily/mental energy or libido.
11 Stephen Heath, 'Introduction' to Roland Barthes, *Image, Music, Text* (London: Fontana, 1977), p. 10.
12 Ariel Salleh, 'On the Dialectics of Signifying Practice,' *Thesis Eleven*, 1982, No. 5/6, pp. 72–84. This usage of the 'negative dialectic', with its negative (nonpredicated) 'essence', comes from Theo Adorno, *Negative Dialectics*, trans. E. Ashton (London: Routledge, 1973); and from Adamo's *Minima Moralia*, trans. E. Jephcott (London: New Left Books, 1969).
13 Ashis Nandy, *The Intimate Enemy* (Delhi: Oxford University Press, 1983), p. 113. Italics added.
14 Alda Britto da Motta and Inaia Maria Moreira de Carvalho, 'Pauperization and Women's Participation in Social Movements in Brazil', in M. and G. Dalla Costa (eds.), *Paying the Price* (London: Zed Books, 1995), p. 87.
15 Minnie Bruce Pratt, 'Identity: Skin, Blood, Heart', in E. Bulkin et al. (eds.), *Yours in Struggle: Three Feminist Perspectives on Anti-Semitism and Racism* (New York: Long Haul Press, 1984). Refer also to Chandra Mohanty et al. (eds.), *Third World Women and the Politics of Feminism* (Bloomington: University of Indiana Press, 1991); bell hooks, *Yearnings: Race, Gender, and Cultural Politics* (London: Turnaround, 1991), pp. 145–53; Marilyn Frye, *The Politics of Reality: Essays in Feminist Theory* (Trumansburg, NY: Crossing Press, 1983).
16 Adorno, *Negative Dialectics*, p. 203; Adlorno, *Minima Moralia*, p. 73.

17 Ulla Terlingen, 'Women in the Ecology Movement, Ecology in the Women's Movement', in E. Hoshino Altbach et al. (eds.), *German Feminism* (Albany: SUNY, 1984), p. 319; reference is made to Ilona Ostner, *Beruf und Hausarbeit* (1978).

18 Kate Fillion's problematic criticism of feminism in *Lipservice* (New York: Harper, 1995) amplifies the pitfalls of treating terms like 'feminine/ masculine' as individual traits rather than sociologically relational notions.

19 This is one reason why Maria Lugones and Elizabeth Spelman, 'Have We Got A Theory For You! Feminist Theory, Cultural Imperialism and the Demand for The Woman's Voice', *Women's Studies International Forum*, 1983, Vol. 6, pp. 573–81, misses the mark. Identities are inscribed by biological and phenomenological experiences as much as by discursive ones.

20 Lourdes Torres, 'The Construction of the Self in US Latina Autobiographies', in Chandra Mohanty et al. (eds.), *Third World Women and the Politics of Feminism* (Indianapolis: Indiana University Press, 1991), p. 275.

21 On positivism, see: Ariel Salleh, 'Contribution to the Critique of Political Epistemology', *Thesis Eleven*, 1984, No. 8, and Paula Gunn Allen, *The Sacred Hoop: Recovering the Feminine in American Indian Traditions* (Boston: Beacon, 1986).

22 Maxine Hong Kingston, *The Woman Warrior* (New York: Vintage, 1977), p. 35.

23 Salleh, 'Dialectics of Signifying Practice'; Gregory Bateson, *Steps to an Ecology Mind* (Frogmore: Paladin, 1973); R. D. Laing, *Self and Others* (Harmondsworth: Penguin, 1961). It would be more useful to our collective liberation, perhaps, if existing psychotherapies were replaced by socio-political analysis.

24 Jim Cheney, 'Post Modern Environmental Ethics: Ethics as Bioregional Narrative', in M. Oelschlaeger (ed.), *Postmodern Environmental Ethics* (Albany: SUNY Press, 1995), p. 24. Also, on situated knowledges, see Donna Haraway, *Simians, Cyborgs and Women* (New York: Routledge, 1991).

25 Gloria Anzaldúa, quoted by Chandra Mohanty et al. (eds.), *Third World Women and the Politics of Feminism* (Bloomington: Indiana University Press, 1991), p. 37.

26 Susan Griffin, *Made from This Earth* (London: Women's Press, 1982), pp. 340–4; reprinted from the closing passage of *Woman and Nature.*

27 The thesis for an embodied materialism is sketched out in Salleh, 'Dialectics of Signifying Practice'. The stance has similarities to and differences from Sandra Harding's standpoint epistemology: see *The Science Question in Feminism* (Ithaca: Cornell University Press, 1986).

28 Ariel Salleh, 'Deeper than Deep Ecology', *Environmental Ethics*, 1984, Vol. 6, pp. 339–45.

29 Hilkka Pietila, *Women as an Alternative Culture Here and Now* (Rome: ISIS, 1986).
30 Vandana Shiva, *Staying Alive* (London: Zed Books, 1994), p. 10.
31 Maria Mies, *Patriarchy and Accumulation on a World Scale* (London: Zed, Books, 1987).
32 Torres, p. 275; according to Bateson, a failure to negotiate such contradictions can be associated with schizophrenia.

12. BEYOND VIRTUAL MOVEMENTS

1 Ariel Salleh, 'Contribution to the Critique of Political Epistemology', *Thesis Eleven*, 1984, No. 8, p. 27
2 Michael Redclift and Ted Benton, *Social Theory and the Global Environment* (London: Routledge, 1994), p. 18. Italics added.
3 Ibid., p.29.
4 Antonio Contreras, 'The Two Faces of Environmentalism: The Case of the Philippines', *Capitalism Nature Socialism*, 1994, No. 19, p. 77.
5 For a gender-aware overview of the field, see Jan Pakulski, *Social Movements: the Politics of Moral Protest* (Melbourne: Longman, 1991).
6 Ulrich Beck, *Risk Society: Toward a New Modernity*, trans. M. Ritter (London: Sage, 1992).
7 Jurgen Habermas, 'Modernity: An Incomplete Project', in H. Foster (ed.), *The Anti-Aesthetic* (Port Townsend, WA: Bay Press, 1983).
8 Ferenc Feher and Agnes Heller, 'From Red to Green', *Telos*, 1984, No. 59, pp. 35–44.
9 Ernesto Laclau and Chantal Mouffe, *Hegemony and Socialist Strategy* (London: Verso, 1985).
10 David Harvey, in *The Condition of Postmodernity* (Cambridge: Blackwell, 1989), discusses this compression of space and time under late capitalism.
11 Anne Phillips, *Democracy and Difference* (Cambridge: Polity Press, 1993); Paul James, *Critical Politics* (Melbourne: Arena, 1994).
12 Alain Touraine, *The Voice and the Eye* (Cambridge: Cambridge University Press, 1981). Also in this tradition: Ronald Inglehart, *The Silent Revolution: Changing Values and Political Styles Among Western Publics* (Princeton: Princeton University Press; 1977); and on movements as collectively negotiated cognitive praxis, see R. Eyerman and A. Jameson, *Social Movements: A Cognitive Approach* (Cambridge: Polity Press, 1991).
13 For example see Ingolfur Bluhdorn et al., *The Green Agenda* (Keele: University of Keele Press, 1995), which concentrates on state policy, economic interests, trade unions, and environmental pressure groups.
14 E. P. Thompson et al., *Exterminism and Cold War* (London: New Left Books, 1982); Rudolf Bahro, *Building the Green Movement*, trans. M. Tyler (London: Heretic, 1986).

15 Claus Offe, 'New Social Movements', *Social Research*, 1985, Vol. 52.
16 Alberto Melucci, *Nomads of the Present: Social Movements and Individual Needs in Contemporary Society* (London: Radius, 1989), pp. 206, 216.
17 Malini Karkal, 'Indian Women and Globalisation', Forum for Women's Health, Bombay, unpublished paper, 1996.
18 Tarja Cronberg, quoted in Hilkka Pietila, 'Women's Reflections on the European Community', Helsinki, unpublished paper, 1992, p. 1.
19 Garrett Hardin and John Baden (eds.), *Managing the Commons* (San Francisco: Freeman, 1977); Robert Heilbronner, *An Inquiry into the Human Prospect* (New York: Norton, 1991); William Ophuls and Stephen Boyan, *Ecology and the Politics of Scarcity Revisited* (New York: Freeman, 1992).
20 Compare the parallel arguments in Christopher Stone, *Should Trees Have Standing?* (Los Altos, CA: Kauffman, 1974).
21 Murray Bookchin, *The Ecology of Freedom* (Montreal: Black Rose, 1991); Bill Devall, *Simple in Means, Rich in Ends* (Salt Lake City: Peregrine Smith, 1988); Peter Berg, ed., *Raise the Stakes!*, newspaper of the Planet Drum Foundation, San Francisco; Kirk Sale, *Dwellers in the Land* (San Francisco: Sierra Club, 1985). These delinking efforts are quite distinct from the regional 'mercantilism' of the EU or APEC.
22 Helen Forsey, 'Two Kinds of Power: A Different Experience at Oka', in C. and J. Plant (eds.), *Putting Power in its Place* (Philadelphia: New Society Publishers, 1991), p. 135.
23 Helen Ross, 'Aboriginal Australian's Cultural Norms for Negotiating Natural Resources', *Cultural Survival Quarterly*, 1995, Fall.
24 This hands-on materialist approach should not be confused with eco-psychological efforts to restore integral personhood by means of Jungian archetypes or deep ecologists' use of transpersonal psychology to achieve cosmic identification.
25 Serge Latouche, *In the Wake of the Affluent Society* trans. M. O'Connor and R. Arnoux (London: Zed Books, 1993), p. 201.
26 The literature includes Mary O'Brien, *The Politics of Reproduction* (Boston: Routledge, 1981); Sara Ruddick, *Maternal Thinking* (Boston: Beacon, 1989); Hilary Rose, 'Hand, Brain and Heart: A Feminist Epistemology for the Natural Sciences', *Signs*, 1983, Vol. 9, pp. 73–90.
27 Compare Dorothy Smith, *The Everyday World As Problematic: A Feminist Sociology* (Boston: Northeastern University Press, 1987).
28 See John Andrews, *Political Dreaming: Men Politics, and the Personal* (Sydney: Pluto, 1995); Robert Lawlor, *Earth Honouring: The New Male Sexuality* (Sydney: Millenium, 1990); Barbara Ehrenreich, *The Hearts of Men* (New York: Anchor, 1983).
29 For a full ecofeminist critique of this problem in eco-socialism, social ecology, deep ecology, and postmodern feminism, see www.arielsalleh.info.

30 Mathias Finger, 'Politics of the UNCED Process' in W. Sachs, (ed.), *Global Ecology* (London: Zed Books, 1993), pp. 41–7. Italics added.

31 Adapted from Ariel Salleh, 'Politics in/of the Wilderness', *Arena Magazine*, 1995, No. 23.

INTERVIEW

1 Timothy Morton, *Ecology Without Nature: Rethinking Environmental Aesthetics* (Cambridge, MA: Harvard University Press, 2007); Judith Butler, *Bodies that Matter: On the Discursive Limits of Sex* (New York: Routledge, 1993).

2 Donna Haraway, *Simians, Cyborgs, and Women: The Reinvention of Nature* (New York: Routledge, 1991).

3 Ariel Salleh, 'Deeper than Deep Ecology: The Ecofeminist Connection,' *Environmental Ethics* 6 (1984): 339–45.

4 Ariel Salleh, *Ecofeminism as Politics: Nature, Marx, and the Postmodern* (London: Zed Press and New York: Palgrave, 1997), 150–82.

5 Ariel Salleh, 'Contribution to the Critique of Political Epistemology,' *Thesis Eleven* 8 (1984): 23–43.

6 Stacy Alaimo and Susan Hekman (eds.), *Material Feminisms* (Bloomington: Indiana University Press, 2008).

7 Stacy Alimo, 'Trans-Corporeal Feminisms and the Ethical Space of Nature' in Alaimo and Hekman (2008), 237. The reference is to Julia Kristeva, *Powers of Horror: An Essay on Abjection* (New York: Columbia University Press, 1982), 1–4.

8 Clearly there are as many ways of performing a masculine identity as there are versions of the feminine, but I am referring to hegemonic masculinity here.

9 Michael Hardt and Antonio Negri, *Multitude: War and Democracy in the Age of Empire* (London: Penguin, 2004), 132–149, 172–75.

10 Clay Grantham, 'Re: collapses of historical civilizations may have been socially optimal,' ENVIROSOC@listserv.brown.edu.

11 Robert Brulle, 'Psychological Factors Help Explain Slow Reaction to Global Warming, Says APA Task Force', ENVIROSOC@listserv.brown.edu.

12 Gerd Johnsson-Latham, *Initial Study of Lifestyles, Consumption Patterns, Sustainable Development and Gender* (Stockholm: Ministry of Sustainable Development, 2006); also Ariel Salleh, 'Climate Change—and the Other Footprint,' *The Commoner* 13 (2008): 103–13.

13 Ariel Salleh, 'Sustaining Nature or Sustaining Marx? A Reply to Foster and Burkett,' *Organization and Environment* 14 (2001): 443–50. The paper was a response to John Bellamy Foster and Paul Burkett, 'The Dialectic of Organic / Inorganic Relations: Marx and the Hegelian Philosophy of Nature,' *Organization and Environment* 13 (2000): 403–25.

14 Namely, John Clark, 'Marx's Inorganic Body,' *Environmental Ethics* 11 (1989): 243–58. Other idealists according to Foster and Burkett are physicist Fritjof Capra, philosophers Kate Soper, Val Routley, John O'Neill, and ecofeminist Salleh.
15 Neil Smith, 'The Production of Nature' in G. Robertson et al. (eds.), *FutureNatural* (London: Routledge, 1996).
16 Peter Dickens, *Reconstructing Nature* (London: Routledge, 1995); Jurgen Habermas, *Knowledge and Human Interests* (London: Routledge, 1983).
17 Bertell Ollman, *Dialectical Investigations* (New York: Routledge, 1992).
18 The term 'reproduction' is used here in its generic sense, applying to the maintenance of biological processes, economic relations, or cultural practices – and it dovetails with sustainability. The phrase 'reproduction of capitalism' is a specific usage characteristic of marxism and it is at odds with sustainability.
19 Salleh, 1997; and Editorial, 'Moving to an Embodied Materialism,' *Capitalism Nature Socialism* 16 (2005): 9–14.
20 Diana Fuss, *Essentially Speaking* (London: Routledge, 1989); Ariel Salleh, 'The Politics of Representation,' *Arena* 91 (1990): 163–69; 'Essentialism—and Ecofeminism,' *Arena* 94 (1991): 167–73.
21 Michael Zimmerman, 'Feminism, Deep Ecology, and Environmental Ethics,' *Environmental Ethics* 9 (1987): 21–44; Daniel Faber and James O'Connor, 'The Struggle for Nature,' *Capitalism Nature Socialism* 1 (1989): 1–10.
22 Salleh 1984a. Subsequently, Noel Sturgeon, *Ecofeminist Natures* (New York: Routledge, 1997), following Zimmerman 1987, went on to use the piece as an essentialist prototype.
23 Chris Cuomo, 'Still Fooling with Mother Nature,' *Hypatia* 16 (2001): 149–52. On transgenders: Salleh 1984b.
24 Herbert Marcuse, *One-Dimensional Man* (London: Abacus, 1964).
25 Ariel Salleh, 'Eco-socialism/Ecofeminism,' *Capitalism Nature Socialism* 2 (1991): 129–34.
26 Ariel Salleh, 'Editorial: "Towards an Inclusive Solidarity on the Left", Symposium: Ecosocialist-Ecofeminist Dialogues,' *Capitalism Nature Socialism* 17 (2006): 33–8. The paired contributors were: Maria Mies and Victor Wallis, Ana Isla and Robert Chapman, Silvia Federici and Salvatore Engel-di Mauro, Terisa Turner, Leigh Brownhill and Stuart Rosewarne, Phoebe Godfrey and Jesse Goldstein, Ariel Salleh and Alan Rudy.
27 Eco-socialist International Network, EI-Netork-subscribe@yahoogroups.com.
28 Ariel Salleh (ed.), *Eco-Sufficiency and Global Justice: Women Write Political Ecology* (London: Pluto Press and New York: Palgrave Macmillan, 2009).
29 REDD stands for Reducing Emissions from Deforestation and Degradation.

30 On the epistemology of meta-industrial labour: Ariel Salleh, 'Is Our Sustainability Science Racist?', Ockham's Razor program, ABC Radio National, October 4, 2009, www.abc.net.au/RN.

31 Slavoj Žižek, *In Defense of Lost Causes* (London: Verso, 2008); Andre Gorz, *Paths to Paradise* (London: Pluto Press, 1985). The opening chapter of Salleh 1997 carries a discussion of candidates for historical agency in a time of ecological crisis.

32 Hardt and Negri, 2004, 88–9, 236–28, 349–50.

33 Peoples' World Conference on Climate Change and Mother Earth Rights, Cochabamba, Bolivia, April 19–22, 2010, www.bolivia.un.org/cms.

34 CGIAR stands for Consultative Group on International Agriculture Research.

35 Ingunn Moser and Vandana Shiva (eds.), *Biopolitics* (London: Zed Books, 1995).

36 Sharon Astyk, 'A New Deal or a War Footing? *Ruminations for a New Future,*' casuabonsbook.com, November 11, 2008.

37 For example, World Watch Institute, *Toward a Transatlantic Green New Deal: Tackling the Climate and Economic Crises* (Brussels: Heinrich-Boell Stitung, 2009); ACF et al., *Joint Statement Towards a Green New Deal*, www.acf.org.au.

INDEX

'Ariel Salleh sets the standard for intersectional study of the crises we face in nature, economy and society. Her praxis epistemology – based on labour in the humanity–nature metabolism – speaks the most passionate, humbling truths.' – **Patrick Bond, University of Witwatersrand; author of *Politics of Climate Change***

'This ecofeminist challenge is sustained by a deep knowledge of struggles on the ground by women's, worker's, indigenous, and ecological groups. Integrative actions call for multi-dimensional theory, and here is Salleh's contribution.' – **Lau Kin Chi, Lingnan University, Hong Kong; co-founder Global University for Sustainability**

'*Ecofeminism as Politics* has pioneered the integration of social movement debates, and its dialectical approach to these as internally related is path-breaking. Salleh is a must-read authority on how to challenge twenty-first century capitalism in theory and practice.' – **Adam David Morton, University of Sydney; author of *Revolution and State in Modern Mexico***

PRAISE FOR THE FIRST EDITION

'One of the main points of the book is discussion of the stereotype that "women are closer to nature" ... Salleh develops her arguments at several levels of analysis, with a wealth of empirical material.' – **Joan Martinez-Alier, Autonomous University of Barcelona; author of *Ecological Economics***

'I place Ariel Salleh's scholarship in the front rank with the work of other socialist ecofeminists such as Vandana Shiva, or ecofeminists generally like Rosemary Ruether and Susan Griffin.' – **Max Oelschlaeger, author of *Caring for Creation*; co-editor of *Postmodern Environmental Ethics***